The Developn
of
Western European
Stringed Instruments

Ephraim Segerman

PEACOCK PRESS LTD

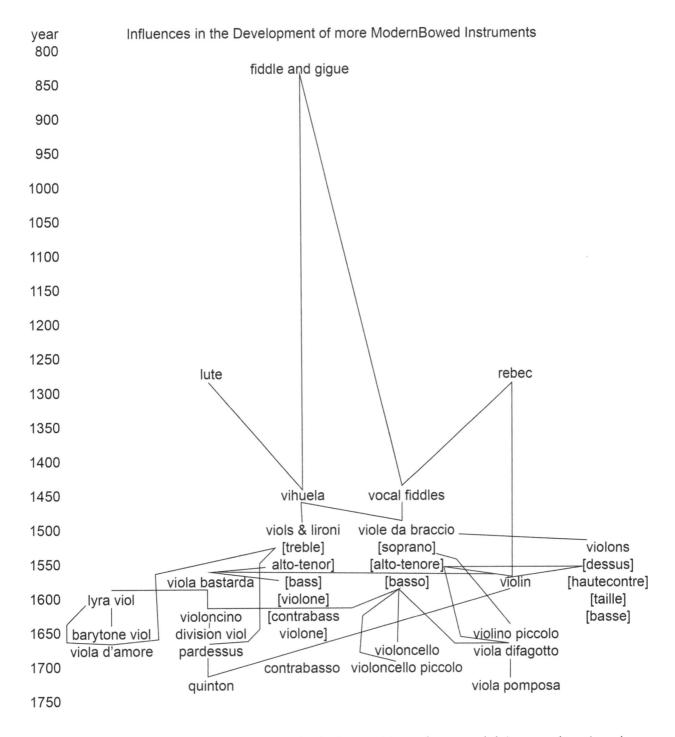

year

800	Influences in the Development of more ModernBowed Instruments

fiddle and gigue

lute   rebec

vihuela   vocal fiddles

viols & lironi   viole da braccio   violons

[treble]   [soprano]   [dessus]

alto-tenor]   [alto-tenore]   [hautecontre]

viola bastarda   [bass]   [basso]   violin   [taille]

[violone]   [basse]

lyra viol   violoncino   [contrabass

barytone viol   division viol   violone]   violino piccolo

viola d'amore   pardessus   viola difagotto

contrabasso   violoncello

quinton   violoncello piccolo   viola pomposa

Names in brackets [ ] are size names for the instrument type above, and date rows do not apply

1

The Development of Western European Stringed Instruments
© Ephraim Segerman

Published by

PEACOCK PRESS LTD
Scout Bottom Farm
Mytholmroyd
West Yorkshire, HX7 5JS (UK)

ISBN: 978-1-912271-89-4

First Published by Northern Renaissance Instruments, Manchester 2006, republished in May 2021 by Peacock Press Ltd.

The Development of Western European Stringed Instruments

Introduction

This book offers no new discoveries of historical evidence, but many new interpretations of the available evidence. It differs from previous histories in the questions I ask and how I try to answer them. The main questions I ask of the evidence are how the instruments (and their names) developed, and how they were tuned, played, made and sounded. Much historical information is not relevant to these quests, such as outstanding composers, players, makers, surviving instruments and repertoire, and so these issues are not discussed. Previous histories have answered most of the interesting questions for which the evidence clearly allows only single answers. The questions I ask go further, including those which may have more than one possible valid answer.

There is no objective way of choosing what questions to ask, but in evaluating answers, some ways are more objective than others. The usual way in the music world is to judge whether it makes sense in terms of what one believes one knows, and how much evidence it can explain. My approach, which is more objective, is to judge how well the answer (i.e. theory) can explain every bit of the relevant evidence. The difference is discussed in Chapter 1a.

Many of my suggested answers will be considered by some to be wild speculations, since the evidence does not unambiguously support them. I consider them to be valid theories (because they can reasonably explain how all of the evidence came to be what it is), and I accept that other valid theories could possibly answer the questions just as well. A collection of valid theories answering each question would be a much greater contribution to knowledge than concluding that the question is unanswerable (i.e. it remains a mystery) with the evidence available. In most cases, I strongly doubt whether there are many other theories with as much explanatory power as the ones I offer.

I have been trained as a scientist rather than as an historian or musician, so my indoctrination does not include the traditions of music scholarship, making my approach to how scholarship is performed different from most music historians in some crucial ways. One way is that I am more determined than most to avoid letting my enjoyment of performances of the music that I hear (or can imagine) to influence my judgements concerning the interpretation of evidence. It could be considered that this makes me rather old-fashioned. Westrop wrote that

> "A friend of mine was once shown, by Johannes Wolf, a piece of old music. He remarked, innocently enough, that it ought to sound well, only to receive the austere reply: 'I'm not interested in how it sounds'".[1]

Wolf was a music historian, and apparently was aware that any attempt to judge how well it sounds involves modern criteria which would obscure the only relevant historical question about sound, which is how it was expected to sound when written.

Most music historians since Wolf's time have been too interested in how it sounds to modern ears, considering that the major purpose of their work is to contribute to the enjoyment of music by the listening public (with the cooperation of early music performers). Making music enjoyable is the job

---

[1] J. A. Westrop, 'Practical Musicology', *Music Libraries and Instruments* (Hinrichsen, 1961), p.25.

of musicians, not historians. It is right and proper for musicians to exploit what the historians do when it suits their own purposes. But the music historian's job is to contribute to building the most probable picture of the sounds of what was performed and enjoyed then (as well as the cultural environment around such performances), based on as full and objective an interpretation of all of the evidence as can be mustered. It is not the historian's job to support the fantasy that many musicians and instrument makers have, that they are closely imitating the original musicians and makers, nor to support the fantasy that many listeners have, that they are hearing just what their ancestors heard. The historians have been giving this support by indulging in their own fantasy of expecting that the more historically accurate a performance of old music is, the more enjoyable it should be to modern ears. To protect this fantasy, they have avoided the pursuit of any scholarship that might reduce the attractiveness of the music, and by resisting acceptance of any research leading to such results.

Since development is my major theme, I pay rather more attention to chronology than most - what changes appear to have happened when. Thus, while most histories concentrate on characterising main-stream instruments, I am just as concerned with transitional instruments. Ordering the evidence in chronological sequence has allowed my suggested answers to development questions to include some detailed stages.

From my scientific training, I am more numerate than most in the field, and so am more likely to use quantitative methods whenever the questions are quantitative. These methods have mainly been applied to questions about the sizes of instruments, for which as a measure of size, I have focussed on the vibrating open-string length.[2]

There is an attempt here to be somewhat comprehensive, so an amount of rehashing of familiar material cannot be avoided. But I don't adhere to the convention that the space given to each topic should be related to a judgement of its importance, either then or now. The space I give to each instrument is mostly related to how much I have to say about its main characteristics and its development.

In the current culture of music historians, it is commonly felt that the great scholars of the past have established a fairly complete broad picture of music history. This is no-doubt true. But it is very often also considered that what is not known are 'mysteries', not knowable with the evidence available, and that all that modern scholars can expect to do is to collect new evidence to fill in the details. Those with this view may not welcome my reinterpreting the evidence on some historical questions, considering that these issues were either settled ages ago, or if not, they should remain as mysteries. I am sure that the revered early scholars would have been much more generous in considering and debating alternatives. And they would have been more willing to correct their mistakes when pointed out to them.[3]

---

[2] For a long time, I have been calling this 'string stop'. Since others have not appreciated the advantage of this terminology, in this book, I am reverting to the term more universally used but less precise 'string length', meaning 'vibrating open-string length'.

[3] Two mistakes pointed out here are: - assuming the equivalence of the *lirone* and the *lira da gamba* (by all historians who mention both names, going back at least to Hayes in 1930), and assuming that baroque fiddle tunings and sizes applied to 16th century *viole da braccio* (by Boyden in 1965).

I never intended to write a book since my writing style is not as readable as most. My work involves trying to answer historical questions that haven't been adequately answered before. Since I could not have confidence that I had adequately considered all alternatives to my answers, initial publication in *FoMRHI Quarterly*, which always welcomed incomplete and controversial studies, has been appropriate. With the publishing of Quarterlies halted by the current leadership of FoMRHI, this no more provides an outlet for my work. Indeed, some of my interpretations published as Communications (Comms) in *FoMRHI Q* have had to be revised, but a surprising number of others have stood up to further consideration, and it would be appropriate to combine these into longer articles in a journal of record that has a wider distribution in academic circles. This view is apparently not shared by such journals. A recent such article offered to one of these journals was rejected on the basis that the ideas had previously been published in *FoMRHI Q*. It was suggested that publication in a book would be more appropriate. With both of these outlets effectively closed, I really have had no choice but to write a book.

Many people consider that a book has more authority than other scholarly publications. That is only true to the extent that the time it takes to produce a book is great enough for second thoughts to modify ideas and how they are expressed, and to correct errors. Every book I have seen that was supposed to be the final word on its topic has turned out not to be so. This one will most certainly not be the final word on any topic. This could be especially true here since many of the ideas presented have not had the luxury of previously appearing in *FoMRHI* Comms, and so they have not had the benefit of such further reconsideration.

If there is interest, I hope soon to produce an improved illustrated edition of this book. Readers are requested to help this improvement in any way they can, especially by informing me of whatever errors I've made (such as where there is evidence that contradicts any of my theories) and of omissions (such as alternative valid answers to the questions I have addressed).

I have greatly enjoyed putting this book together, and I hope that the reader will find the ideas presented stimulating, even if there is some reluctance to incorporate them into one's views of instrument history. I expect few immediate converts to my methodology, but expect that there will be many more when fashions of thinking about scholarly questions in this field swing towards more logical and quantitative analysis, objectivity, and more respect for the evidence and for valid theories attempting to explain it.

May 2004, revised May 2006

The Development of Western European Stringed Instruments

Contents

Chapter 9: **Renaissance and baroque plucked wire-strung fingerboard instruments**

The Development of Western European Stringed Instruments

Chapter 1a: Methodology - Approaches in scholarship

The scholarly method I follow

Everyone agrees that the purpose of scholarship in any field is to create knowledge, which is composed of evidence and theories. Evidence is the raw material worked with, and theories are generalisations that provide explanations of the evidence and apply beyond it. The basic criterion for acceptance of a theory is that it is consistent with the evidence. Beyond such basics, methodology can vary. My approach follows that most commonly followed in the sciences, where a theory is falsified (proved untrue) when it cannot explain any piece of evidence in a way that has a reasonably acceptable probability of being true. A falsified theory then has to be either abandoned or modified to remove the falsification. Scientists design experiments to obtain the critical evidence that will falsify one or more of the competing theories. No theory can be proven true because it is always possible that a new piece of evidence will appear that falsifies it. Knowledge is not to be believed as true, but is to be trusted as the closest to truth that scholarship can offer with the evidence available and the valid (i.e. non-falsified) theories that have been offered.

The job of a scholar, while collecting all of the relevant evidence, is to imagine the various possible theories that might explain the evidence, and to eliminate those that are falsified by evidence that cannot be adequately explained by them. The remaining theories are then evaluated according to the probability of each one's least probable explanation of any piece of evidence. This is the criterion for how well a theory explains all of the evidence. If that probability is clearly much higher for one theory than for the others, it is chosen and added to current knowledge. If anyone suspects that this particular theory should not be the chosen one, he or she tries either to collect new evidence that could falsify it, or to create a new theory (or to modify a preexisting one) that explains all of the evidence at least as well as the chosen one does.

If two theories equally well explain all of the evidence, the simpler one is preferred. This principle goes by the name 'Occam's razor'. 'Simpler' is defined by having fewer assumptions unsupported by evidence. A common misapplication of this principle is to pre-judge how simple the theory should be and reject one that works just because it is more complicated than expected. Another common mistake is to interpret Occam's razor so that a simpler theory is to be preferred regardless of how comprehensively the competing theories can explain all of the relevant evidence.

The probability of a theory's explanation of a piece of evidence is a matter of judgement. Since scholarship is supposed to be as objective as possible, the effect of bias in judgement should be kept to a minimum. Bias is difficult to avoid in judgement, and to be able to come to conclusions in the process for scholarship, judgement at some point is unavoidable. The process of judging the historical probability of a theory's explanation of a piece of evidence resonates much less strongly with the unavoidable biases of previous expectations and almost-unconscious vested interests than the usual alternative - judging the probability of a theory being true. The former allows one to be more rational and fair, thus maintaining a higher level of objectivity.

Maximum respect for the evidence is basic in this approach to scholarship, so the evidence should have maximum control over the choice of theory. When one piece of evidence is apparently in contradiction with another, the theory must be able to explain both reasonably well. A theory that explains both without assuming error is preferred to one that assumes one is in error. But mistakes in evidence do occur, and conflict with other evidence is the only way to detect it. The mistake could be the result of the source's incompetence, bias or misunderstanding, or it could not be what it seems to be, or it could be an error in methodology or recording, or be deliberately misleading. A theory's explanation for it would present a scenario of how it could have become what it is, citing support from other evidence for similar problems in that source or similar ones. The probability of the explanation reflects how readily such a problem could occur, which makes falsification of theories by mistaken evidence remarkably rare. It is also very rare for sources to deliberately mislead.

Trust is usually given when we perceive that the probable consequences of not trusting are more undesirable than living with the perceived probability that the trust would be betrayed. For example, we trust doctors properly to diagnose and treat our illnesses, though we know that there is some probability that errors will be made. They have our trust because it is considerably more probable that our health will be preserved by trusting them than by following any alternative course. It is in this spirit that we trust the evidence (unless there is other evidence that suggests otherwise), and we trust that the chosen theory is as close to truth as is currently possible (unless we have some good ideas that could lead to replacing the chosen theory with another one).

Accepting that knowledge is no more than the best that scholars can do with the evidence available and the theories they had been able to dream up, with no objective way to determine how close to truth the theories might be, there is no inhibition to forming theories when there is very sparse evidence indeed. This allows a large majority of realistic questions historians want to ask to have answers in theories. With little evidence, the decisive evidence that falsifies some theories might be lacking, but having a set of possible theories is a better position to be in than keeping these questions open as mysteries to which there are no possible answers.

The methods usually followed in music scholarship

In music scholarship, theories are usually treated quite differently. Training does not include the falsification of theories by contradictory evidence, so there is no way to clearly disprove any theory with decisive evidence that invalidates it. Since there is no recognised objective criterion for settling disputes, controversy is rather futile and so is frowned upon, with gentlemanly behaviour the rule. The approach is to try to 'prove' that a theory is true by arguing rhetorically that the theory must be true because of the impressive amount of evidence that is consistent with it. Some evidence can be mistrusted, requiring 'confirmation' by other evidence to be taken seriously, so evidence that contradicts one's theory can easily be rejected as probably wrong, without taking responsibility for showing how it could have become wrong. A theory is incorporated into knowledge when the leading authorities in the field are convinced of its truth and include it in their books. When they are not convinced of the truth of a theory, they usually just ignore it, but when pressed for a response, the reaction is 'it is not proven'.

The main model for this process appears to be the law. The law aims to make quick clear decisions punishing (and deterring potential) wrongdoers or settling disputes within currently acceptable criteria of fairness. Since there is lots to gain or lose, much testimonial evidence is expected to be false or misleading. The weight of evidence and its trustworthiness are paramount. Evidence is readily rejected if one can raise any doubt about its reliability, and the decision is made on the basis of judgement by a jury or judges. That judgement is considered to be the proof. Since the outcome of the proceeding is very often dependent on judgements concerning the truth of evidence, it is strongly influenced by the persuasiveness of the performances of witnesses and advocates.

Because the knowledge that music scholars produce is strongly based on judgement and consensus, it is subject to change when a new generation wants to make its mark, and thus knowledge is a creature of fashion. Recent fashions have been deconstruction (which attempts to 'debunk' accepted judgements), and the politically-correct promotion of the contributions of women and members of minority groups. Whether truth could or should be a matter of fashion is a matter of debate. Post modernism is rather popular in our modern culture, and it postulates that there is no truth other than what is believed to be true. No distinction is made between subjective truth, which is what is believed, and an objective truth, which is a reality out there that is independent of what anyone thinks about it. Having unreserved conviction that one's insights are true is an advantage for success in many fields, including being a musician. Many music scholars have it too, and their scholarship is what they

do to convince others of this. A statement attributed to Howard Mayer Brown[4] (though I know of no evidence that he followed it) illustrates this: 'Musicology is what you indulge in when you know something is true, and have to go out and prove it'. To members of this school of music historians, the only function of evidence is to bolster their claims.

Other schools accept that there is a truth independent of what is believed to be true. One is a school that is at the opposite pole, being skeptical about most theories. The members of this school will only give acceptance to a theory if it is an unambiguous consequence of the evidence. Theories that cannot qualify (including those that are needed to answer most of the interesting unanswered historical questions) are to be avoided. Scholars in this school (and H. M. Brown was an outstanding practitioner) are renowned for collecting evidence and presenting it in useful ways.

The majority of music scholars I've met belong to a third school. They believe that scholarship produces truth that they can believe, and they seek answers to the important historical questions. The only way to achieve both of these objectives is to rely on consensus amongst their peers as the criterion for worthiness of belief. They may be somewhat independent thinkers in their own narrow fields of study, but otherwise, they follow the crowd. To them, the evidence and theories that are agreed to be true by the consensus are considered 'facts', and theories that don't have such agreement are considered 'speculations'. Speculations are opinions that everyone is entitled to have and promote, no matter how

---

[4] H. Meyers, private communication

well or poorly they can explain the evidence. This seems quite appropriately liberal-democratic, but liberal democracy only works if there is controversy and free debate. But in this field, these are discouraged as unseemly. Speculations offered by respected scholars that are not challenged for some time slide into being considered facts, and are thus added to knowledge that can be believed in. Once a theory is so accepted, any new competing theory faces an enormous struggle just to be considered seriously.

Professional success in any field depends on communication skills, charisma and a reputation for competence. In a field like this one, that finds controversy embarrassing, anyone not superbly endowed in such ways who disputes issues that are considered settled, or engages in disputes of any sort, will be mistrusted and considered a loose cannon that might lower public respect for the field.

Some questions in music history present difficulties for music scholars when the surviving evidence conflicts with their aesthetic understanding of the music (i.e. when the objective truth indicated by the evidence conflicts with subjective truth, which is strongly related to aesthetic expectation), so these areas are consigned to the category of 'mysteries'. One example of this is the level of improvisatory deviation from the written music in early performances. Another, which I will discuss now, is the history of tempo standards:

It is a tribute to the objectivity that musicologists can muster is the general acceptance that till well into the baroque, contrary to modern practise, tempo markings referred to tempo standards. When some of the evidence concerning what those standards were was discussed by eminent musicologists in the 20th century, some of it was disbelieved and some misinterpreted. The problem was that when the musicologists performed the music at the tempi indicated by the evidence, it moved much more slowly than they expected, and they could no more enjoy it or understand it in the way they were used to. They couldn't imagine how it could possibly ever have been appreciated that slowly. Musicologists seem to have convinced themselves that their understanding of the surviving music, which includes aural acceptability, is objective truth, and so evidence indicating otherwise cannot be trusted and must be wrong. That is probably why the topic was not seriously studied till my two papers published in 1996, where I analysed all of the evidence I could find up to 1700,[5] and I linked all of the evidence in a theory explaining the evolution of tempi from the beginning of mensural notation. I consider this to be my most important contribution to music history.

I thought that the papers would be of interest to early music performers as well as musicologists, so I submitted them to a journal they both read. There was a question as to whether the papers would be accepted for publication, since the journal's policy has always been advocacy for the early-music movement, and my results contradicted the tempo assumptions of the movement, which were at least twice as fast. There was only one response to my study, a highly critical one, but the editor didn't publish it because she wanted to avoid an extended debate. To accommodate her concern for brevity, I suggested that my critic and I presented single position statements from each of us in full

---

[5] E. Segerman, 'A re-examination of the evidence on absolute tempo before 1700 - I and II', *Early Music* XXIV/2 (May 1996), pp. 227-48 and *Early Music* XXIV/4 (Nov. 1996), pp. 681-9.

knowledge of what the other was writing, and she accepted the suggestion. We submitted the position papers, but they were never published. This was probably because he could not fault my analysis according to historical criteria. Tempo history will continue to be considered a mystery by the field until either someone can find an interpretation of the evidence that is felt to be believable (hoping that new evidence emerges which contradicts that which is known), or a new generation of music scholars demands more objectivity in their field. The study of music history is often primarily considered to be a service to our current music culture, with much less interest in it as an application of general principles of scholarship to the evidence on the history of music.

In my papers since, I have been promoting (with some resistance from editors) my more disciplined approach (based on how scientific scholarship is performed) to bringing more objectivity into the way theories relate to evidence in music history. I have had no indication of success in convincing others, (and have noticed a deterioration in my acceptance in the scholarly community). This is to be expected, especially in a culture in which the need for re-examination of one's ideas is rare. If one is satisfied with how one does one's job, one's colleagues agree, and then someone from a different tradition comes along with a different set of rules for doing it, claiming that those rules would make the job better, it is much simpler to dismiss him as a crank rather than to seriously consider the issues raised.

Whenever a new conclusion presented here differs from what people in the field prefer to be true, it is likely to be widely rejected as 'unproven', or just ignored.

The Development of Western European Stringed Instruments

Chapter 1b: Methodology - Determining the original sizes and pitches of instruments

Size clearly affects what an instrument sounds like. I focus on the vibrating string length as a good measure of instrument size since it can be related to string properties and pitches. It can be estimated from interpreting measurements of pictures, surviving early written measurements, the evidence on surviving instruments, finger stretches in surviving tablature music and the reported pitches that the strings were tuned to (converted to pitch frequencies by knowledge of the history of pitch standards).

Measuring pictures

Estimating an instrument's string length by measuring it in an undistorted picture is straightforward if the strings are close to being parallel to the plane of the picture, and for comparison, there is something else of known dimension at the same apparent distance from the viewer. Let us call S_p the string length measured in the picture, R_p the apparent length of the reference object measured in the picture, R_f the known full-size real length of the object and S_f the full-size string length we want to find. Then by proportionality, $S_f = R_f(S_p/R_p)$, where / means divide, no symbol means multiply and parentheses () enclose values that are calculated before being multiplied or otherwise operated on by what is outside. The most obvious reference object in a picture of an instruments being played is some dimension on the player. One possibility is total height, which for a fully grown male could, I would suggest, be about 160 cm, with perhaps an uncertainty of maybe 20%. Another possibility would be a dimension of the head, which could be better because we have reason to expect that variation in head size would be less than variation in total height. But hair styles and head clothing usually obscure direct measurement of head size in the pictures, so I mostly use visible components of head size, namely the distance between the eyes or the distance between the mouth and the centre between the eyes, whichever distance line is closest to being parallel to the plane of the picture. From averages in a small study performed on my acquaintances, I use 6.2 cm for both of these reference dimensions, and expect that the uncertainty would be about 15%.

The above assumes that the artist accurately depicted what would be realistic, as if the picture was a photograph. Even those pictures that look photographic could be distorted for various reasons. One is that the artists often worked from pattern books rather than copying from life, and they could have altered pattern-book designs with other design components from memory, forming unrealistic hybrids. Another is that the artist could contract, expand or distort items in a picture to give a more desired visual balance, to fit into a space or to provide emphasis for symbolic or other purposes. Some instrument depictions are unrealistic since they would not work as musical instruments as shown (but we should be careful about assuming this because some instruments could work in ways that we are not familiar with). And, of course, some pictures have been changed by over painting at a later time to update the subject matter or to attempt to 'restore' it.

Clearly unrealistic depictions can sometimes be due to amateur incompetence of the artist, or it was intended to be an instrument of fantasy. The latter can become evident from what the picture appears to represent. In early times, artists were not respected for their creativity, and their objectives were to meet the expectations of the people for whom they made the pictures, which were to depict reality when there was no good reason to do otherwise. In many cases, the artist was trying to be more realistic than a photo-like image would be, by twisting design components around to show their most interesting and informative aspects. Picasso said that art is the lie that reveals the truth. How the lie reveals the truth involves using a visual language that needs to be understood by the intended viewers, who in earlier times would usually have been members of the affluent classes, and with modern art they are the artistic cultural elite.

When trying to use pictures for measurements, it is necessary to be aware of the methods, the culture and the probable objectives of the artists when making the pictures. When choosing an instrument for measurement, one should first survey other pictures of people playing what seems to be the same instrument, and pick those that appear competent, undistorted and typical.

I have encountered some historians that argue that there is no technical information of value to be had from early pictures of instruments. There are makers who research and service the instrument needs of early-music performers, and they routinely scale the dimensions of surviving instruments in their 'copies' to meet customer requirements. They emphasise uncertainties in scholarship (as a basis for rejection) when the evidence indicates that a typical historical instrument characteristic, such as size or pitch level, differs from what is considered normal in the modern culture they share with their customers. It certainly is difficult to distance oneself from the culture of music and history we are immersed in, and to try to be fair about scholarship that challenges any of it. Training in scholarship should develop such objectivity (learning to distinguish between subjective and objective truth), but it rarely goes beyond encouraging trainees generally to be skeptical. Skepticism and cynicism, generally popular nowadays, are towards any claim of authority, but rarely towards one's own judgements. In this spirit, many of these historians can only accept studies that use evidence and techniques that they have been trained to handle (based on surviving instruments), and reject other evidence and techniques that are at least as relevant to their conclusions.

The other group is scholars with the responsibility for cataloguing collections of instruments or pictures[6], who agonise about how sure they can be about the information they put in their entries. I sympathise with their predicament. They are expected to produce catalogues that are authoritatively correct, and they feel that any needed subsequent modifications could raise doubts about their competence. The modern history of historical scholarship shows that almost all of the studies of topics that attempt to be complete and definitive are not, often needing modification after publication. One can't write anything that is 'fireproof', and it is best to accept the disappointment with equanimity when one has missed something. I am not sure which is sadder, being able to convince oneself (with the hope of convincing others) that one has achieved the wanted perfection, or realising that one cannot meet the standard of perfection that one thinks is expected. History is an ongoing research project approaching truths, not a collection of truths.

---

[6] e.g. M. Tiella, 'On musical iconography', *FoMRHI Quarterly* 90 (Jan. 1998), Comm. 1551, pp. 14-7.

Size estimation from fingering stretch

There has been some controversy about the size of the English cittern used for playing the solo repertoire published by Holborne and Robinson and in surviving manuscripts from that period (c.1600). The contenders are the small English cittern depicted by Praetorius with a string length of 35 cm and the smallest size of surviving Italian citterns with a string length of about 45 cm. A way to estimate the maximum string length is to find the biggest stretch indicated by the tablature in the repertoire, and compare it with an assumed maximum stretch for a average hand. I have assumed that my hand is of average size, and my maximum stretch between the first finger on a barré and the stretched-out little finger is about 11.5 cm.[7] If we assume equal-temperament fretting for simplicity, and n is the fret number of the index finger and m is the fret number of the little finger, then the stretch = string length

times $(2^{-n/12} - 2^{-m/12})$, where the higher symbols are powers to which 2 is raised (the calculation can be done on any school scientific calculator). In the case of this repertoire, the biggest stretch occurs between a barré on the 2nd fret and the little finger on the 9th fret. It occurs in a printed book of cittern lessons, so it is unlikely to be intended for a player with a particularly large hand.[8] Then the maximum

string length = $11.5/(2^{-2/12} - 2^{-9/12})$, or 39 cm. This is enough less than the 45 cm string length of of the majority of Italian citterns to strongly favour the small English cittern.

This approach is useful in estimating the string length of the lyra viol used to play Corkine's (1610) tablature. The greatest stretch is between the 1st and 5th fret. The maximum string length then calculates to 59 cm. That was the size of a tenor viol. This should be compared to the lyra viol played later in the 17th century. Mace's (1676) lyra viol music had the greatest stretch from the 3rd and 7th fret. The maximum string length calculates to be 66 cm. By the end of the century, the Talbot ms (c.1694) indicated that the string length of a lyra viol was 71 cm. This indicates that the most valued sizes of lyra viols increased during the 17th century.

Evidence from surviving instruments

Surviving early instruments are the most dramatic evidence of instrument history. They provide invaluable information on materials, making methods and details of design and construction. As with any other type of evidence, care needs to be taken in its interpretation. During an instrument's centuries of coexistence with people interested in music, it is most likely that there had been very many attempts to find out what it sounded like. If the sound was found interesting, it is also very likely that it was used for performances of some kind. For such performances, any deterioration in its integrity would probably have been repaired, during which it could have been modified to better suit the playing technique of the player. These modifications could easily be detected now if the repairs and alterations were either incompetent or in a very different style or it used different materials than the rest of the instrument, but some other modifications could be undetectable.

---

[7] A recent study on finger stretch involving 50 people by Eric Franklin (The *Lute* No. 78 2006, pp. 19-20) led to a mean value of 11.3 cm, with a standard deviation of 1.5 cm.

[8] A. Holborne, The *Cittharn Schoole* (London, 1597), 'Bonny Sweet Robin'

The question of which aspects of a surviving instrument are original is important for instrument historians. One often finds components of instruments that clearly had previously been parts of other instruments. There was a thriving 19th century instruments antique industry, mostly in Italy (the most famous firm that did this was that of Franciolini), in which parts of surviving instruments were used to create instruments that differed from the originals but were most in demand by the collectors. One remarkably influential overreaction to the uncertainties resulting from such fakes, has suggested that some well-known 16th century museum instruments that used worm-eaten wood or were composites were also later fakes.[9] The problem with this suggestion is that good well-seasoned wood has always been highly prized by makers because of its greater stability. So wood with a few non-active worm holes that present no threat to structural integrity would gladly be used in making a new instrument (even by many modern makers), and parts of irreparable or redundant instruments were gladly recycled.

Instruments have been most likely to be discarded when they lost respect when fashions changed, and they had no function to perform in the new fashion. Many more instruments that could be used without modification survived than those that needed modification for use, while very few (other than those of high decorative value) survived if they had no musical use. The rate of loss with time decreased when they became uncommon and gained value as curiosities and antiques. When instruments came in different sizes, we can expect that the numbers of each size that survived were usually very unrepresentative of what they originally were.

Lutes, citterns and bandoras were very popular in Renaissance and baroque England, yet not a single example of any of these instruments made in England survives. Nevertheless, many dozens of English viols from then have survived. The vast majority of these viols were small bass soloistic ones that survived because they could be used later as cellos. Some original tenor viols have survived because they could be used as small cellos. Treble viol bodies have survived because they had been in demand from the late 17th to the 20th centuries for conversion to violas. Only one viol that approaches consort bass size (converted to a small double bass) has survived. When the playing of viol music in sets was revived late in the 19th century, the written evidence on original sizes was either unknown or disbelieved. The disbelief was because they thought they knew what the sizes of bass viols were from the predominant number of surviving ones of cello size. They then invented tenor and treble viol sizes by scaling down from the basses they knew. This new set of viol sizes, 20% smaller than the originals, became standard then, and they still remain standard in the current early-music culture.

The current viol culture does not deny the clear written evidence on original larger viol sizes, but modern sizes 'work' well at the modern early-music pitch standard of $a' = 415$ Hz, and original sizes would not because of excessive breakage of gut top strings. This issue is avoided as much as possible by scholars as well as musicians. The listening public would be annoyed (at least) if it was made aware of aspects of the performances it enjoys that are knowingly historically inaccurate, and it would not thank anyone who informed it of this. Very occasionally, musicians attempt to emulate the rich sonorous sound of viols of original sizes by playing the music on sets composed of modern tenors as

---

[9] E. Segerman, 'Review: "Problems of Authenticity of 16th Century Stringed Instruments", by K. Moens, *CIMCIM Newsletter* XIV (1989), pp. 41-9', *FoMRHI Quarterly* 98 (Jan. 2000), pp. 19-25.

trebles, modern basses as tenors and double bass viols as basses.

Many instrument historians (who are often makers) are so enamoured by the sound of music played on restored surviving instruments (or accurate copies) that they are much more willing to trust interpretations of measurements on such instruments than any other type of evidence. Surviving instruments are real, able to be appreciated by sight and touch as well as by sound, while pictorial and written evidence is, by comparison, very remote and lifeless. Subjective truth, associated with the perception of attractiveness, is confused with objective truth. When there is apparent conflict between a piece of evidence of each of two different types, these historians are biassed towards trusting the type of evidence that they are most familiar with, and tend to reject or ignore the other. I will illustrate this below with the interpretations of evidence on Praetorius's Cammerthon pitch by organ and wind-instrument specialists. This issue is important for my estimation of sizes of various stringed instruments.

If we apply the more objective approach I have outlined above, one has the obligation to present a scenario for how every piece of relevant evidence that is apparently inconsistent with what one's theory expects could have possibly became what it is. One cannot reject evidence because one does not trust it without presenting a good case based on other evidence for how it became 'wrong'.

Praetorius's pitch - organ evidence

Important examples of poor standards in current scholarship are concerned with the question of Praetorius's Cammerthon pitch standard[10]. Its frequency is essential for my calculations of limits on string lengths from nominal pitches outlined below. At the end of the book about instruments written by Praetorius[11], after the Index, and before the list of errata, is a 2-page addition entitled only 'NB'[12]. It includes a diagram giving dimensions for making a chromatic octave of square wooden and round metal pitch pipes. The stated intention was to define his primary pitch standard, which he called *rechten Chormass* or *rechten Thon*, for organ makers and singers to tune to.[13] This appears to have been a more precise version for organ tuning of the pitch standard he generally called *Cammerthon* (or the usual or *rechte Chorthon*).

In the 19th and 20th centuries, various scholars have used the dimensions specified to find the frequency of that standard either by measuring it from pipes made, or by calculating it directly from the physics of the air vibration in an open cylindrical organ pipe with a mouth opening. The earliest determination of Praetorius's pitch from the pitch-pipe diagram was $a' = 423$ Hz (0.7 semitones below

[10] E. Segerman, 'Praetorius's *Cammerthon* Pitch Standard', *Galpin Soc. J.* L (1997), pp. 81-108.

[11] M. Praetorius, *Syntagma Musicum* II *(De Organographia)* (Wolffenbüttel 1619 & 1620)

[12] M. Praetorius, ibid pp. 231-2, translated in S. Heavens, 'Praetorius's pitchpipe *Pfeifflin zur Chormass*', *FoMRHI Quarterly* 78 (Jan. 1995), Comm. 1328, p. 60.

[13] Clear evidence that these were the same as Cammerthon is given in S. Heavens & E. Segerman, 'Praetorius's Brass Instruments and *Cammerthon*', *FoMRHI Quarterly* 78 (Jan. 1995), Comm. 1327, pp. 56-7.

modern) by A. J. Ellis[14] in 1880. Early in the 20th century, A. J. Hipkins[15] mistakenly assumed that the pitch standard represented by the pitch pipes was the Chorthon of Catholic churches that Praetorius preferred to his own, and so Hipkins assumed that Praetorius's Cammerthon was a tone higher than Ellis's determination, i.e. a' = 475 Hz.

The apparent origin of the modern early-music pitch standard of a' = 415 Hz is in Bessaraboff's famous 1941 book[16]. His suggestion was that, for practical purposes, we should approximate the original pitches with the closest pitches to whole semitone steps from modern a' = 440 Hz. Thus, accepting Hipkins's erroneous conclusions, Bessaraboff assigned Ellis's 423 Hz for Praetorius's Chorthon to a' = 415 Hz and his Cammerthon to a' = 466 Hz. He claimed that the Chorthon pitch 'is the tonality of the musical system of the classical period, which lasted from about 1600 until 1810-20'. We now know that this is a gross distortion and oversimplification[17], but the grain of truth here is that Praetorius pitch of the pitch pipes continually remained as the usual standard for string ensembles in north and much of south Germany though the period stated.

One problem with Bessaraboff's proposal is that it was based on Ellis's determination of the pitch-pipe pitch. If he made the proposal later, when better determinations of the pitch (see below) indicated that it was up to 10 Hz higher, his pitches would have been 440 Hz for Chorthon and 494 Hz for Cammerthon. This highlights the other problem with his proposal, which is that the important pitch standards of the time fall near the middle of his semitone ranges, so a small shift such as this one is grossly amplified.

The great attraction of Bessaraboff's proposal to early musicians is that it blurs the picture enough that they can justify the use the same instruments for all baroque and classical music, including copies of the superior later-baroque French woodwinds which played at about a semitone lower than Praetorius's pitch.

Bunjes[18] built a set of reproduction pipes with the resultant pitch being a' = 430 Hz, and Bormann[19] did the same with the resultant pitch being a' = 427 Hz. Thomas & Rhodes[20] calculated the pitch using the method of Ingerslev & Frobenius[21], with the resultant pitch being a' = 426 Hz. D. Gwynn[22] surveyed previous determinations and added his own corrections to that of Bunjes, which he considered most reliable, with the resulting pitch being a' = 433 Hz.

---

[14] A. J. Ellis, 'The History of Musical Pitch', *Journal of the Society of Arts* XXVII (Mar. & Apr. 1880); and XXIX (Jan. 1881), pp. 109-12.

[15] A. J. Hipkins, *Encyclopaedia Britannica*, 11th ed., xxi, p. 660.

[16] N. Bessaraboff, *Ancient European Musical Instruments* (Harvard Univ. Press, Boston, 1941), p. 378.

[17] E. Segerman, 'A Survey of Pitch Standards before the Nineteenth Century', *Galpin Soc. J.* LIV (2001), pp. 200-18.

[18] P. G. Bunjes, *The Praetorius Organ* (Concordia, St Louis, 1966), Chap. XIV, pp. 772-866.

[19] K. Bormann, *Die gotische Orgel zu Halberstadt* (Merseburger, Berlin, 1966)

[20] W. R. Thomas & J. J. K. Rhodes, 'Schlick, Praetorius and the History of Organ Pitch', *Organ Yearbook* II (1971), pp. 58-76.

[21] F. Ingerslev & W. Frobenius, 'Some Measurements of the End-Corrections and Acoustical Spectra of Cylindrical Open Flue Pipes', *Transactions of the Danish Academy of Technical Sciences* I (Copenhagen 1947), pp. 7-44; see review and summary by E. Segerman, *FoMRHI Quarterly* 99 (Apr. 2000), pp. 9-12.

[22] D. Gwynn, 'Organ Pitch, Part 1 - Praetorius', *FoMRHI Quarterly* 23 (Apr. 1981), pp. 72-7.

Organ historians try to follow an organ's pitch history by studying its records of repairs and alterations, and on each of the pipes, studying the nominal pitch names written on them, the styles of that writing, the signs of pitch alteration and the final pitches. When the pitch of an organ is changed, pipes can be shifted to be activated by different keyboard keys and their lengths can be shortened by trimming (or cutting scoops) or lengthened by adding an extension. Smaller changes can be made by widening or narrowing the tops of pipes. When a pipe was shifted to a new key, the new nominal pitch was sometimes marked. The trimming of pipe lengths can rarely be detected, nominal pitches on pipes are often missing and records of an organ's repairs and alterations are notoriously incomplete. Occasionally, original decoration on some pipes or the space inside an original organ case can put limits on some original pipe lengths. The original pitch of an old organ is usually estimated from the pitches of pipes with the earliest pitch-name markings that show the least evidence of alteration.

Some experts on German organs made in the 17th and 18th centuries make the generalisation that their original pitches tended to be at about a semitone above modern throughout that period. There is no question that this was the case late in the 17th century, but we are concerned with the situation on Praetorius's time, early in that century. One very highly regarded organ, in mostly original condition, is the 1616 Compenius organ in Frederiksborg. Its very unusual all-wooden piping resists the tinkering with pitch that metal pipes have always been subjected to, and it fits neatly into an original case so original pipe lengths couldn't have been longer. It appears to have been made originally at a pitch of about a semitone above modern, and Praetorius was consulted on its design. These experts are very impressed by the sound of this organ and its association with Praetorius, and so they are very skeptical about Praetorius's pitch-pipe evidence, which implies that his pitch standard was about a semitone lower than the pitch of this organ.

Praetorius wrote that most of the organs in his time were tuned to his pitch (Cammerthon or proper Chorthon), but that there also were many at a tone higher and lower, and 'not a few' a semitone higher.[23] He mounted a spirited argument against the tendency in his time to raise the currently fashionable pitch to a semitone higher[24]. A likely scenario is that he lost the battle against the higher pitch for the Compenius organ, but hoped (vainly, it turned out) to win the war with the arguments in his book. That organ is the only one amongst the about three dozen organs he esteemed (listing their stop dispositions) that have survived well enough for modern researchers to be able to estimate what their original pitches were. The vast majority of his esteemed organs could easily have been at the pitch he specified. There are three other German organs that Praetorius could have known when writing the book that have had their original pitches estimated. We have no idea about what he thought of them. Two had the pitch of a semitone above modern, and one was approximately at modern pitch. Since the pitch of the first two remained in fashion later in the century, the probability of their survival would be greater than others. In conclusion, there can be no statistical case made from the pitches of the few early 17th century German organs estimated that the most prevalent pitch was different from what Praetorius claimed.

---

[23] M. Praetorius, ibid p. 103.
[24] M. Praetorius, ibid p. 15.

There is also written evidence indicating that the most popular organ pitch level early in the 18th century was a tone higher than Praetorius's pitch, and that it dropped by a semitone late in that century. This change in pitch recognition is not reflected in the general conclusions of the organ specialists. In my analysis (that accepts all of the written evidence), the fashion of German organ pitch changed as follows: Early in the 17th century (Praetorius's time) it was a semitone lower than the constant level assumed by the organ experts, it was at that level (a semitone higher than in Praetorius's time) later in that century (when Schnitger was the major maker), it went up another semitone around 1700 (to follow the pitch of the ancient organs), and it dropped a semitone about two-thirds into the 18th century. We would expect these organs to be at the organ experts' pitch levels by late in the 18th century. I would be very surprised if the organ experts can tell the difference between the pipes remaining where they were during all of the 18th century (which they claim) and their being shifted a semitone at the beginning of the century (with the longest pipes unused) and back again later in the century.

The two competing theories are that Praetorius's pitch was as deduced from his pitch-pipe diagram, and that his pitch was about a semitone higher, as usually found in the surviving German baroque organs. The subjective choice that is usually taken is to decide which evidence one trusts more. A more objective choice between them should depend on the relative probabilities of how well the pitch-pipe evidence can be explained assuming the higher pitch theory, and of how well the surviving organ evidence can be explained by the lower pitch-pipe theory. It was shown above that there is no statistical case for inconsistency between the surviving organ evidence and Praetorius's lower pitch-pipe pitch.

The organ specialists have not attempted to explain how the pitch-pipe evidence could be consistent with their higher-pitch theory, but a harpsichord specialist who supports that theory has attempted this[25]. He noted that Praetorius had neither specified the wind pressure nor the mouth dimensions of his pitch pipes, and he proposed that these could have been high enough to get a pitch a semitone higher. As a model, he picked a late 16th century Innsbruck organ with pipes having extraordinarily large mouth dimensions, which has been restored with an extraordinarily high wind pressure of 90 mm water column. Assuming room temperature, these parameters and Praetorius's dimensions, he got a good part of the way towards pushing the pitch up a semitone on a test pipe he made.

To support his theory that the mouth dimensions were larger than expected, he also presented the mouth dimensions and diameters of 19 pipes (marked with the same nominal pitch as one of the pitch pipes) from surviving German organs roughly contemporary with Praetorius (their lengths have most probably been altered, so that is not relevant evidence). I calculated the averages of the pipe diameters and the mouth dimensions. Assuming Praetorius's pipe length, a wind pressure of 75 mm water column (considered to be the maximum expected by a specialist on early German organs, who happens to advocate the higher-pitch theory for Praetorius's pitch) and the annual average temperature of 10 degrees Celsius in Praetorius's region in Germany (churches were not heated), I calculated the

---

[25] J. Koster, 'Praetorius's Pfeifflin zur Chormass', presented at the Conference 'Pitch and Transposition, 16th-18th Century' organised by Internationale Musikprojekte, Hochschule für Künste, Bremen (October 1999).

pitch of a pipe with the average mouth dimensions and Praetorius's diameter. The method of Ingerslev & Frobenius was used, with a slight correction for the average mismatch between their test pipes and their theoretical calculation.[26] The result was $a' = 437$, 436, 435 and 434 Hz for the temperament being equal, sixth comma, fifth comma and fourth comma meantone respectively. If I use the average diameter of the pipes instead of Praetorius's diameter the results are 2 Hz higher. If I assume a wind pressure of 55 mm water column (like on the Compenius organ) instead of 75 mm, the results are 3 to 4 Hz lower.[27] The uncertainty in the calculation method is about ± 6 Hz.

Thus the pipe information not given by Praetorius cannot provide an explanation of how the pitch-pipe evidence is what it is in a way that has a reasonable probability of being true. Koster seems to believe that just showing that a theory's explanation is a possibility is enough to give it validity.

Praetorius's pitch - wind-instrument evidence

The semitone-higher theory for Praetorius's pitch has been an article of faith amongst wind-instrument specialists since Anthony Baines suggested it in his famous book on woodwind instruments[28]. He wrote that "Recorders at Verona identical in shape and in size with those in Praetorius's scale drawings at 'chamber pitch', sound a good semitone above modern pitch; say about $a' = 470$". His criteria for being 'identical' must have been rather fuzzy since I (and others) have found that there is a systematic error in the sounding lengths of the recorders in Praetorius's drawing, so that as depicted, the pitch standard varies, with the smallest ones at a standard about a semitone lower than the largest ones.

We have reason to expect that a large fraction of the surviving wind instruments would sound about a semitone above modern because they were made in Venice, where they were played with organs, and that was the pitch standard of Venetian organs. Woodwind instruments made there were used extensively throughout Europe, and the woodwind specialists interpret this as suggesting that this pitch standard was largely universal (including the German regions Praetorius knew). This could well have been true for most bands of Venetian woodwinds, but the expectation of these specialists that this carried over to the pitch standards of string bands does not have any supporting evidence, and is unlikely because wind bands and string bands rarely played together (the difference in pitch standards probably was a factor). Praetorius's insistence that both types of instruments played at the same standard was very unusual for his time. A minority of surviving instruments (mostly transverse flutes and mute cornetts) were made at lower pitch standards, apparently for playing with stringed or keyboard instruments at lower standards.

The pitches of woodwind instruments other than recorders cannot be determined from Praetorius's drawings with enough accuracy to distinguish between the two theories a semitone apart.

---

[26] E. Segerman, 'Spreadsheet I & F calculation of organ pipe pitch', *FoMRHI Quarterly* 107-8 (Apr-July 2002), Comm. 1800, pp. 7-8.

[27] The Compenius organ at Frederiksborg castle has a wind pressure of 55 mm water column according to the 'Compenius' entry by H. Klotz in *The New Grove Dictionary of Musical Instruments* I (Macmillan, 1984), p. 449.

[28] A. Baines, *Woodwind Instruments and their History* (1957, revised 1962), p. 242.

There is uncertainty concerning pitch-affecting factors that can't be seen, such as the plug positions on transverse flutes and the reed characteristics in reed-blown instruments, but in addition, the pitch can be varied rather more on them than on recorders by the way it is blown.

An instrument for which there are no uncertain pitch-affecting factors, except for how it is blown, is the trombone (or sackbut). From measuring the lengths of the vibrating air columns in Praetorius's drawings of the trumpet and 5 sizes of trombone, Steve Heavens and I have shown that, as expected, they played at the same pitch standard, if the method of blowing was the same.[29] We then showed that the pitch reported by modern blowing of a surviving Nuremberg trombone contemporary with Praetorius (who preferred such a trombone), when scaled to the length of Praetorius's trombone, would sound just over a semitone higher than it would sound if $a' = 430$ Hz.[30]

Assuming the theory that the pitch deduced from the pitch-pipes is true, the only explanation for this result is that the modern style of trumpet and trombone blowing (the same in modern and early music ensembles) produces a pitch about a semitone higher than in the blowing style at Praetorius's time. Modern blowing technique is characterised by what has been called the 'keyhole principle', in which the vertical direction in an old-style keyhole (having a vertical slot with a wider round top) represents the possible pitches, and one blows to pitch at the round top. Above the round top, the pitch breaks into the next higher harmonic of the vibrating tube. At the round top, the sound is richest (with more contribution of higher harmonics to the sound quality), is the most resonant, and it is easiest to blow a stable pitch. This can be called 'playing on the resonances'. In that explanation, in the early style of playing the trombone and trumpet (in non-military circumstances), they were played about a semitone lower than at the resonances. The softer sweeter sound of playing lower than the resonances could well have been considered to confer a more vocal quality.

There is early evidence that supports the hypothesis that wind instruments that could be played off the resonances often did. The virtuoso music for 17th century trumpet includes short ornamental notes that could only be played by lipping both a tone above and a tone below their normal notes. The evidence on early reeds indicates that they were much stiffer than the reeds that modern players use in both modern and early music. Stiffer reeds transfer much of the control over pitch from the fingering to the lips, with more effort in playing and more concentration needed to play in tune. A good reason for normally lipping a semitone lower than the top of the pitch range for a note is that instruments that could imitate the vocal appoggiatura strove to do so (a modern equivalent is that instruments than can imitate the vocal vibrato, usually do so). According to Tosi[31], the appoggiatura was a continuous slide in pitch. The slurring between two fixed pitches on keyboard and fretted instruments would be an inferior imitation. A practice of normally lipping below the resonance would give the continuous pitch range for lipping that accommodates the appoggiatura from above. This appoggiatura was a very

---

[29] S. Heavens & E. Segerman, 'Praetorius's brass instruments and *Cammerthon*', *FoMRHI Quarterly* 78 (Jan. 1995), Comm. 1327, pp. 54-9.

[30] E. Segerman, 'Praetorius's and surviving Nuremberg sackbut lengths and playing pitches', *FoMRHI Quarterly* 80 (July 1995), Comm. 1371, pp. 34-6.

[31] P. F. Tosi, *Observations on the Florid Song*, trans. by Mr. Galliard (London 1743), pp. 29-33; discussed in E. Segerman, 'The appoggiatura, early vocal style and instrumental imitations', *FoMRHI Quarterly* 103 (Apr. 2001), Comm. 1756, p. 27.

important component in music performance from the middle of the 16th century onwards through the baroque and later.

If we allow ourselves the subjective luxury of judging the trustworthiness of the evidence, without accepting responsible for having to present a reasonable case (based on other evidence) for what could be wrong with what we do not trust, then of course, we would prefer Praetorius's pitch-pipe evidence to be wrong, rather than modern lipping on the trombone to be wrong. We enjoy the music that modern early music groups produce. We want to trust that the wind players are playing in a reasonably accurate simulation of the original style, and would prefer to avoid considering that this may not be true. But the only admissible evidence for evaluating an historical theory should be historical evidence, and we should maintain the scholarly discipline of considering this modern evidence to be historically irrelevant. The very popular expectation of early musicians that an instrument of authentic design will automatically lead the player to authentic performance practices is pure fantasy.

A majority of the people presently interested in Praetorius's pitch are organ and wind-instrument specialists, who make broad generalisations about original pitch standards from pitch evidence collected within their specialisms, ignoring other kinds of evidence. They believe that it was a semitone higher than modern. That theory remains falsified by Praetorius's own way of communicating that pitch, the pitch-pipe evidence. The evidence of the limits on the relationship between string-length and pitch (the theory of which is given below), as given for gut strung instruments in this book, is consistent with the pitch given by Praetorius's pitch pipes, and not with the semitone-higher theory.

Pitch and string-length limits from string properties and Praetorius's evidence

String physics can relate the vibrating string lengths of instruments to the range of pitches that the strings can be tuned to. The highest string has to last long enough for the musician to get on with making music, and the lowest string needs to sound well enough to be musically useful. The breaking stress (i.e. tensile strength) of the string material is closely related to string longevity, but how close to the maximum stress that a string can 'safely' be tuned to is a matter of judgement, which could (and has) varied in different historical circumstances. The deterioration in the sound of strings made of any particular material as they get thicker and are tuned to lower pitches is largely understood in terms of inharmonicity (loss of harmonics, leading to loss of pitch focus and dullness of sound), pitch distortion (sharpening on fretting) and pitch instability (the variation of pitch with changing vibrating amplitude), but again, how bad is too bad is a matter of judgement in the culture of the time. I will quantify what these judgements were for gut-strung instruments by analysing historical evidence, and then present a table of acceptable ranges. Rather rougher estimates of the ranges of metal strings will also be made.

<u>The highest-pitch longest-length limit</u>

For a uniform string, according to the Mersenne-Taylor Law, the fundamental pitch frequency (f) of a string times the vibrating string length (L) equals half the square root of the string stress (S) divided by the density (ρ), or $fL = (1/2)\text{sqrt}(S/\rho)$. Stress in a string is defined as the stretching force (tension) divided by the cross-sectional area. The tensile strength of the string material is defined as the stress at which breaking occurs. The tensile strength of plain metal strings can depend on diameter since the process of drawing a wire through successively smaller die holes introduces dislocations in the structure that inhibit the crack propagation that is necessary for breaking. In fresh well-made gut strings, the tensile strength depends mainly on the average angle between the gut fibres and the string axis. That angle results from the twist that is put into the string when it is made. For maximum strength in thin treble strings tuned near the breaking stress, they have normally been made with the minimum twist necessary to produce cylindrical strings out of the few membrane-like pieces of gut each is made from. These are called 'low-twist' strings.

We can then consider that there is a maximum working stress for a treble (low-twist) gut string that represents the stress at which the rate of string breakage of the highest-pitched string is just tolerable. With strings of the same material, density is constant, so we can consider that there is a highest acceptable product of the frequency and the vibrating string length, or 'fL product', which is proportional to the square-root of the highest acceptable stress. Some musicians find it difficult to accept that gut string breakage depends only on the string length and frequency, and not on the diameter and tension. They associate higher pitches with thinner strings and expect that a thinner string can go to a higher pitch. But if they did the experiment of tuning a low-twist gut violin 1st string until it broke and then did the same with a low-twist gut violin 2nd, they will find that the 2nd will break at a much higher tension, but the pitches at breaking would be as close to the same as can be expected from the variability of a natural product.

To determine the maximum fL product tolerable in a historical period, we need to consider instruments that push the pitch limits by having an exceptionally large open-string range, and for each we need to know simultaneously its vibrating string length, the nominal pitch of its highest string and the pitch standard that applied to that nominal pitch. A source that provides all of this information is

the book *Syntagma Musicum* II by Michael Praetorius.[32] Scaled drawings of most of the instruments discussed in the text provide the vibrating string lengths, tables of tunings provide the nominal pitches, and the basic pitch standard used is defined by the speaking lengths and cross-sectional dimensions of diatonic octave sets of cylindrical and square pitch pipes, indicating that his standard was about $a' = c.$ 430 Hz[33].

The gut-strung instruments in the book with the large open-string ranges are the lute in chorthon (2 octaves + 5th on 61.8 cm), the short neck of the Paduan theorbo (2 octaves + 4th on 97.2 cm), the large 5-string bass *viola da braccio* (2 octaves + major 3rd on 75.0 cm) and the *viola bastarda* type of viol (2 octaves + 4th on 72.9 cm).[34] The fL products calculated for the highest strings on these instruments are respectively, 211, 209, 207 and 209 metres/sec, indicating that a good estimate of the maximum fL product acceptable in the early baroque was about 210. In the middle of the 19th century, when orchestral woodwinds were asserting their power by pushing pitch standards up to sound more

---

[32] Michael Praetorius, *Syntagma Musicum II* (Wolfenbüttel 1618-20).

[33] E. Segerman, 'Praetorius's *Cammerthon* Pitch Standard', *Galpin Society Journal* L (1997), pp. 81-108.

[34] E. Segerman, 'Further on the pitch ranges of gut strings', *FoMRHI Quarterly* 96 (July, 1999), Comm.1657, p. 58.

brilliantly, many violinists had to live with an fL product of over 220. It was mainly pressure from the rate of breaking of violin 1sts that lowered the pitch standard, as a compromise, to $a' = 440$ Hz later in the 19th century. At 440 Hz, the violin 1st fL product became about 216.

The metal-strung instruments tell us about the highest fL products of some of the metals involved. The fan-shaped fretting of the bandora suggests that the string length of the top course was at its maximum when the design was developed in the 3rd quarter of the 16th century. For the iron of that time, the top course was 5 semitones lower than it could be with gut. By 1580, when the orpharion was invented, much stronger ferrous metal was available from Meuler in Nuremberg, and this was reflected in the top course being 1 semitone higher than it could be with gut. After 1600, Meuler apparently perfected his process and the top course of the theorboed lute was almost 5 semitones (and of the gittern-tuned small English cittern over 4 semitones) higher than it could have been with gut.[35]

There are indications that after Meuler's success in achieving dramatic increases in tensile strength of ferrous wire, the other Nuremberg wire drawers improved their processes so that the subsequent highest fL product for iron was increased by about 2 semitones, being about 3 semitones lower than that for gut. They apparently did the same for brass, resulting in a highest fL product about 6 semitones below that for gut.[36]

<u>The lowest-pitch shortest-length limits - pitch instability and pitch distortion</u>

In pitch instability, the pitch sharpens in strong playing. The frequency changes because the string length and the string tension changes while playing. When that is because of the high amplitude of vibration, the frequency change (Δf) divided by the frequency (f) equals a quarter times the ratio of the elastic (or stiffness or Young's) modulus (E) divided by the string stress (S), times the ratio of the maximum stretch of the string due to strong playing: (ΔL) divided by the vibrating string length (L). In symbols only, $\Delta f/f = (1/4)(E/S)(\Delta L/L)$. The maximum stretch divided by the vibrating length ($\Delta L/L$) for a plucked string is $[1/(2(r-r^2)]$ times (d^2/L^2), where r is the fraction of the vibrating length that the distance of the plucking point from the bridge represents, and d is the initial displacement of the string at that plucking point. For the bowed string, r is 1/2 and d is the displacement at the mid-point of the vibrating length. The Mersenne-Taylor formula can substitute for the stress, $S = 4\rho f^2 L^2$. Then the pitch instability ($\Delta f/f$) equals the product of a constant (1/32), times a term of properties of the string material (E/ρ), times a term of how the string is used on the instrument $[1/(f^2 L^4)]$, times a term of how the string is played $[d^2/(r-r^2)]$.

To modern ears at least, the maximum tolerable pitch instability is about a third of a semitone, or $\Delta f/f = 0.02$ (2%). On plucked instruments, the maximum amplitude occurs at the pluck, after which the pitch decreases as the amplitude dies away. If the ear's initial judgement of pitch is not confirmed immediately afterwards, the perception is of a twang with only an impression of pitch. This happens mostly with low-tension iron or steel stringing. On such ferrous metal strings, E/ρ is very high (about

---

[35] E. Segerman, 'Praetorius's plucked instruments and their strings', *FoMRHI Q* 92 (July 1998), Comm.1593, pp. 33-7.
[36] E. Segerman, 'Praetorius's plucked instruments... op cit.

25 Km^2/sec^2), but on gut strings, with E/ρ less than 5 Km^2/sec^2, inharmonicity becomes serious well before pitch instability or distortion does. On bowed instruments, when there is pitch instability, strings have to be fingered flat to stay in tune in very strong playing. This happens particularly on some modern cello C strings.

In pitch distortion the string stretches and sharpens because of pressing the string against the fingerboard, $\Delta f/f = (1/2)(E/S)(\Delta L/L) = (1/8)(E/\rho)(1/(f^2L^2))(\Delta L/L)$. This pitch sharpening on fretting is the main reason for changing string type to one with a lower E/ρ for lower strings on metal-strung fretted instruments. If for different instruments we consider that the action is equally-well adjusted, $\Delta L/L$ will be constant. Then for a constant maximum tolerable pitch distortion, we can deduce that the fL at the bottom of the range is proportional to the square root (sqrt) of (E/ρ). This is constant for a particular metal, and since the maximum fL is roughly constant for a particular metal, the pitch range for that metal is the same for different string lengths.

An estimate of the bottom of the range for early Renaissance iron can be made from Tinctoris's statement that the cetra could be strung all in iron. The open-string range was a fifth (7 semitones). If we accept the highest fL was that for Praetorius's bandora, 5 semitones below the highest fL of gut, the lowest fL would be an octave below the highest fL of gut. Using published values of E and ρ[37], the values of sqrt(E/ρ) for iron, brass or copper, silver and gold are about 5100, 3100, 2800 and 2140 m/sec respectively. Then the lowest fL for brass or copper, silver and gold would be lower than that of iron by 7.5, 10 and 15 semitones respectively.

<u>The lowest-pitch shortest-length limits - inharmonicity</u>

Inharmonicity is the effect that limits acceptability of the sound of low gut strings. In the inharmonicity of a uniform string, the real frequency of the harmonic called 'the nth mode' (the fundamental is the first mode), which we represent by f_n, divided by the in-tune frequency of that harmonic, which is n times the fundamental frequency (f_1), equals $1+B(n-1)^2$, where B is the 'inharmonicity constant'. In symbols only, the inharmonicity of the nth mode $f_n/(nf_1) = 1+B(n-1)^2$. The constant $B = (\pi^2/32)(D/L)^2(E/S)$. If, as above, we substitute for the string stress using the Mersenne-Taylor formula, we find the inharmonicity constant B is equal to the product of a constant $(\pi^2/128)$, times a term of properties of the string material (E/ρ), times a term of how the string is used on the instrument $[D^2/(f^2L^4)]$.

We assume that there is a maximum inharmonicity in the sound of the lowest gut string that is tolerable in a music culture, but that may vary with the type of instrument family (especially when, as with the lute or *lira da braccio*, it is played together with an octave string). Maximum inharmonicity is expected on the lowest string of the member of that family with the maximum open-string range. In the Praetorius evidence, it is the *viola bastarda* for the viols and the large 5-string bass *viola da braccio*

[37] E. Segerman, 'Some theory on pitch instability, inharmonicity and lowest pitch limits'. *FoMRHI Q* 104 (July 2001), Comm. 1766, pp. 28-9.

for the fiddles. To find how this maximum inharmonicity in each family affects the pitch range in other members of each family (or set) with different vibrating string lengths, we invoke the Tension-Length principle, which states that the tension of corresponding strings in members of different sizes is proportional to the string length[38]. This is an empirical principle that is reasonably consistent with most of the evidence of the stringing of historical and contemporary instruments.

Combining this principle with the Mersenne-Taylor formula, we get D^2 proportional to $1/(f^2L)$. For constant maximum inharmonicity, D^2 is proportional to f^2L^4. Thus $1/(f^2L)$ is proportional to f^2L^4, so f^4L^5 is a constant for the lowest possible string in members of the family of instruments. Then if f_0 and L_0 are the frequency and string length of the lowest string of the family member at the limit, for a different string length L, the lowest frequency is $f_{min} = f_0(L_0/L)^{(5/4)}$, and for a given lowest frequency f, the minimum string length is $L_{min} = L_0(f_0/f)^{(4/5)}$. The viol with the largest range in Praetorius's data, on which the lowest string is expected to have the maximum inharmonicity, is the *viola bastarda*. This instrument provides $L_0 = 72.9$ cm, and $f_0 = 53.7$ Hz, which is the frequency of *AA* at $a' = 430$ Hz. It turns out that the same maximum inharmonicity applies well for fiddles as well. When the lowest string is supported by an octave string, as with the lute, more inharmonicity is acceptable, so a lower pitch can be tolerated. On Praetorius's lute, $L_0 = 61.8$ cm and $f_0 = 56.9$ Hz, which is the frequency of *C* at $a' = 383$ Hz. It was called a *Chor Laute*, implying that it was in his preferred Chorthon, a tone below Cammerthon.

With this relationship, if there is a factor of 2 in L, it leads to a difference of 15 equal-temperament semitones of f (such a semitone has the frequency ratio of a twelfth root of 2, which is 1.0595), 3 more than with the fL product. If there is a factor of 2 in f (12 semitones or an octave), it leads to a ratio of 1.74 in L. This reflects the observation that when a member of a family had a larger open-string pitch range than the others, it was the bass, and when the ranges were the same, there was more variability in the bass sizes.

If the lowest string pitch is somewhat below the range calculated from the above relationship, it can be brought into the range by violating the Tension-Length principle and using a thinner string. For each 6% thinner, the inharmonicity constant is raised by 12%. The tension is then reduced by 12%, which reduces the amount of sound energy that string can produce. Such a weaker lowest string can be tolerated in a smaller member of a set that plays together because notes on that string rarely need to sound strongly in the ensemble. It would usually not be tolerated on a bass member of the set or on a member that plays full-range solos.

Around 1580, new lutes started to appear with the lowest string a 4th lower than before, and the *viola bastarda* appeared, which was a viol that used the same range expansion. The expansion appears to be associated with a kind of thick gut string (called 'catlins' or 'catlines' in English sources) that newly became generally available. With constant D, L, and inharmonicity constant B, the drop of a

---

[38] E. Segerman, 'Strings through the ages I: the history of strings and their construction', *The Strad* Vol 99 No 1173 (Jan. 1988), pp. 52-5.

fourth (a decrease of a factor of 3/4 in f) can be accomplished by decreasing E/ρ by the square of the change in f (9/16), or about a half.

It has been suggested that the range expansion was due to an increase in density by the string being loaded with heavy metal particles or salts as it was twisted up[39]. Such a string would be completely opaque, while several sources indicated that, at least when new, it was clear or translucent in transmitted light. The only hypothesis that can reasonably explain all the evidence is that the string elastic modulus was reduced by rope construction. There is clear evidence that this kind of construction was used on thick musical instrument strings[40].

As with tensile strength, the elastic modulus of a gut string depends mainly on the angle generated by twisting between the gut fibres and the string axis. To get a specific average angle, the number of twist turns is inversely proportional to the diameter. String makers usually varied the number of turns less than this, automatically making the twist angle greater with thicker strings, but keeping within the twist limit above which the string takes the shape of a corkscrew or helix. Near this limit, the string is called a 'high twist' string, and we assume that before catlins became available, the lowest string was of the high-twist type. On the strings we make, we have found that the elastic modulus of high-twist ones is about half that of low-twist ones, and that of roped ones (catlins) is about half that of high-twist ones.[41] These measurements are consistent with the theory.

The following tables give the calculated string-length limits for gut strings on bowed instruments with a single lowest string and on lutes with an octave-pair lowest course. It is likely that the limits for a single lowest string would apply to plucked as well as bowed instruments, and those for an octave pair lowest course also apply to bowed as well as plucked instruments. The string lengths in the left table (with a low-twist highest string) are calculated from 21000 (210 m/sec in cm/sec) divided by the frequency. The string lengths in the right table (with a catlin lowest string) are calculated from equal inharmonicity with the lowest string of the viola bastarda for instruments with a single lowest string, and of the lute for instruments with an octave-pair lowest course. When the lowest string is of high-twist gut, its pitch limit is a fourth higher. If one wants to extrapolate beyond the range given, there is a factor of 2 in the longest string lengths in the left table for every 12 semitones, and in the shortest string lengths in the right table for every 15 semitones. The approximation of equal temperament is used in these calculations.

Let us be clear that the ranges presented here represent the judgement of Praetorius's musicians about how long a top string should last while still being musically useful, and how dull a lowest string can sound and still be musically acceptable. All that the string physics contributes is the extrapolation of individual worst cases from Praetorius's evidence to the full range of string lengths and pitches.

---

[39] M. Peruffo, 'New Hypothesis on the Construction of Bass Strings for Lutes and other Gut-Strung Instruments' *FoMRHI Quarterly* 62 (1991), Comm.1021, pp. 22-36.

[40] A. Ramielli, *Le Artifiose Macchine ...* (Paris 1588); translated by M. T. Gnudi as *The Various and Ingenious Machines of Agnostino Ramielli* (Dover, 1994); the relevant quote concerns a component of a trebuchet that is 'a thick double rope made in the same way as the thick strings of large bowed instruments'.

[41] E. Segerman, 'Measuring the elastic modulus of gut', *FoMRHI Q* 105 (Oct. 2001), Comm. 1775, p. 10.

Table: Gut string limits of pitch and string-length from Praetorius

Longest string length for highest pitch

string type: low-twist pitch	Mersenne 375 Hz. (cm)	Chorthon 383 Hz. (cm)	Cammerthon 430 Hz. (cm)
c'''	24	23	21
b''	25	24	22
	26	26	23
a''	28	27	24
	30	29	26
g''	31	31	27
	33	33	29
f''	35	35	31
e''	37	37	33
	40	39	35
d''	42	41	37
	44	44	39
c''	47	46	41
b'	50	49	44
	53	52	46
a'	56	55	49
	59	58	52
g'	63	62	55
	67	65	58
f'	71	69	62
e'	75	73	65
	79	78	69
d'	84	82	73
	89	87	78
c'	94	92	82
b	100	98	87
	106	104	92
a	112	110	98
	119	116	103
g	126	123	110
	133	130	116
f	141	138	123
e	150	146	130
	158	155	138
d	168	164	146
	178	174	155
c	188	184	164

Shortest string length for lowest pitch

catlin low-twist pitch	high-twist pitch	Mersenne 375 Hz. single (cm)	octaves (cm)	Chorthon 383 Hz. single (cm)	octaves (cm)	Cammerthon 430 Hz. single (cm)	octaves (cm)
c'	f'	23	21	23	20	21	19
b	e'	24	22	24	21	22	19
		26	23	25	22	23	20
a	d'	27	24	26	23	24	21
		28	25	28	25	25	22
g	c'	29	26	29	26	26	23
	b	31	27	30	27	28	25
f		32	29	32	28	29	26
e	a	34	30	33	30	30	27
		35	31	35	31	32	28
d	g	37	33	36	32	33	29
		39	34	38	34	35	31
c	f	41	36	40	35	36	32
B	e	43	38	42	37	38	34
		45	40	44	39	40	35
A	d	47	41	46	41	42	37
		49	43	48	43	44	39
G	c	51	45	50	45	46	41
	B	54	48	53	47	48	43
F		56	50	55	49	50	45
E	A	59	52	58	51	53	47
		62	55	61	54	55	49
D	G	65	57	63	56	58	51
		68	60	66	59	61	54
C	F	71	63	70	62	63	56
BB	E	74	66	73	65	66	59
		78	69	76	68	70	62
AA	D	81	72	80	71	73	65
		85	76	84	74	76	68
GG	C	89	79	88	78	80	71
	BB	93	83	92	82	84	74
FF		98	87	96	85	88	78
EE	AA	102	91	101	89	92	82
		107	95	106	94	96	85
DD	GG	112	100	111	98	101	89
		118	104	116	103	106	94
CC	FF	123	109	121	108	110	98
	EE	129	115	127	113	116	103
		135	120	133	118	121	108
	DD	142	126	139	124	127	113
		148	132	146	129	133	118
	CC	155	138	153	136	139	124

The Development of Western European Stringed Instruments

Chapter 2: Performance practices: early compared to modern

The evidence has been sketchy on how performance practices, including the use of instruments, varied over time and place in historical musical cultures. If we had more of such evidence, our understanding of early practices would certainly be more complex than it now can be, but that in no way invalidates the understanding we can gain from what is available. In the process of scholarship, one formulates theories as generalisations that go beyond the evidence, and how far they go in time and place is only limited by the existence of contrary evidence. One popular generalisation nowadays is to apply modern performing traditions while trying to understand and perform surviving music from previous cultures. The sparse contrary evidence is considered inconclusive since it cannot exclude the modern way as an historical possibility. This can be effective in generating attractive early music, but is not good history. In history, we consider all of the possibilities not excluded by the evidence, and then try to objectively evaluate the probabilities of the occurrence of each on the basis of evidence. The modern way feels so natural that many consider it to be neutral, without bias with respect to the performance practice of any place or time. On the contrary, this is highly biassed, and to combat that bias, it is desirable to initially ignore the modern way and explore the other possibilities, and then consider it only if there is evidence to support it.

Let us consider some aspects of early performance practices that are largely inconsistent with the modern way of doing things. One difference is the very much greater respect we now give to the composer's contribution to music than to that of the performer. Musicologists work very hard to establish the version of a piece of music that most closely represents the composer's original creation. Then this version is slavishly reproduced in performances. Musicians in pre-classical Europe also respected the composer's contribution (since the composer was very often identified), but they not only felt free to modify the music in their own ways, but they apparently were moved to do so to demonstrate individuality and professional competence. There was not the clear distinction between professional composers and performers that there is today. Composers of repute mostly earned their living as performers, and most performers of repute also had to demonstrate composition skills in their performing.

Embellishment

The modification of pitch by *musica ficta* will not be discussed here. Neither will the varying of pitch by less than a semitone, which is likely to have occurred very often in individual interpretations, but was not systematic enough to have left other than occasional evidence in instruction manuals. The modifications I will discuss are various type of embellishment. That involves colouring individual notes, usually by simple slurred pitch variation around it (gracing), replacing a sequence of notes in a melody by many more shorter ones (division), and more complex modifications. Most surviving music gives very little indication of embellishment. The theory supported here is that it was expected to be added by the competent performer to all music (including that which we now consider to be great music). Many musicologists believe in the competing theory that when a composer did not notate embellishment, it was considered unnecessary. Their view is that added embellishment in performance obscures what the composer created, and is thus undesirable. Such musicologists cannot accept the clear evidence on original tempi because its slowness also deprives music of the movement they expect it to have. If they combined original tempi with embellishment, that could provide a degree of movement that would be more acceptable to them.

The occasional evidence of composers objecting to embellished versions of their work by others has been considered to be evidence in favour of the theory that embellishment was optional. But that evidence is quite ambiguous as to whether the objection was to all embellishment or only to a particular type such as division. The identical objection can be heard today concerning the self-indulgence of musicians in modern jazz.

Almost all of the highly embellished surviving music is for lute and harpsichord, and this has been interpreted as the result of their being plucked instruments, in which the notes die away quite soon after sounding. Embellishment would then be the way to extend the effective duration of the notes. An alternative explanation is that these instruments had to play several polyphonic voices simultaneously, and though instruments responsible for only a single voice could easily improvise embellishment, doing it while also playing other parts is more difficult, and thus more likely to have needed to be planned beforehand, and thus notated. This explanation is supported by considerable evidence of embellishment in organ music, and in vocal performance, which don't have this limitation.

There is much evidence of embellishment throughout the period, but fashions in embellishment changed. The occasional evidence of avoidance of embellishment involves changes in fashion (usually complaints about excessive use of division), not the avoidance of all embellishment. Advice on the choice of embellishment survives, but none for when not to use any embellishment at all. This all implies that some sort of embellishment was considered natural in all performances.

There was a hierarchy in the ways that musicians embellished compositions. Gracing is the simplest, and particular graces could usually be learned by imitation after hearing it. Lute books occasionally showed how a newly popular grace could be fingered in tablature, but instruction manuals usually considered it unnecessary to describe them. Almost everyone could improvise graces in a performance, and the question of usage (i.e. which one, just how it was done and where it was applied) was mainly a matter of spontaneous expression and personal style within a context of good taste at the time. There is no evidence of early objection to excessive gracing.

Division was not as easy to do, since there were many manuals to teach readers how to do it. The manuals provided a catalogue of divided versions for each single long note leading to the next one or a sequence of a few such notes, usually in a cadence. The student wanting to divide such a sequence would find it in the catalogue, and replace it by a choice amongst the variety of divided versions that it offered, and thus assemble his or her own divided version. We can expect that some did no more than this cut-and-paste procedure, while others gained manual and aural experience with sequences that linked notes, and eventually could improvise their own divisions. Most divisions were slower than the fastest ones, and these slower divisions were most probably subjected to other embellishment types like gracing and time alteration.

Most of the objections to embellishment referred to excessive or distasteful division, to which no division would be preferred. In the Renaissance and the baroque, some performed harmonic division, with new harmonies inserted between the original ones (and occasionally replacing them), and this may have led to more objection than ordinary division.

The next step up in musical accomplishment was to add an independent new part to a polyphonic composition or to replace a preexisting part with a new one. In the common circumstance of the new part being higher than the others, this has been called 'descanting'. The new part could have note lengths similar to the other parts, or more notes of shorter lengths (essentially a divided part). To do this well required a good knowledge of (and/or feel for) the rules of polyphony and harmony. Some musicians had reputations of being able to do this spontaneously, but most had to work it out beforehand.

When musicians performed together in ensembles, there usually was some agreement to keep the embellishment from getting out of hand. This mainly referred to division. Of the ways of keeping order that there is evidence of, one was for the different lines to take turns. Another was for only the top line to embellish, with the proviso that only one musician embellished when more than one was playing the line, and when the first line was resting, the next line down was free to indulge. 'Heterophony' is the term for the simultaneous sounding of embellished and unembellished versions of a tune, and very early evidence for it is the probable performing style on the ancient Greek aulos when the two pipes were of equal length. There is evidence for it in the Renaissance and the baroque, and it was probably usual when there was more than one musician on a part.

Fastest notes[42]

The mid-14th century author Vetulus wrote that there were 54 *athomi*, which were the indivisible units of time, in an *uncia*, of which there were 480 in an hour (24 of which are in a day). Also, there were 27 *particulariter vocis,* which were the indivisible units of vocal time, in an *uncia*. Thus, there were 7.2 *uncia* and 3.6 *particulariter vocis* in a second. The fastest written note in the music at that time was a minim in minor prolation, of which there were 1.6 in a second. It is likely that Vetulus determined how small *athomi* were by the fastest one could play on an instrument, and that this was twice as fast as the fastest that singers could sing, which was about twice as fast as as the fastest written note.

In the early Renaissance, one occasionally finds smaller note values than one finds normally, and we presume that these were performed as fast as could be expected. In instrumental music, that was the demisemiquaver in alla semibreve time, of which there were 9.6 per second, and in vocal music, that was the fusa (quaver) in C stroke (cut) time, of which there were 4.8 per second. These

---

[42] E. Segerman, 'A re-examination of the evidence on absolute tempo before 1700 - II', *Early Music* XXIV/4 (Nov. 1996), pp. 681-9.

speeds are 33% faster than that in the above medieval evidence.

In the baroque, Quantz wrote that competent musicians could play up to eight notes per pulse beat (which he stated was 80 beats per minute) 'with double tonguing or with bowing', which is 10.7 notes per second. This is 11% faster than the above fastest speed for early Renaissance instrumentalists. Mersenne wrote that instrumentalists 'who are esteemed to have a very fast and light hand, when they use all the speed possible for them', when playing divisions or graces (*aux passages & aux fredons*), could play up to 16 notes per second. That is 50% faster than what was expected of Quantz's competent musicians.

While practising up to be able to play very fast was done only when one wanted to specialise as a musician who was able to astound by fast playing, in the 19th and 20th centuries, being able to play almost as fast as Mersenne's speed specialists became a necessary aspect of music training for the profession. Heifetz was clocked at 14 notes per second playing spicatto.[43]

Tempo[44]

Hearing is the first sense that develops in the human embryo, and by the time we are born, we have already been powerfully influenced by the sounds heard in the womb. Dominating those sounds are the sounds of the beating heart. Those sounds involve alternating long and short beats. The steady repeating rhythm of the heart is once for every uneven pair of heartbeats, and that is the pulse of the blood. Its rhythm is between 60 and 80 beats per minute for normal people at rest. In all of the historical evidence on tempo, one note value in the most popular type of tempo corresponded with the pulse.

The earliest clear quantitative evidence of tempo was from Vetulus in the middle of the 14th century, and then the note that corresponded with the pulse was the minim in major prolation. Before then it must have been the perfect semibreve, and before then (at the beginning of mensural notation) the breve. By late in the 15th century, it was the minim in minor prolation, and in the 16th and 17th centuries it was the crotchet in the duple cut *alla semibreva* time (or the minim in *alla breve* time). In the 17th century, it was common to distinguish between a slow tempo at the bottom of the pulse range and a faster tempo at the top of the pulse range. Later in the baroque, reliance on time signatures to specify tempo deteriorated in favour of Italian time and expression words, so tempo indications became rather vaguer. Without such Italian words, a default standard tempo still pertained. In 1756, the physicist-musician Tan'sur indicated that the usual duration of a crotchet was a second (60 per minute).[45] By the 19th century, Beethoven complained that 'we can hardly have any *tempi ordinari* any more, now we must follow our free inspiration'.

These early tempi are considered much too slow by musicologists, though none has been able to fault the analysis of the evidence, nor to offer an alternative analysis that fully respects the evidence.

---

[43] F. A. Saunders, *Benchmark Papers in Acoustics* (1946).
[44] E. Segerman, 'A re-examination of the evidence on absolute tempo before 1700 - II'... op cit.
[45] W. Tan'sur, *New musical grammar* (1756), third edition

General tempo standards were abandoned in music of quality, but they have persisted in fragmented form in many aspects of music, subject to modification by cultural changes. It has recently been reported that in modern pop songs, it was at 120 beats per minute in the 1980s, but it has since increased to 130 today, largely as a result of the use of Ecstasy in the clubs.[46]

The observed sequence of tempo augmentations through the centuries has defied a simple convincing explanation. It is possible that it could have been driven by new schools of musical innovators who made increased use of the shortest note values used at the time. When their compositions became popular, musicians would want to improvise divided versions, but this was inhibited by the short note values in the originals. The solution was to augment the tempo, leaving room for the divisions (the tunes, being already familiar, would be easily recognised performed at slower speed). Eventually, a new shortest note would begin to be used, and this cycle could be repeated.

Time alteration

Alteration (from that indicated by the music) of the time when melodic notes start and how long they last is mainly confined to rubato in modern performance practices. In modern rubato, the tempo is smoothly tugged slower and faster. There is no evidence for such smooth tempo changes in pre-classical music except for rallentandos at cadences. Stepped tempo changes were notated by changes in time signature throughout the period, and changes in smaller steps became common in the baroque. Expressing these steps was the initial use for Italian tempo/expression words. Much more frequent in our period was the old meaning of the term 'rubato', which was to keep the basic measure (of several pulse beats) steady while otherwise varying when the notes started and how long they lasted. There was much greater freedom to vary the time of notes than modern musicians are comfortable with. Dotted rhythms are examples of such variations in a repeated simple pattern.

Because of this freedom of shifting the notes in between the beats of the basic measure, previous planning would be needed to avoid clashes when there was more than one musician to a part. Amateur musicians rarely had group rehearsals, so they rarely performed with more than one to a part, but professional ensemble musicians had to rehearse, largely for this reason. Comfortably fitting the words of subsequent verses of songs (when the setting is just for the first) was eased by such time variations plus readily adding or subtracting notes. While exploring original fingering indications in cittern music, I found very large changes in position after the shortest of notes, which suggests that time was probably taken from an adjacent note to provide the time needed.

When more than one note was written to sound simultaneously, this was often not the case when played. Arpeggiation was common when playing such notes on the lute and other single instruments. It could start from the top or the bottom or the middle (in either direction) or a mixture of these, so it is unlikely that simultaneity when different instruments were involved would have been as necessary accurate as it is nowadays.

---

[46] M. Stock, 'On song', *New Scientist* Vol 180 No 2423 (29 Nov. 2003), p. 48.

Note production on viols and voices

A major aspect of developing modern viol technique is to suppress the grating transient noise that is made between when the bow first contacts the string and when the string sorts out its stable vibration modes. This is done by starting the bow stroke softly and then swelling the sound as soon as the stable tone has developed.

This type of note production is clearly not what one would expect from the word 'strike' in the phrase 'Strike the viol' in Purcell's famous *Come ye Sons of Art* ode to St. Cecelia. Similar evidence comes from French sources. Mersenne wrote that viols 'have a percussive and resonant sound like the spinet'.[47] English viol playing was the most respected in Europe at that time. Though Mersenne wrote about various differences between the French and English in how they used their viols, he would certainly have mentioned a difference in note production if there was any.[48]

About a century after Mersenne's comment, Le Blanc similarly wrote that viol 'bow strokes are simple, with the bow striking the string as the jacks pluck the harpsichord strings, and not complex like those of the Italians, where the bow, by the use of well-connected up- and down-bows whose changes are imperceptible, produces endless chains of notes that appear as a continuous flow such as those emanating from the throats of Cossoni and Faustina.'[49] He also wrote 'Using a smartly-drawn and plain bow stroke which resembles so much the plucking of the lute and guitar, the kind of sound that le Pere Marias had in mind for his pieces, he varied it into six different types of bow strokes.'

That plain basic bow stroke was called the *coup de poignet*, meaning 'blow of the wrist'. It was described by Loulié, who indicated that at the beginning of the stroke, the wrist was bent to lead the hand in the direction of the stroke, with the middle finger of the bowing hand pressed heavily against the hair[50] 'as though you want to grate or scratch the string', and as soon as the string began to sound, the excess tension on the hair is released, and at the same time the wrist moves to lean in the other direction.[51] Loulié mentioned that some variants on this basic stroke had only a beginning and not a middle nor end. The *soutenu* had the middle and end the same as the beginning. The *enflé* had a minimal beginning and then swelled. When Marais wanted this stroke to be used, he notated it by putting a letter 'e' over it or soon after it. It was a special effect, not the usual way to produce a note, as modern viol players assume.

Mersenne wrote that the viol 'imitates the voice in all its modulations'.[52] This most probably included how notes were produced. In vocal technique we would then expect the sound would be strongest on the first consonant with a fall-off of intensity as the syllable progressed. This was

---

[47] M. Mersenne, *Harmonie Universelle* III, The Books on Instruments (Paris 1636), Third Book, Prop.1.

[48] ibid, Fourth Book Prop. VII.

[49] H. De Blanc, *Défense de la basse de viole contre les entreprises du violon et les prétensions du violoncel* (Amsterdam 1740), translation in J. Hsu, 'The use of the bow in French solo viol playing of the 17th and 18th centuries', *Early Music* 6/4 (1978), pp. 526-9.

[50] Robinson's bow hold, where the middle finger is on the frog, is more likely to have been used by the English in playing their popular early 17th century repertoire.

[51] E. Loulié, *Methode pour apprendre à jouer la viole* (Bibl. Nat. Paris, MS fonds fr. n.a. 6355, fol. 210-220).

[52] M. Mersenne ibid Fourth Book Prop. V.

probably a major reason why the syllable 'ut' was dropped from fasola singing in England (probably before the middle of the 16th century), as it was the syllable that did not start with a consonant. Voices and viols were quite interchangeable in England around 1600. Untexted part music was apparently deliberately ambiguous as to whether it was performed on viols, sung fasola with voices, or mixed. About half of the published books of the English madrigalist school indicated on the title page that they are apt for voices or viols. So the stylistic equivalence between the sound of the viol and voice is well supported in England as well as France.

Phrasing and style

There has been no attempt to study the history of phrasing. There is no doubt that in all music, there has always been concern for the dynamic shapes of units of all time spans, from the individual note to a whole programme of music. Yet most attention is given to a particular unit which one shapes most carefully. In the modern cantabile style of music performance, that is the 'musical phrase', which usually corresponds with a line of text or what can be performed in one breath. This concept of phrasing appears to be quite modern. Well on in the 19th century, C. Engel wrote: 'A phrase extends over about two bars, and usually contains two or more motives, but sometimes only one'.[53] A motive is equivalent to what was called a 'point' in the baroque. The verbal phrase, which is the basic unit for expressing ideas, usually corresponds to one or two points.

It seems that in the Renaissance, the French baroque and the early Italian baroque, the musical phrase was the same as the verbal phrase. In the late baroque, Quantz, when comparing French with Italian style, wrote that 'The French manner of singing [has] ... a spoken rather than a singing quality. They require facility of the tongue, for pronouncing the words, more than dexterity of the throat'. The French style was declamatory. Many Renaissance and baroque writers compared the performance of music to the oratory of public speakers. They sometimes suggested writing the words of pieces of vocal origin into the music of instrumental versions so that the instrumentalist could phrase it properly.

In this declamatory rhetorical style, emotion was expressed by the meaning and imagery of the words, combined with a dramatic delivery. It is rarely heard nowadays (chances are greatest from the pulpit) because it seems ludicrously exaggerated, pompous and unnatural. Yet that is the authentic way to perform Shakespeare. Modern theatrical interpretations wisely neither attempt nor claim authenticity in performing style. This style was developed for orators to be able to sway crowds in situations of poor acoustics and still be understood. Pronunciation had to be very clear, so consonants had to be emphasised, as well as important words. The articulation obviously had no time spaces between syllables of a word, a small space between words, a bigger space between verbal phrases, and a bigger space yet between sentences. Delivery was considerably slower than in conversational speech.

This applied in musical performance except that gracing or short divisions were often substituted for greater sound volume as a method for providing emphasis for important syllables or words. Important words occur in most verbal phrases, so the dominant phrasing involved the shaping

---

[53] C. Engel, *Introduction to the Study of National Music* III (1886), p. 82, cited in *O. E. D.*

of verbal phrases, with peaks at the important words. These peaks interfere with the smooth shaping of modern phrasing, and this is one reason why gracing is usually avoided (when fidelity to the composer allows) in modern performances. Others are that the improvisatory skills involved are discouraged, and that the very much faster tempos taken make it difficult to perform and to listen to such embellishment. Extended division appears to have been a musical artifice that departed from trying to convince by declamation, and was a display of invention while contributing momentum to the performance.

In the contrasting later baroque Italian style, the vocalisation was supposed to express emotion more directly, stringing together ornate versions of the sounds associated with emotion such as sighs, sobs, cries, gasps, groans and chokes, with the words being quite subsidiary. Public display of emotion (without artifice that shows that it is under control) was still not socially acceptable (as it is in the visual media today), but the vocal agility demonstrated in the decorated music provided enough artifice to avoid embarrassment. Its use in Monteverdi's *Lamento d'Arianna* became very popular, and it became an increasingly standard feature in Italian opera (arias of this type were interchangeable in different operas to some extent). By late in the baroque, this shift of emotional expression from full words (with strong consonants) to vowels led to the common use of a standard swelling type of note production called *messa di voce* for both voices and instruments. Modern vocal and instrumental style is strongly influenced by this Italian baroque tradition, with the emphasis still on the vowels, but shifted from vocal agility and expressive variety to pitch accuracy and a beautiful powerful tone. The long modern musical phrase also seems to hark back to this tradition.

Standards of precision

In my youth, in the middle of the 20th century, many opera singers often slid up to the written note without necessarily reaching it. The intended note was obvious from the musical context, and the pitch tension created by this practice added to the enjoyment of performances by many listeners. Around that time, the critics were engaged in a concerted campaign to raise 'standards', apparently mainly concerning precision in pitch, precision of playing together in ensembles and clean accurate playing in fast passages. Record companies, attempting to produce the 'best' recordings of popular works, had recording engineers eliminate these blemishes in the cutting room, and since some musicians and ensembles could produce such technically perfect performances most of the time, the critics insisted that this should be expected in every public performance.

The musical conservatories system rose to the challenge, and by late in the century, the critics didn't have reason to make this complaint any more. All the conservatories apparently did was to give greater priority to the skills in precision and clean fast technique in choosing applicants and in training them, at the expense of musical flexibility and inventiveness. The early music movement grew mostly in this period. Aspiring professional early music performers sought acceptance as a branch of 'serious' music, rather than going the more informal way of folk music or jazz. The musicologist critics encouraged them to go in this direction to provide a showcase for the results of their research. Also, respectability and income promised to be higher. This required conforming to the standards in the field, thus largely leaving skills in improvisation and invention undervalued and undeveloped. The 'best' early musicians succeeded in meeting those standards.

Initial attempts at playing and making early instruments were mostly by amateurs. Some sought out the historical evidence and explored how to interpret it. Being more authentic than had been attempted before conferred status. Others felt that they understood the spirit of the original practitioners and they invented their personal versions of it. When the professional performers achieved commercial success, the amateurs were expected to rally around these heroes, and the field had to be stabilised. Both of the above groups of creative amateurs largely evaporated. The remaining amateur players were those who were happy to be pale imitations of the professionals. The makers who gave the professional players what they wanted flourished and became professional makers. The professional players also convinced professional makers of modern instruments to service their instrument needs as well. Many of the conservatories hired the professional musicians to teach early music performance, and making schools hired the professional early-instrument makers to teach their craft.

When the field became professionalised, the players had a playing technique and style and instrument designs that served their purposes well and were acceptable to their customers and to the musicologists and critics. They invested much time in practising to meet standards, and invested much money into appropriate instruments, so it is understandable that they would not welcome any subsequent research that would suggest that a different performing style or technique or a different instrument is more historically accurate. If following any new research results would make what they did obviously more attractive, they would of course seriously consider the further investment. Otherwise, they would only take such research seriously if their respected musicologist mentors did as well. This didn't happen because the musicologists were equally concerned about rocking the boat (everyone was apprehensive about whether or when the early-music 'bubble' would burst). The musicologists were happy that modern early music style is different enough from modern standard style to convince most that an effort has been made to be historically accurate, and this was accepted by the listeners. Keeping that style, and expanding repertoire would be a much more useful contribution to modern musical life than properly exploring historical performing styles. Historical research that expands repertoire and provides material for programme notes and record sleeves has been all that is welcome.

Early in the early music movement, there was an attempt to be authentic by using singers with good voices but not trained in the modern style of vocal production. This situation was not stable. Some critics steeped in the modern tradition considered that the early music singers sounded amateurish. Singers with modern training wanted to include early music in their performance options, and opera managers saw a promising expansion into early operas. A compromise was reached to keep almost everyone involved happy. Early opera performances employed loads of early-music instrumentalists in their orchestras, while voices trained in modern vocal production became acceptable as long as vibrato was noticeably reduced. Such singing now completely dominates, and the original singing in the 'naive' style no more has a place in professional performance. Singers in that early style have had to acquire modern training to remain acceptable.

In the history of pre-classical music, there is occasional evidence of ensembles which had the reputation of playing with exceptional precision, and performers with the reputation of playing exceptionally fast. But there is no evidence indicating that these were considered to be practices that were generally aspired to. Most of us will admire a juggler or acrobat for his or her skilled accomplishments, but are not willing to invest the effort needed to try to do it ourselves, because these skills are not necessary for doing what we want to do. We can safely claim that standards of what was necessary for acceptability in technical perfection then were considerably lower then than they are now. Some now will say that improved quality can't be objected to. On the contrary, one can object if the criteria for quality suppress spontaneous improvisation and 'out of tune' pitches, a very important original avenue of early musical expression, and modern standards do that.

Sensitivity to technical perfection varies in the population, and there has always been a minority that have had particularly sensitive ears for tuning and ensemble precision. In the last century, these people have become dominant in all aspects of music training and in the music industry, and they dictate the standards for professional involvement. Previously, when the arbiters of public taste were members of the affluent classes, public taste was satisfied with rather more relaxed standards.

Concluding comments

Modern early music seems to be about what the music should have sounded like according to modern performing traditions and expectations. Since the primary responsibility of any performer has always been to provide that which the consumers appreciate, what is being offered is fully justified by its commercial success. A problem early in the movement was that the performers led the audiences to expect historical accuracy in what they heard. The compromises with modern practices that made performing practical and the performances enjoyable were hidden, and indeed the audiences were happier not to have been told about them. More recently, the dubious morality of this practice has largely been eliminated by the performers claiming only that what they offer is 'historically informed'. With reduced dependence on authenticity and fidelity to the the composer's intention as seen from the narrow viewpoint of music historians, performers now have some more freedom.

Exploration of original performance practices essentially stopped when the early music movement became professionalised. Most performers since are convinced that the pioneers had worked out all of the historical problems, and they don't worry about it. I strongly suspect that further exploration of historical practices would uncover some other aspects of the music that would be pleasing to modern ears. Such exploratory interpretations of the music would usually not lead to runaway commercial success, but I am sure that there are many open-minded cultural-tourist listeners who will get much out of serious minimum-compromises attempts to recreate the sounds of the music their ancestors enjoyed. There is a 'slow food' movement to better appreciate the preparation and eating of food, so why not 'slow music' (with verbal phrasing)? The people who can do it would have to be able to explore the implications of the historical evidence while being skeptical about their modern aesthetic judgements. They should exist amongst music historians, but indeed are very hard to find.

The Development of Western European Stringed Instruments

Chapter 3: Stringed instruments before the 15th century

Ancient stringed instruments

Any stringed instrument requires a resonator of some type to convert the energy of each string's vibration into vibrations of air that can readily be heard, and some mechanism to bring each string up to its desired pitch. Before the appearance of the tuning peg in the first few centuries AD, all stringed instruments were tuned by gripping and twisting each string around a stationary arm. The end of the string was tied to a stick or bead or to a collar already twisted around the arm. To give enough room for the twisting hand, that arm needed a considerable amount of space around it.

The earliest evidence of stringed instruments comes from Mesopotamia in the 3rd millennium BC, when three types were played (the names used here are modern terminology). One was the lyre, where the tuning arm (called a yoke) was supported away from the resonator by two other arms, one on each side. Another was the arched harp, which was like an archery bow with one end expanded into a boat-shaped resonator, with the strings extending from along the resonator to along the rest of the bow. The third was the long lute, where the tuning arm was a continuation of a long neck. That neck was plugged into the resonator and was used for stopping the strings,. By the 2nd millennium BC, the angled harp appeared. It had the tuning arm sticking out of one end of the boat-like resonator like a mast. During that millennium it replaced the arched harp in Mesopotamia. These early types of harp did not have pillars supporting the far ends of the tuning arms that more modern harps have had. Both types of harps as well as the lyre and long lute, became popular in Egypt. In the 1st millennium BC, under Greek influence, lyres became dominant, but long lutes and harps (mainly angled) were still played.

The tuning peg apparently appeared in the first few centuries A.D. It made tuning easier and allowed much more compact instrument designs. New instruments exploiting the tuning peg developed in the Near East, and spread east and west. One was the psaltery, in which the tuning pegs were inserted directly into the resonator. Another was the short lute, in which the tuning pegs were inserted into a peg head at the end of the handle part of the club-shaped resonator that was used for stopping the strings.[54] A finger-plucked instrument seen in sculptures on Roman sarcophagi from a few centuries A.D. had the tuning mechanism hidden.[55] It was over half a metre long and about 12 cm wide with 4 to 10 strings of equal length. It seems to have been a combined short lute and psaltery before they

---

[54] There are statuettes of club-shaped instruments in the Louvre presumably from a few centuries BC, illustrated as Fig. 173, 174 and 175 in H. Panum, *The Stringed Instruments of the Middle Ages* (London, 1940). The end of the fingerboard and the tuning mechanism were missing in the first (from Tanagra), which (from later photos) had been 'restored' in the 20th century to look like a medieval fiddle. The second and third, appear to have had bent-back lute-like pegboxes, but the carvings do not show any pegs. If tuning pegs actually were used in these classical Greek times, they were so well hidden that they were not widely copied till centuries later.

[55] shown as Fig. 185, 186 and 187 in H. Panum op. cit. and Fig. 28 in F. Harrison & J. Rimmer *European musical instruments* (London, 1964).

became differentiated. This instrument seems not to have survived past the Empire. No Latin name for it has been identified. Versions of the lyre using tuning pegs spread across Roman-influenced Europe.

Medieval instrument names and development

The first concern of an instrument historian is to associate the names of instruments that appear in early written sources with evidence of other instrument characteristics, including what can be seen in depictions. Instrument names mentioned in history have almost always been those used by the musicians, and they usually distinguished between instruments according to different techniques used in playing them.[56] Another factor that has influenced the choice of name was a claim that it was a revival of a earlier instrument that had a particularly high reputation. Sometimes the revival was of the name without any relationship with the original instrument. This could result in instruments with very different techniques from different periods using the same name. There also were generic names as well as specific names, and generic names were often used either to be deliberately ambiguous or to distinguish between the instrument in question which did not have a specific name and one that did, but belonged to the generic category. Also, the name used for a particular instrument varied to some extent with locality and time.

Fiddle names have the structure f/v*(d)*l*, where a stroke / denotes alternatives on each side, a star * denotes a variable vowel and the brackets ( ) enclose a dispensable part. This includes the names viola, vihuela, viol and vielle as well as fiddle. The name appears to have originally come from the Latin. The entry under 'fiddle' in the Oxford English Dictionary says "The ultimate origin is obscure. The Teutonic word [Middle High German 'videle'] bears a singular resemblance in sound to its medieval Latin synonym 'vitula, vidula'." My Collins pocket Latin dictionary lists 'vitula' as 'cow-calf', and 'vidulus' as 'trunk, box'. Many boxes of the time were made by carving the body out of a piece of wood, with the lid on top made separately, just like medieval fiddles were made. This makes this possibility of the origin particularly attractive.

It is clear that this name was associated with fingerboard instruments that were primarily bowed when bowing became established in Europe. The name applied to instruments of a variety of shapes, the most common ones having an oval body clearly differentiated from the neck, and the ones having a club or pear shape with the body blending smoothly into the neck. There were a variety of playing positions (including the figure-8 shaped ones played with the neck above the body), but the most common was with the body against the shoulder, arm, neck or chest. The numbers of strings was usually from 3 to 5, but it could be up to 7. Fiddles with 5 strings often had one of them, called a *bourdon*, that lay off the fingerboard/neck. Tuning was mainly in fifths with pairs often in unison or octaves, and the strings were gut.

Gigue names with the structure g/z(h)*g(h/j)* were used for instruments closely related to the

---

[56] S. Potter & L. Sargent, Pedigree: *Essays on the Etymology of Words from Nature* (London 1973) shows that in medieval times, animals with very different appearances would be given the same name if they moved in the same way, or were functionally equivalent (from the human point of view). Moving the same way and functional equivalence amongst musical instruments (with varied appearance) involves how they were played.

fiddle. Some 12th century sources refer to the *trichordum giga.*[57] A 14th century source concerned with the number of strings on various instruments (not including the fiddle) stated that the *zigga* had 4 strings.[58] Some sources apparently show both names being applied to the same instrument,[59] but both appearing in lists of instruments in other sources implies that they were in some way different. It is likely that both names varied in usage as to whether it had a generic meaning or it referred to instruments with specific characteristics.

One of the few medieval sources that shows instrument drawings with names has both 'giga' and 'viola' names.[60] The 'viola' is clearly associated with a fiddle with a fingerboard and a clearly delineated neck and body, but the name 'giga', together with 'lira', is next to a harp. There are two unnamed instruments in the vicinity, a gittern and a symphony. An explanation of this evidence is that 'giga' referred to the symphony, and could have meant any bowed instrument other than a viola in that source. Some modern historians have speculated that the gigue was a club-shaped fiddle. A playing characteristic (such as gigues not having a bourdon or having fewer strings) is more likely to have been a distinguishing characteristic when there was one.

Names for the **rebec** have the structure r*b*b/c*. The bowed fiddle-like instrument and its name came from the Arabs to Christian Europe in the 13th century, and it initially had only 2 gut strings. It had an Arabic pegbox (with the pegs coming into it from the sides). The body and neck had a narrow club shape. Various writers indicated that the rebec was smaller than more common fiddles.

The Latin name *symphonia* referred to the hurdy gurdy (the modern name, that dates from the 18th century), which was a high-tech fiddle bowed by a rosined wheel and fingered by keys that push against the strings. The alternative name *organistrum* was used for the same instrument in German areas. The instrument first appeared around the middle of the 12th century, when it had 3 gut strings. I shall use the English **symphony** name for these instruments.

Bowing appeared in Europe by the end of the 10th century. Fiddle and gigue names first appear in the 9th century, and we expect that the plectrum-plucked instruments of similar appearance in earlier depictions probably went by the same names. By the beginning of the 13th century, a fiddle that usually had a more ornamental design than most and remained plectrum-plucked was called by **citole** names, derived from the Latin *cithara*. Citoles had 4 gut strings plucked by a plectrum, and its tuning seems to have been in fourths with a second. During that century, beside the rebec, other Arabic fingerboard instruments (with Arabic name origins and pegboxes with pegs coming in from the sides) were imported to Christian Europe from the Arabs, and they were called by **lute** and **gittern** names (the gittern and citole names both derive ultimately from the Greek *kithara* via Arabian and Latin intermediates respectively). They were usually plucked by plectrum or quill and differed in size, with the gittern having about the same range of string lengths as the fiddle, while that of the lute was

---

[57] W. Bachmann, *The Origins of Bowing* (OUP 1969), p. 83.

[58] C. Page, *Voices & Instruments of the Middle Ages* (Dent, London, 1987), p. 123.

[59] C. Page, ibid, p. 241 and pp. 169-70.

[60] British Library, *Sloane 3983* (f 13), an early 14th century Dutch astrology treatise; reproduced as Plate II in J. Montagu, *The World of Medieval and Renaissance Musical Instruments* (David & Charles, 1976), p. 25.

considerably larger. They both usually had 4 gut courses and were tuned mainly in fourths.

Psaltery names had the form (p)s*(l)t*r*(n), and applied to shallow-box instruments with brass or silver strings stretched above a soundboard on the top. The name came from the Latin *psalterium* but the instrument came from the Arabic *kanun* or Persian *santir*, and appeared in Christian Europe in the 11th century. Initially it was in triangular, truncated triangular or rectangular shape, the latter often having several bridges. After the 13th century it usually had a pig-snout shape, though the triangular and truncated triangular shapes survived. A 13th century source is the earliest to mention metal stringing, which was usual afterwards.[61]

The earliest surviving use of **harp** and **cruit** names was in a poem from around 600 by Venantius Fortunatis, the bishop of Poitiers. He wrote '*Romanusque lyra plaudat tibi, Barbarus harpa, Graecus arcilliaca, chrotta Britanna canat*'. There was little variation in harp names but the chrotta names had the form (c)(h)r*(w)*d/t(h)* (the cruit version is the one used here). It is clear that the Roman instrument was a lyre, and most probably so was the Greek instrument (in ancient Greece, the lyre was similar to the kithara, but was smaller and appeared earlier). The only plucked Germanic instrument that there is evidence for at that time was a lyre, so that probably was what the *harpa* was there. Earlier, Roman historians reported that the Celtic bards sang to and played the lyre (without giving the Celtic name for it), so it is likely that the *chrotta* was one too, like the others. But Sachs suggested[62] that it was the pillar harp, because later Continental evidence associated the chrotta name with an instrument that developed from the triangular psaltery and was played like a pillar harp.

I suggest that when the fiddle (still plucked) appeared in Europe within the next couple of centuries after Venantius, it competed with the lyre, which had a playing range of only about an octave. The extra half octave of range provided by the fiddle's fingerboard contributed to its success. Increased range could have been an advantage because it allowed some melodic fragments to be repeated in different octaves. To respond to the new taste for greater range, the Celts first made many of their lyres asymmetric so they could have shorter higher strings, allowing more of them. They then transformed that asymmetric lyre into the pillar harp[63]. Both of these new increased-range open-string instruments used gut strings (as the lyre did). To distinguish the new instrument from the cruit (old lyre), the name adopted were those used for the lyre in German region, the **harp**. I can imagine a Celt saying to a Norseman 'you call your cruit a "harp", but we now have a harp that is much better than yours'. After the psaltery appeared, Continental musicians adapted old triangular-shaped ones to have strings on both sides to be played vertically like a harp. They used a name they hadn't ever used but had heard about, the cruit name **rotta**. The original names for the lyre persisted in their regions for some time as vernacular generic terms for plucked or stringed instruments.

After the fiddle (still plucked) appeared, some lyres increased their range by adding a fingerboard bisecting the hole in the lyre through which the left hand usually operated. I shall call this cross between a cruit and a fiddle by the cruit name most usually applied to it, the **crowd** (**chorus** in

---

[61] C. Page, ibid, p. 217.

[62] C. Sachs, *The History of Musical Instruments* (New York, 1940), p. 262.

[63] Depictions on 8th and 9th century Irish monuments look like asymmetric lyres, part way towards a proper pillar harp.

Latin). And when bowing appeared, both the types (with and without a fingerboard) adopted it. During this change, the original cruit or crowd name persisted. As harps developed, Irish ones acquired larger bodies and adopted brass or silver strings. Welsh ones often used horsehair strings. Harps diffused to the continent easily and quickly, but rottas didn't diffuse significantly to Britain, where they were occasionally imitated by harps with a double row of strings. Such double-row harps appeared on the continent as well.

The Latin names **cithara** and **lira** referred to the ancient Greek kithara and lyre which were considered to be the original highly-successful stringed instruments. Thus these names were sometimes used instead of vernacular names to claim historical respectability. They were often used generically for all stringed instruments, and for any particular one that had a naming problem. The latter might be why it was particularly common for the harp to be called a cithara when it became popular in Germanic and surrounding areas, to avoid confusion with the original Germanic use of the harp name for a lyre.

More details of the instruments follow:

Cruit and crowd

The original cruits (lyres) had, from the pictures, 5 to 8 strings according to Galpin's count.[64] There is no evidence on tuning. We should not automatically assume that it was diatonic, since some lyres of non-European cultures have had pentatonic tuning, and even re-entrant tuning. In the pictures we see cruits sometimes plucked with the fingers of either hand alone or with both hands. We also see the left hand spread out with the fingers apparently touching all of the strings. Possibilities are that the fingers were plucking, selectively damping the strings or stopping the strings (with perhaps fine tuning by finger pressure). Other pictures show the left hand holding the top of the instrument, with the tips of the fingers on the strings in a position that does not allow them to pluck. Selective damping is most likely when the right arm was bowing all of the strings. When we see the right hand holding a plectrum with these left-hand positions, it is likely that the plectrum was strumming across all the strings, since important styles of playing would most probably have carried over when the bow was adopted.

There is a famous 11th century 'St Martial Troper' picture of a 3-stringed crowd which had an extraordinarily high flat bridge apparently placed on top of the strings. The player held the bow with it crossing the strings below the bridge. This picture is often used to demonstrate how ridiculously unreliable medieval art can be. An observer who has some understanding of the traditions of information transmission in early drawings will appreciate that when the artist drew the bridge, it is most likely that he was interested in showing where it went and what was special about it. How it really would look on that instrument, as if in a photo, was of much less importance to the artist, and to the viewers. Also, an observer who trusts the evidence more than his expectations, will try to imagine how such an instrument could be played. One question is why the bridge was so high. It would make stopping by pressing the strings onto the fingerboard particularly difficult. It is likely that when this special bridge was used on the instrument, the strings were not pressed onto the fingerboard. The

---

[64] F. W. Galpin, *Old English Instruments of Music* (Methuen, London 1921-65), p. 5.

distance between the bridge and the tail attachment of the strings was close to half the distance between the bridge and the tuning pegs, implying that the string parts below the bridge vibrated an octave higher than those above it. So this instrument offered two sets of constant-pitch strings an octave apart, for bowing, strumming or percussion (hitting with the bow). A 15th century source[65] gave the name 'chorus' (otherwise applied to the crowd) to the string drum, which suggests that there was a percussive component to crowd playing. Then a high bridge helps.

Harp

According to Galpin, early harps usually had 11 or 13 individual strings, but the number could range from 8 to 18.[66] The tuning appears to have been generally diatonic. When a harp was passed from one player to another, or when a performer played a different piece, the harp was often retuned. What was important was how the semitones were distributed amongst the tones. Many pictures (usually of King David) show the harp being tuned with a tuning hammer. This fuss made of tuning was apparently to demonstrate musical learning more than just having a good ear. It is probable that the tuning hammer was used to divide the vibrating string into proportional sections (as the bridge on a monochord does), to generate harmonics for accurate tuning of octaves and fifths. It may have been used at times to stop a string in mid air while playing. This could have been what was implied in the drawing of a 4-string harp in the Berkeley ms on which a number of letters are displayed along one of the strings.[67]

A c. 1300 source indicated that on the harp, 'one hand continually (*iugiter*) plucks the lower strings, while the other hand plucks the higher strings, not continually, but at intervals and in turn (*non iugiter sed vicissim et interpollatim*)'.[68] 'Continuously' here apparently meant without pitch change and at regular intervals of time, and this implies a repeated low drone below a melody or figuration. A repeatedly plucked drone apparently had an attractive affect that was different from a bowed drone since the bourdon was added to the fiddle to have both.

In the 1180s, Gerald of Wales (who provided the first evidence that the Irish used metal strings) wrote that the playing of the Irish was 'not slow and solemn as it is in Britain .. but is rapid and lively, although the sound is soft and pleasant. It is astonishing that with such a rapid snatching of the fingers, the musical proportion (*proportio*) is preserved'.[69] The proportion could have referred to pitch, but from the context, it more probably was to tempo. If there were no standards of absolute tempo (as pertains today), this could mean that tempo changes were done properly while playing usual kinds of music at a faster tempo. But with the tempo standards we expect were followed then, it meant that the usual tempo changes were properly observed in spite of the many more notes produced by faster finger motions, i.e. a more divided performance at normal tempo. This is the only evidence I know of for

---

[65] Jean de Gerson, *Tracitus de Canticis* (1423), quoted in C. Page, 'Early 15th-century Instruments in Jean de Gerson's Tractatus' ..., *Early Music* vi (1978), p. 339; a string drum is shown in the Angers Tapestry of the Apocalypse of 1380 illustrated as Fig 67g in *European musical instruments* (London, 1964) by F. Harrison and J. Rimmer.

[66] F. W. Galpin, ibid, p. 11.

[67] Plate III in C. Page, 'Fourteenth-century Instruments and Tunings: a Treatise by Jean Vaillant? (Berkeley, MS 744)' *The Galpin Society J.* XXXIII (1980), pp. 17-33.

[68] C. Page, ibid, p. 120.

[69] C. Page, ibid, p. 230.

particularly fast playing in this period, and the earliest evidence for division in instrumental performance.

Psaltery

Galpin's count of the number of strings on the psaltery was 8 to 20.[70] The tuning was diatonic. One source said that it had a string for all of the notes of the gamut (i.e. 15 notes covering 2 octaves).[71] In quite a few pictures, instead of these being single strings, they were courses with multiple strings. There are indications[72] that in a few of the multiple-string courses, some of the strings were tuned a semitone away from the others, providing the alternatives that harps retuned for. The hands are shown plucking with fingers or with plectra or quills. One often sees a finger plucking the lowest-pitched string with the hand position not conducive to plucking any other string, implying that it was a drone.

Rotta

One early 14th century source discussed the stringing of the rotta[73], saying that there were 22 strings on each side, and that there were 11 'more notable' (*notiores*) strings, which I assume meant diatonic pitches. This rotta seems to have had double courses. We would expect that any instrument at that time should be able to play in the drone style, so one hand should be able to be devoted to a repeated drone on one side while the other hand (on the other side) is free to play a melody or figuration. This leads to the suggestion that each side was in itself tuned diatonically, but they differed in the distribution of tones and semitones, to have available (without retuning) two of the distributions that harps tuned to. With such diatonic tuning and 11 notes on each side, the range of this rotta was an octave and a fourth. I haven't seen multiple-string courses on rotta pictures, but 11 strings on each side is quite typical.

Fiddle and gigue

In the first few centuries A.D., the invention of the turning tuning peg facilitated the development of much more compact stringed instruments. Small highly-portable instruments with their pegheads, necks and bodies carved from the same piece of wood appeared. Those with the pegs plugged into a peghead from the top were what later were called fiddles or gigues, while those with the pegs plugged into a pegbox from the sides were the early gitterns (which later became rebecs when bowed) and larger ones were the early lutes.

---

[70] F. W. Galpin, ibid, p. 45.

[71] C. Page, ibid, p. 123.

[72] see Fig. 1 in M. Tiella, *FoMRHI Q* 90 (1998), Comm. 1551, p. 15, which shows string groupings of variable number, with greater numbers apparently showing both chromatic alternatives, as presented in my analysis in *FoMRHI Q* 91 (1998), Comm. 1571, p. 31; Page's paper on the Berkeley ms 744 ibid Plate V shows a diagram of a 10 course double strung psaltery with the courses grouped in pairs, with virtual chromatic alternatives shown between groups. There was no indication whether the alternatives applied to one or both strings in each course.

[73] C. Page, ibid, p. 123-4.

Early European plucked fiddles were played with plectra. The neck had no frets, and this usually pertained to subsequent fiddles. Three pictures of these plucked fiddles are shown in Bachmann's book[74]. Since we rarely see such a plucked fiddle after the bow was introduced before the 11th century, we can expect that replacing the plectrum with the bow did not significantly change the basic style of how musicians made music on their instruments. So that basic style with the plectrum most probably involved stroking most of the strings, since the basic bowing style involved simultaneous bowing of most of the strings.

In the above-mentioned pictures, the left thumb is bent over the lowest string of the 3-string fiddles and the lowest pair of strings in the fiddle with 5 or 6 strings. It is possible that these were all 3-course instruments tuned in fifths with the left thumb stopping the lowest one at the tone, so it would sound an octave lower that the highest one. A melody, melodic fragment or figuration would be fingered on the 2nd and 1st courses. The open 2nd course is the root of the tonality, with the 1st and 3rd courses at the fifth. The obvious alternative full-stroked mode is with the thumb off and the 1st course always fingered. Then, the open 3rd course is the tonality root, a fifth lower than in the first mode.

Another possibility for the 3-stringed instruments is that the first two strings were tuned in unison. The musician could finger only the first (leaving the second amongst the set of drones), or finger both for emphasis. Bending the thumb would still switch from one tonality to the other. The loss of fingered pitch range would be compensated for by security. Bachmann has suggested that doubling the highest course was valued 'so that playing was not interrupted if one of the strings broke'.[75]

Of the early bowed fiddles, up to the 12th century, most of the pictures show 3-stringed instruments, with a sprinkling of fiddles with 4 and 5 strings. Sharp bending of the thumb is not seen again, but a few pictures show the thumb over the last course. The string spacings on one 4-string instrument shows it to have had two courses, but others could well have had three. String spacings on some of the 5-string fiddles indicate they had three courses. Several pictures of 12th century fiddles of Germanic origin show only one or two strings. In the 13th century there was a considerable increase in popularity of 5-string fiddles.

From the first half of the 12th century, we see the growing use of a new modification, in which one string of a 4- or 5-string fiddle avoided the fingerboard, extending from the bridge to the side of the peghead before getting to its peg. The thumb of the fingering hand usually stuck out between this string and the fingerboard. Possible things that the thumb could do with this string would be to pluck it (when it is not touched by the bow), damp it, stop it or leave it alone either to be bowed or not (when the bow is tilted enough to avoid sounding it).

Jerome of Moravia
Around 1300, Jerome of Moravia called this string the bourdon (*bordonus*).[76] He listed three

---

[74] W. Bachmann, *The Origins of Bowing* (OUP 1969), plates 16-18.
[75] W. Bachmann, ibid, p. 83.
[76] C. Page, 'Jerome of Moravia on the *Rubeba* and *Viella*', *Galpin Soc. J.* XXXII (1979), pp. 77-98. All of the information and

relative tunings for the 5-string fiddle. The lowest note on each of these was given as *G* (*Γ*). That was the lowest note (Gamma ut) of the normal scale at the time, and does not imply that the lowest note in each tuning was actually at the same pitch. The tunings given were 1st: *d/Gg d'd'*, 2nd: *d Gg d' g'* and 3rd: *G/G d c'c'*, with the slash (/) denoting that the string on the left was a bourdon.[77] These pitches were very far from the absolute pitches according to any pitch standard we would recognise today.

Since the 1st and 2nd string of the 1st and 3rd tunings were unison pairs, we can expect that in these tunings they were most important in carrying the melody or figuration. With no doubling in the 2nd tuning, the melody would be distributed more evenly amongst all of the strings. This expectation is consistent with the *d* string being on the fingerboard to be fingered as well, and Jerome's mentioning that this 2nd tuning was for wide-ranging melodies. With the melody embedded in the stack of *d*s and *g*s, those strings not fingered for melody acted as constant drones. For the melody to be aurally distinguished from the drones when its note was on an open string, it would probably have needed ornamental pitch movement of some sort, such as shaking.

Jerome wrote that the 1st tuning could be used for melodies in all the modes, and indicated where on the fingerboard (confined to first position) all of the notes (from *G* upwards) could be fingered.[78] It is not clear how much this fingering exercise was for fulfilling Jerome's stated objective of applying to the fiddle the musical theory previously presented in his book, and how much the lower pitches were actually used for melodies in practical fiddle playing. His only comments on the 3rd tuning were that compared to the 1st tuning, the *d* string was on the other side of the *G* string, and that the fingering of the notes could be found in the same way.

Finally, Jerome wrote that 'that which is most difficult, serious and excellent in this art [is] to know how to accord[79] with the *borduni* in the first harmonies any note from which any melody is woven'. The marginal note by Pierre de Limoges on this was 'Because the *d bordunus* must not be touched with the thumb or bow, unless the other strings touched by the bow produce notes with which the *bordunus* makes any of the aforesaid consonances namely fifth, octave and fourth, and so on.'

Pierre's note clearly implies that the bow could be controlled so that it does not touch the bourdon when its pitch is not consonant with other strings being bowed, and that there could be reason for the thumb to touch it if there is consonance. The bow can avoid the bourdon by bowing far from the bridge (where the bourdon slants away from the average plane of the other strings), but in the often-seen bowing far from perpendicular to the string, some of the bow stroke must have been close to the bridge.[80] The other possibility for avoiding the bourdon is for the strings to be high enough above the soundboard so that that the bow could tilt enough to miss it. It is rare to see a depiction of a fiddle with

---

translations from Jerome's book are from this paper.

[77] Actually, Jerome didn't mention that any of the *G*s in the 3rd tuning was a bourdon, but his contemporary Pierre de Limoges, the owner of the only complete surviving copy of Jerome's book, mentioned it in an explanatory gloss in the margin. I am aware of no evidence implying that Pierre was any less competent an observer of current musical practices than Jerome, so I see no basis for Page's rejection of the evidence this comment offers.

[78] For the notes *e* and *f*, which are unavailable in first position on the fingerboard between the *G* and *g* strings, the octave above was substituted.

[79] Page changed the translation of *respondere* to 'reply' in *Voices and Instruments*.

[80] This is explained below.

a bourdon that doesn't also have a raised fingerboard. Adding a raised fingerboard would be necessary for comfortable fingering if the bridge height was increased to allow the bow to change angle enough to not touch the bourdon. When this is possible, the only sensible thing that the thumb could do with the bourdon when there is consonance is to pluck it. This source offers no support for the alternatives of the thumb stopping or damping the bourdon. It appears that the repeated plucked drone as played on the harp was a valued component in the sound pallet of the fiddle.

In Jerome's final statement about consonance between melody notes and *borduni*, there is a question about the meaning of *borduni*, which is plural. If it is understood as the bourdon strings of fiddles collectively, as Pierre seems to have, there is no problem, except for two questions: why was the plural used here and nowhere else, and how can this be difficult, as Jerome wrote it was. There is also the question of whether Jerome's 'any' note referred to every melody note or whether it referred to any melody note that the player decided was musically important.

Page[81] suggested that Jerome's 'any' note meant 'every' note, and that the consonances were not between different strings on one fiddle but between the melody played on a fiddle and either the voice or another fiddle, ending up with 'fifthing' or organum, a primitive form of polyphony. This could occur with fiddle playing, but it is very far-fetched to consider that this was what Jerome had in mind when he was writing about *borduni*, a word used for off-fingerboard strings on the fiddle and for low drone strings on harps. If the harp usage is relevant here, organum can be played on a single fiddle with the complex fingerings sometimes seen in the pictures (while usually avoiding or damping the bourdon). Such fingerings can be used for other things fiddlers could have done. One is to provide a set of consonant notes as drones for a singer pitching the song at an odd pitch level. Another is to shift the set of drones to another pitch within a song if the player wants to treat that part of the song as being in a different mode (a kind of modal modulation). Another could have been if the note requiring consonance (that Jerome referred to) was that of a tenor melody, above which the fiddler improvised a faster-moving descant.[82]

Jerome's 1st tuning obviously caters for fifths and octaves based on *g*, which I shall call its 'tonality', but with a finger stopping the *G* and *g* strings (either together as a course or with two fingers) at the tone, it caters for a *d* tonality. This tonality flexibility mirrors what was suggested above for the original plucked fiddles. Playing in a host of other tonalities is possible (avoiding the bourdon by tilting the bow) by fingering all of the other strings in either of the above patterns in higher positions. There may be fingers left to also finger a descant melody or figuration. The 2nd tuning caters for only the *g* tonality. The 3rd tuning obviously allows a *g* tonality with the first two strings fingered at the tone. A *c* tonality can also be played by fingering the 3rd and 4th strings together at the fourth. Other tonalities are possible by fingering those strings together at other places, with the 1st and 2nd strings fingered appropriately together.

---

[81] C. Page, *Voices & Instruments...*, pp. 71-4.

[82] How to generate a descant from a tenor was discussed in a 1320 treatise by Petrus Dictus de Palma Ociosa, as cited in D. Fallows, 'Embellishment and urtext in the fifteenth-century song repertories', *Basler Jahrbuch für Historische Musikpraxis* XIV (1990), pp. 59-85.

Other considerations

From the pictures, it seems that fiddles with a bourdon were never the most popular. After the middle of the 14th century, it is hard to find one until the end of the 15th century when they were revived, leading to the *lira da braccio*. Also from the middle of the 14th century we start to find some fiddles adopting pegboxes like on the rebec or gittern.

Fiddle soundboards, as seen in surviving sculptures[83], were either flat or very gently arched, and it is very unlikely that there were any internal supports. These would have not been necessary since pressure of the bridge on the soundboard depends on string tension and bridge height, and the bridge height was low enough to avoid excess soundboard compression.[84] The amount of string vibration that the bridge transmits to the soundboard, and thus can be converted to sound, also depends on bridge height, and the low bridge height of most medieval fiddles implies that they were considerably quieter than later fiddles with higher bridges. This is discussed in Appendix 2.

The player that wanted to play an end string without any others by tilting the bow would need the end strings to be near the soundboard edge. This was accomplished either by having the bridge of average width but on a very narrow body, or by having a very wide bridge on a body of average width. Both approaches were used since there were many narrow fiddles and a few of the latter design.

Since the baroque, the place on the string where the bow rubs has usually been within the first fifth of the distance from the bridge to the nut. This bow placement creates a sound with strong harmonics, giving a rich and incisive sound that can be soft or swelled. As the bow placement moves away from the bridge and approaches the centre of the string, the sound loses harmonics, giving it a less focussed type of sound, rather like humming. Many more pictures of medieval fiddles show the bow in the second fifth of the open string length than in the first fifth. It appears that a humming non-projecting bowed string sound (that is not heard today) was highly appreciated in medieval times[85]. When bowing at such distances from the bridge, trying to swell the volume by increased bow velocity and bow pressure has very little effect.

Another aspect of the modern bowing position close to the bridge is that each string is stiff in its resistance to being pushed towards the body by the pressure of the bow hair against it, so that the relative positions of the different strings on the bridge are largely preserved where the bow rubs. Little experience with modern bowing is relevant to medieval bowing. Let us consider the artificial question of bowing all the strings at once near the bridge on an instrument where that bridge is flat. For each string to sound, it needs a minimum amount of bow pressure. Bow pressure is proportional to the hair tension times the angle (deviating from straight) that the bow hair makes over the string. So there must be a minimum angle in the bow hair at each string it bows. The shape of the bow hair is a polygon with a corner at each string, and to create that shape, the end strings have to sustain more bow pressure to

---

[83] e.g. L. Wright, 'Sculptures of Medieval Fiddles at Gargilesse', *Galpin Soc.J.* XXXII (1979), p. 71

[84] Violins and viols made today have arched soundboards that can withstand the much higher bridge pressure without the support of a bass bar and soundpost, but makers and players usually find it hard to imagine that this can be true.

[85] W. Bachmann, op cit. On p. 139 he wrote 'The bow was applied to the strings roughly in the middle or the first third of its length, presumably producing, on medieval fiddles, a weak, veiled sound.'

depress them towards the body than the middle strings. Bowing near the bridge might not allow enough depression on the end strings to meet the pressure required for the middle strings to sound.

The higher the hair tension, the smaller the minimum angle in the hair at each string needed, and the easier it is to get the middle strings to sound when bowing near the flat bridge. There are indications that medieval bows only had a fraction of the number of hairs that modern bows have, so the maximum hair tension was much lower. Consequently, to bow all strings together near the bridge, it is best to have a curve on the tops of the strings where they sit in the bridge grooves. In most medieval bowing, the bow was much farther from the bridge, and there the strings provide much less resistance to being pushed towards the soundboard by the bow pressure. Then, the details of the bridge shape become much less important.

There has been much discussion about flat vs round bridges, with the implication that the choice was between bowing the strings all at once when the bridge is flat and bowing individual strings without the others when the bridge is round. The real situation was rather more complicated. Each of the two strings of a rebec could be played individually, mainly since the instrument was narrow. All strings could be played individually on a 3-stringed fiddle if the bridge was curved and high enough (relative to the body width) and the bowing was close enough to the bridge. The player could play all the strings simultaneously by bowing farther from the bridge. With more strings, the choices tend to reduce to either playing all of the strings or avoiding the end string.

While we are on technical subjects, it should be pointed out that for bowing to bring out the tone of the string (rather than other noises), the hair of the bow needs to be moving in a direction close to perpendicular to the string. If the direction in which the bow is held is not at this angle, as is often seen in the depictions, the above condition can still be met when the direction of bow movement is not the same as the direction in which the bow is held. In this side-swiping motion during the bow stroke, the place on each string at which the bow rubs moves towards or away from the bridge. The resultant change in tone during the stroke could have been musically useful.

Rebec

It is very unfortunate that instrument historians of the last century assumed that when instrument names from Renaissance and medieval times were linguistically related, that implied that they referred to instruments with similar shape (rather than to the training to play it). So if the body outline of a medieval plucked instrument had any hint of a waist, it was called a gittern, and if it had a club or pear shape with no sharp distinction between body and neck, it was called a mandora if plucked, and a rebec if bowed. In 1977, Wright showed conclusively[86] that what they had been calling a gittern was originally called a citole, and what they had been calling a mandora was originally called a gittern. It is just as unfortunate that the leading historians then believed so deeply in their previous 'knowledge' that it took decades before they could accept Wright's work.[87]

---

[86] L. Wright, 'The Medieval Gittern and Citole: A case of mistaken identity', *Galpin Soc. J.* XXX (1977), pp. 8-42.

[87] e.g. M. Remnant, *English Bowed Instruments* (Clarendon, Oxford 1986), p. xx, and A. Baines, *The Oxford Companion to Musical Instruments* (OUP 1992), pp. 62-3.

The rebec name also needs re-evaluation. Some, like Baines[88], appreciate that most of the medieval instruments that we would now call rebecs because of their shapes would not have been called that at the time. Most of what we know about what a rebec was in this period is what Jerome of Moravia wrote. That was that it was smaller than the fiddle, had two strings tuned a fifth apart (the nominal pitches he gave for it were *c* and *g*), and the fiddle was more highly valued. Petrus de Abano (1310) also wrote that it had two strings.[89] Jerome's introduction to his section on bowed instruments indicated that he was to discuss 4- and 5-stringed instruments, but he only discussed 2- and 5-stringed ones. It is possible that the 4-string fiddle that he didn't discuss had two courses a fifth apart. If the high course was in unison and the low course an octave pair, it could be the same as Jerome's 1st tuning without the bourdon. This instrument's tunings would be closely related to both the rebec and fiddle tunings, but whether it would have been called a rebec would have depended on its size and respectability, of which we do not have evidence.

Rebecs most probably always had a narrow club shape since that is the shape of the Arab instrument (rebab) that the name suggests it came from, and of the 3-stringed 15th century instrument of that name with a round-topped higher bridge that it developed into (that was also smaller than fiddles). Both the Arab and 15th century instruments also had the pegs coming into a pegbox from the sides, so it is likely that this was also a characteristic feature of the rebec during all of this period. The fact that there are few surviving illustrations of such an instrument could probably be related to its having lower esteem than other fiddles. With fewer strings than other fiddles, it could have played melodies more than drones.

Symphony or organistrum

A 13th century source[90] stated that the symphony had three strings with the two unstopped drone strings an octave apart and the melody string tuned a fourth or fifth below the high drone. There were 8 tangents that stopped the melody string, providing an octave of 9 notes of a diatonic scale from c with both *b* flat and *b* natural. When the stopped string was a fifth below the high drone (being the mode final), the possible modes that could be played in were mixolydian and dorian (or hypomixolydian), and if it were a fourth below, the possible modes were lydian and hypolydian. The simplest way of changing from the former to the latter would be to tune the melody string up a tone. Tuning it up another semitone would facilitate playing the phrygian and hypophrygian modes, but since this was not mentioned, we can presume that it was less common.

The above was concerned with the original large (about 1.5 metres long) instrument that rested on the laps of two people with the soundboard vertical. The strings were said to be thick. One player turned the rosined wheel with a crank, while the other stopped each note by operating the knobs that protruded from the top of a box that enclosed (and hid) the stopping mechanism. This instrument was mostly associated with religious establishments that were familiar with the monochord and the organ as well as the fiddle, and it was straightforward to want to develop an instrument that combined their characteristics. A second player to turn the wheel was like having one to work the organ bellows.

---

[88] A. Baines, *The Oxford Companion to Musical Instruments* (OUP 1992), p. 279.
[89] cited in C. Page, *Voices & Instruments of the Middle Ages*, p. 123.
[90] *Quomodo organistrum construatur* cited in *New Grove Dictionary of Musical Instruments* 2 (1984), p. 261.

An 18th century copy of a drawing[91] from another 13th century source (since lost)[92] shows a 3-string symphony with the 8-stop mechanism exposed. It appears that all of the strings were stopped by turning the knob on its shaft, which had a protuberance on one side. That protuberance projected from the shaft towards the pegbox and pressed up against the strings when the knob was turned. Since all of the strings were stopped, this is not the same mechanism as that of the instrument discussed above, but an alternative. It could have easily been converted to operate in the other way by adding blobs to the ends of the protuberances under the melody string. The knobs are identified with the pitches associated with them, and they are the same as in the first source discussed.

The drawing shows letters on the soundboard on both sides of the strings, which apparently indicated string tunings. On one side is m   d G , and opposite these on the other side is d   D d . Bachmann[93] suggested that 'm' could mean 'melodia', and that the d and G after it indicated the pitches of the other two strings. He did not interpret the letters on the other side. He concluded that, with the *C* pitch given for the melody string on the neck, the tuning was *G d c*, similar to Jerome's 3rd tuning. This wouldn't work with the stopping of all of the strings simultaneously, so he suggested that the depicted mechanism was mistaken, and only one string was stopped. According to Occam's Razor, an interpretation that avoids assuming a mistake would be preferred.

I suggest that the three letters on one side were associated with the three on the opposite side, so the left pair indicated that the melody pitch (m) was assumed to be *d* in both. Then the middle and right pairs indicated that the other strings were either *d* and *D* or *G* and *d*. This leads to two tunings, both with one other string in unison with the 'melody' string, and the third string an octave lower in one tuning and a fifth lower in the other. In the first tuning *D d d*, all strings would be playing the melody, imitating an octave mixture on the organ. In the second tuning *d G d*, the playing would be in strict parallel organum. The apparent inconsistency between the *C* on the stopping scale and the *d* as the 'melody' pitch is easily explained by each of them intended to be pitches relative to others and not relative to each other. The *C* was relative to the other stopped pitches and it had to be given a pitch name that allowed the others to be normal notes without sharps or flats other than a flat for *b*. The *d* was a pitch normally used with g's and other d's for fiddle strings, as in Jerome's tunings.

The depictions of these large symphonies usually show 6 to 8 knobs. An exception is a sculpture on the Portico de la Gloria in Santiago de Compostela, which had 12.[94] The distance between the tuning-peg end of the neck and the knob closest to the bridge on this instrument was still a bit more than half of the distance to the bridge, as in the others. This implies that the range was an octave like the others, but the stopping was chromatic.

In all of the depictions I've seen, the knobs are shown in quite equal spacing. It is possible that the representations could have been unrealistic, because there was perhaps a tendency for artists to

---

[91] reproduced in H. Panum, *Stringed Instruments of the Middle Ages* (Reeves, London 1940), trans. and revised by J. Pulver, reprinted 1971, p. 295.

[92] M. Gerbert, *Du Cantu et Musica Sacra* II (St. Blasien, 1774), Plate XXXII, p. 16.

[93] W. Bachmann, op. cit., p. 111.

[94] W. Bachmann, op. cit., Plate 80; the knob man seem here to be working two knobs at the same time.

regularise repeating things. This possibility is supported by fret positions on some drawings of citoles not representing any known scales. Competing with this possibility is the apparent tradition on organs that equal musical intervals were mirrored by equal spacing in the mechanism presented to the player. Assuming that the knob spacings were realistic, there must have been offsets allowing stopping at a distance from the knobs. The hiding of the stopping mechanism in a closed box implies that making it mysterious was preferred to letting it be a visual distraction, and offsets could provide such a distraction. If the protuberances on the side of the knob shafts had varying widths, that would have provided the appropriate offsets.

During the 13th century, these large 2-player symphonies faded in popularity as they were replaced by small 1-player symphonies which sounded about an octave higher (like other fiddles). This parallels the rise in popularity of 1-player portative organs. Most of the small ones late in the 13th and early in the 14th centuries tended to have the whole instrument enclosed in a rectangular box about a third to a half a metre long. It was either suspended against the player's chest or resting on the lap. The crank for turning the wheel stuck out from one of the two smallest box sides and a decorative feature stuck out of the opposite one (possibly covering tuning pegs). Instead of turning knobs, the strings were stopped by some mechanism worked by pressing 13 to 15 keys that were evenly spaced along one box edge, from corner to corner. This clearly requires some long-range offsets because some keys must have been on the wrong side of the enclosed wheel.

The box edge with the keys could be along the top, either the edge close to or away from the player, or along the bottom, away from the player. If gravity restored the keys to their resting position, the basic design of the stopping mechanism must have varied.

One possibility is that the string was stopped from below, as with the earlier large symphony. The opposite was suggested by Jeremy Montagu[95]: that the mechanism pressed the melody strings from above onto the wheel as well as stopping them. Then, when no keys were operated, they did not sound. As a key was being pressed, it could make a sound by stopping the string (like on a clavichord) before the string touched the wheel. We can expect there also to have been drone strings that sounded whenever the wheel was turned. For access to the strings, the stopping mechanism and the keys would probably have been built into the box lid. It is possible that the mechanism stopped the melody string against a fretted fingerboard.

Box symphonies lost popularity by the middle of the 14th century, and most later symphonies returned to normal fiddle body shapes with a box covering only the stopping mechanism. Nevertheless there is one from around 1500, having many chromatic keys, illustrated in a stained-glass window of an English church.[96] On the usual later symphonies before the Renaissance, all of the strings went through the box. The number of strings can then be seen, and it was from three to six. The box symphonies could have had also had such a variation in the number of strings. Additional strings could either have been stopped together to give an organ-mixture effect, or tuned in unison but stopped by different sets of keys (as on the earliest clavichords), allowing more than one note to sound simultaneously.

---

[95] J. Montagu, `A Hypothesis on the Symphony', *FoMRHI Quarterly* 10 (Jan. 1978), Comm. 96, p. 25.

[96] Stained glass dated 1501/2 at north transept of the Priory of St. Mary & St. Michael in Great Malvern, Worcestershire; photo reproduced as Fig 60 in M. Remnant, *Musical Instruments of the West* (Batsford, London, 1978), p. 74.

Later hurdy gurdies had their strings stopped from the side by tangents mounted on sliding shafts with the keys on their ends. The organ principle of equal spacing for equal musical intervals was abandoned for simplicity.

Citole

The citole was a revival of the original plucked fiddle with pretensions of being a revival of the ancient Greek kithara. It was popular from about 1200 to 1350, but it lasted in Spain till after 1400. It was referred to with respect by poets for some time after it stopped being played seriously. A characteristic that usually distinguished it from other plucked fiddles was that it had shoulders on the body that were not round, and were either pointed (giving the instrument a spade shape or, if there were points below as well, a holly-leaf shape), or had some protuberance (often a trefoil) on it. It also usually had a protuberance at the tail (also often a trefoil), where the strings were attached. The shoulder decoration apparently was symbolically related to the arms of the ancient Greek kithara. The theory of Winternitz of a direct historical descent from the kithara needs to be modified to have the European round lyre (cruit) combined with the addition of a fingered neck of the fiddle (leading to the crowd) as the appropriate intermediates. Other characteristics usual for the citole were that (like the fiddle with a bourdon) it had a fingerboard on the neck that extended over the soundboard, and (not like that fiddle) that fingerboard had frets on it. Those frets extended over the full length of the fingerboard. Some citoles had a very deep neck, with an elongated hole for the left thumb, giving a side view reminiscent of the two arms of a cruit.

The Berkeley ms is the only source which gave a tuning that can be presumed to be that of a citole. The author presented the development of stringed instruments in terms of an increasing number of strings. The first one mentioned was a 4-string cithara (*citharum*), giving a drawing of an odd instrument with the tuning *c d g c* (the final *c* probably was *c'*) shown on the strings. The instrument's shape, the two pairs of inward-facing C holes in the soundboard and the four pegs plugging into the peghead from above are characteristics of a fiddle. Not characteristic of a fiddle are the tuning, the elaborate carving on the peghead (with a crown on top) and the apparently glued-on bridge, like on a lute. This was supposed to represent an ancient instrument, and it apparently represented the author's imagined cithara, the precursor of a all current stringed instruments with fingerboards. The citole had, for a century and a half, claimed to be its reincarnation, but was losing popularity. On the other hand, the Italian humanists were claiming that the lute was its reincarnation, and it was growing in popularity. The author must have been aware that the citole's recent parentage involved the fiddle, so he hedged his bets and imagined a possible ancestor of both the fiddle and the lute. There is a linguistic argument that his cithara was the citole. The only other instrument using the cithara name then was the harp, and in this source, the harp was referred to as a lyre (*liram*).

This source dates from the middle of the 14th century, when the citole's function, as the common fretted plucked instrument of choice, was being replaced by the gittern. Everyone expects history to repeat itself, so it is not surprising that the author stated that the next historical development was that an 'Arab loosened the lowest string [of the cithara], adjusting a fourth between it and its neighbour, as here:', and then he drew a picture of a gittern.[97]

---

[97] translation from C. Page, 'Fourteenth-century Instruments and Tunings: a Treatise by Jean Vaillant? (Berkeley, MS 744)' *The Galpin Society J.* XXXIII (1980), p. 27.

The tuning, with a tone between the lowest string and the next, and the next string a fourth above that, is very credible to have been that of the citole, since the tuning of the 15th century Italian revival of the citole, the *cetra*, retained this aspect of the tuning. One possible musical use of two adjacent courses on a fretted instrument being a tone apart is to play unisons without the fingers getting in each-other's way, facilitating heterophony (where a melody and a decorated version of it are played simultaneously).

Lute and Gittern[98]

The lute's name comes from the Arabic *ud*. Early in the 7th century, the Arabs apparently adopted a lute-type instrument from the Persians, who previously acquired it from further east. Within a century, it became the most prominent musical instrument in Arab culture. They conquered most of the Iberian peninsula early in the 8th century, and in the next century, that area became a thriving cultural centre. When a few Spanish cities were retaken by Christians in subsequent centuries, the new Christian rulers retained many Arab musicians, but they apparently discouraged integration of the two musical cultures. Thus the Spanish only played a minor role in the spread of the lute in Christian Europe. The major role was played in Italy via Sicily.

In the 9th century, the Arabs conquered Sicily and brought in settlers. By the end of the 11th century, when Norman knights conquered the island, most of the population was Arab. The new Latin rulers kept the peace and prosperity with religious and cultural tolerance and a considerable amount of cultural integration. Within a century, playing the lute and gittern gradually spread to Tuscany and the rest of Italy, and players were using them to accompany singing in Italian. German family connections of Sicilian rulers in the 13th century made these instruments known there as well. During the control of this set of rulers for over a century and a half, Arabs did well at the court and in the army, but not otherwise. Many of the disaffected emigrated while others rebelled, leading to their expulsion.

Arabic lutes had four courses tuned in fourths (with nominal pitches of *A d g c'*), and had frets. There were two types, one with a wide rounded body and wooden soundboard, and the other (a proto-gittern) with a shorter narrow club-shaped body having either a wooden or leather soundboard. Sachs reported the use of the name *qitara* (originally from the Greek) from before 1000 A.D. in North African areas west of Egypt. This was apparently the origin of the gittern name. The lute was played by nobles, professionals and slave girls, mainly to accompany songs. A 9th century treatise on the lute specified double frets of graduated thickness, scordatura tunings varying the lowest string pitch, and thumb-under finger-plucking technique. It was also played with a quill or plectrum. The strings seem to have been in equal tension.[99] Though sizes varied, the most common vibrating string length was a bit over 60 cm (the same as the most common European lute in the Renaissance). At this time we have the first evidence that the lute body was built up of strips of wood attached together, somewhat like on a boat. By the time that the lute diffused to non-Arab players, it mostly had lost its frets and finger plucking. There is no specific evidence about the smaller (apparently less-valued) proto-gittern, but since it was not discussed independently, it was likely to have been played similarly.

---

[98] Much of this section comes from D. A. Smith, *A History of the Lute from Antiquity to the Renaissance* (The Lute Society of America, 2002).

[99] The evidence on this is discussed in E. Segerman, 'Review: *A History of the Lute from Antiquity to the Renaissance* by Douglas Alton Smith (The Lute Society of America, 2002), *FoMRHI Quarterly*, publication delayed.

Late in the 13th century, the lute and the gittern became known in England and France. The gittern quickly spread to widespread use, competing with the citole as a fingerboard plucked instrument, without the citole's pseudo-historical pretensions. It was often associated with taverns and serenading, and was often mentioned in legal proceedings. Lute players were in the employ of the English kings from then onwards, but playing the lute was not popular in that country during this period. The lute was respected by French poets, but the nobility still considered the harp to be the plucked instrument of choice until late in the 14th century.

During the 14th century, the lute spread to be a major instrument throughout Italy (often played by minstrels called *giullari*, who were poet singers) and southern German-speaking areas (often played by students for courting). Its image in Italy changed from being that of an exotic oriental instrument, to become that of the reborn lyre of humanist poetry, which presumably was recreating the ancient Greek and Roman culture. The lute was still played extensively in Spain by Moorish players, and this continued till near the end of the 15th century.

The Berkeley ms is the only source that gave the tuning of the European gittern in this period. The text stated that the tuning was like the *cithara* (citole), given as (*c d f c*), but with the 4th course a fourth below the 3rd, which should then have been *A d f c'*. The diagram shows a standard gittern with 4 double courses, but the notes on the strings were *e b f c*, which is inconsistent with the tuning stated in the text. Page suggests that the inconsistency is due to an error in transmission from an earlier version where the diagram was left-right reversed (another surviving version doesn't have the notes on the diagram, but it is reversed). Then the order of notes should have been *c f b e*. This gives the required fourth between the 3rd and 4th courses, and Page assumed that the notes for the first two courses were flattened to give all strings a fourth apart, like the Arab lute, resulting in *c f b♭ e♭*. There are many uncertainties here, but I can't think of a more likely possibility. The tuning could well have been somewhat variable, as that of the Arab lute was.

There is no evidence on European lute tuning in this period, but a continuation of the Arab tuning is most likely. The lute and the gittern were very closely associated with each other in the Arab culture before coming to Europe, during this period, and afterwards, when it was reported that the stringing and method of playing was the same. We can thus expect that this pertained in this period as well. The pictures from before the 15th century usually show both without frets played with a quill.

A player with a good ear can play a melody more in tune without frets than with them, especially if (as was often with gut) the strings are not completely uniform in weight distribution. (On a double course, it was much easier to get strings to be in tune with each other by finding strings that are not uniform in the same way, than to find uniform ones). When one stops two courses at a time, the in-tune stopping of both courses at the same time without frets gets more difficult. With stopping three courses at a time, one may be more in tune with frets than without (though advanced players might be able to do it without frets). Thus whether an instrument had frets or not is an important clue about what the average player did with it. We can then expect that the basic musical function performed by the lute and gittern then was to play melodies, with perhaps the addition of drones when convenient.

Monochord and keyboard instruments inspired by it

The monochord was a plank or box with at least one string stretched from end to end. Under the strings were two fixed bridges at the ends, and one moveable bridge between them. There were marks on the body used to follow the position of the moveable bridge. It was used by the ancient Greeks as an apparatus for demonstrating that pitch intervals can be associated with proportions (whole-number ratios) of vibrating lengths. I am not aware of any clear evidence that the monochord was used as a musical instrument in ancient and medieval times, but I can't imagine its not being used informally as a drone during singing. Recorded medieval uses of the monochord were to help singers to pitch intervals and to tune organs. The proportions of vibrating lengths were seen as examples of divine principles. The symphony originally appeared in monastery circles in which the monochord was extensively used, and it could have originated as an application to the monochord of the organ keyboard principle of equal finger stretches for equal musical intervals.

From 1360 to early in the 16th century, there were occasional references to a stringed instrument with a keyboard that could be played like an organ, and was called a **chekker**. One source listed instruments in two categories without specifying the criterion for categorisation. An obvious one is whether more than one note could be played on each string.[100] If that is the correct criterion, the chekker was in the category of the symphony and clavichord. It is quite possible that the chekker was an expanded version of the later box symphony but without the bowing wheel, with more keys giving chromatic notes and a greater range, and with more strings allowing more than one note to sound at the same time. If the mechanism was similar to that suggested before for that symphony, it would have been similar to that of the clavichord. It would have differed from the clavichord by its strings being of gut and its stopping mechanism hidden (like the symphony), while the strings of the clavichord were of metal and its stopping mechanism was exposed.

Evidence for the existence of the clavichord and harpsichord started from about 1400. Their development is likely to have been triggered by the new availability of drawn iron wire for strings. In the second half of the 14th century, German wire makers harnessed water power for the drawing of wire, which for the first time allowed the drawing of iron. Previously, iron wire (valued for its strength as wire and stiffness for nails) was hammered to thickness (wrought), but the product was too uneven to be useful as musical strings. I have nothing to add to the further developments of keyboard instruments, which are adequately discussed elsewhere.

Instrument construction

Of the instruments discussed here, some cruits and fiddles have been found in archaeological excavations, and a citole converted to a Renaissance fiddle has survived above ground. Thus much of what follows is supposition extrapolating from these to other types of instruments and from later instruments to earlier ones of the same type.

---

[100] E. M. Ripin, *The New Grove Dictionary of Musical Instruments* I (Macmillan 1984), p. 348.

Medieval furniture and other objects made of assembled pieces of wood did not rely on the tenacity of glue to be held together. The apparent reason is that load-bearing joints that depend on animal glue (the usual type of strong glue available) would fail in prolonged periods of very high humidity, since that glue is somewhat hygroscopic and water soluble. We can thus expect that this pertains to wooden instruments as well (but it is likely that glue was still used to stiffen joints and to avoid unwanted vibration). This is true except for the lute, which had the bridge glued to the soundboard, which was glued to the body, which was made up of ribs glued to one-another. Lute players must have had to be particularly careful to avoid prolonged high humidity, and in such weather conditions, having the lute kept in a room with a continuous fire in it would have been advisable. This tended to limit its location to more affluent environments. Thus, in spite of it respectability, it was usually played only by professionals in aristocratic employment and their amateur students.

Harps were basically made of three pieces of wood assembled in a distorted triangle: a resonator (usually hollowed out from the back, to which the strings were attached), a neck (which held the tuning pegs) and a column (which held the resonator and neck apart against the tension of the strings). These components were all plugged together so that the tension of the strings between the resonator and the neck held the instrument together. In the rotta, which was more accurately triangular, there were two arms, and set in (and clamped by the string tension) between them were one or two soundboards. A column was occasionally plugged into the ends of the two arms (completing the triangle) to help counter the force of the strings. There were no bridges on the soundboards.

The psaltery's soundboard also had no bridges. Its body was hollowed out of a plank of wood cut to the body outline, and the soundboard was set into the top of the space created. The tension of the strings between the two sides to which the strings were attached distorted the body enough to clamp the soundboard in place. On the rotta and psaltery, the tension of the strings slightly buckled the soundboard, and the variation in buckling resulting from the variation in tension due to the vibration of the strings was the main way that audible sound was produced.

The body of the cruit was usually also made of a plank of wood (often oak) cut to the body's outline, including the outer oval and the hole giving the left hand access to the strings. Then the lower part, plus some way up the arms on the sides of the hole, was hollowed out. A soundboard covered the hollowed-out regions to the edges of the body outline and was nailed to the body. Metal nails have been found (as have bridges of amber, bronze and bone or horn). We do not know whether wooden nails and bridges were usual because they would probably not have survived burial.

The fiddle's whole outline (including neck and peghead) was cut out of the plank, and then the body was hollowed out. There was a step cut out of the top of the body so that the top of the soundboard was flush with the top of the neck. The soundboard covered the whole outline below the step. The strings were attached to the tail end of the body in a variety of fashions (with or without a tailpiece), and in each, the string tension clamped the soundboard between that attachment and the step, keeping it in place. The string tension also pressed the bridge against the soundboard, keeping the soundboard pressed against the body. Wooden nails could have been used to help secure the soundboard to the body. When there was a separate fingerboard, it would have been attached to the neck by wooden nails. Some pictures show a tailpiece but no bridge. This could be because the bridge was under the end of the tailpiece, as seen in a few pictures. Then it is likely that the tailpiece was of some tough light material such as leather.

The rebec and gittern were made the same way as the fiddle. If the pegbox was seriously bent back, as with the lute, it was made of a separate piece of wood, rebated into the end of the neck and reinforced with a couple of nails into the end of the neck. When the gittern had a glued bridge, the glued joint was probably reinforced by wooden nails. The citole was made like the fiddle, with nails securing the soundboard against the body at corners where the bridge pressure was not effective for this. The protuberance at the tail aided the clamping of the soundboard against the step at the neck. The frets could have been wooden, set into slots in the fingerboard. As for the symphony, the pressure of the bridge on the soundboard couldn't hold much of it down because of the slot for the wheel cut out of the soundboard, so nails would seem to be what held the soundboard to the body.

Some general points about instrumental music

From the beginning, pitched vocalisation of words appears to have involved either song, which had much pitch movement, or chant, with little or no pitch movement. There was usually one voice involved, but when there was more than one, they were usually in unison. Probable alternatives were singing in heterophony (i.e. simultaneous sounding of the melody and a decorated version of it) and chanting in 4ths, 5ths or octaves. It is possible that the words were sometimes simultaneously sung and chanted. Eventually, a song could be sung in parallel organum (in 4ths, 5ths or octaves), and after that, in polyphony, with parallel 5ths and octaves avoided amongst the independent melodies.

The playing of instruments involved the same components, sounding sequences of pitches recognisable as singable melodies and/or chant-like drones. But in addition, they could play non-melodic sequences of notes, and they could produce percussive effects.

The main use of instruments was to accompany the voice. The more lofty the song's subject matter, the less likely it would have instrumental accompaniment. When there was instrumental involvement, there is evidence for the voice and instrument often sounding alternatively, the instrument providing interludes or punctuation. Duplicating the melody heterophonically and providing drones while singing is probable. The music for dancing was usually sung, especially on refrains (with or without instrumental involvement) rather than played purely on instruments. There is occasional evidence of instruments playing together, but none that they purposely complemented each other. The concept of an instrumental ensemble with each performing a different function had not yet been developed.[101] The many medieval pictures showing a variety of instruments being played in a religious context are better interpreted as each independently praising God than evidence of ensemble playing.

---

[101] These are my conclusions, mainly from the evidence presented by Page in *Voices and Instruments.*

In this period, there was no clear objective of imitating the voice in instrumental playing, so an instrumental melody need not have been the tune of a song, and could be any sequence of notes. There is much evidence for the playing of melodies with the accompaniment of one or more drones on all kinds of stringed instruments. This seems to have been the most common style. There is also some evidence for the performance of parallel organum. Providing a drone accompaniment to parallel organum was possible on many instruments but not specifically indicated. There is no direct evidence that vocal polyphony was played on instruments, either individually or in combination. There is evidence of occasions when multiple instruments played together, when it probably was in unison or organum plus drones.

Instruments were played by people of high status, and by professional entertainers of low status. Some of the latter were music specialists while others, beside singing and playing, told stories, did magic tricks, tumbled, danced, threw knives, juggled, etc. There were also professional musicians of intermediate status rather permanently employed by noble patrons. Except for the rare instrument specialist who was not a singer, there would have been no need to play the instrument in a way that is obviously beyond what ordinary people would imagine that they could readily do themselves with a bit of practice (which today is a necessary badge of professionalism). Just hearing an instrument being played was a privilege.

The Development of Western European Stringed Instruments

Chapter 4: Developments in the 15th century

General points, including developments on the harp, lute and gittern

A major change in music during the 15th century was the extension downwards of the pitch range. In vocal music, the contratenor parts were previously in the same range as the tenor, often extending somewhat beyond the tenor in both directions. The contratenor then split into two parts, one that sang in a range between the tenor and descant, which became the alto, and the other in a range below the tenor, which became the bass. The bass range had not previously been fashionable in music. Organs increased their ranges as well as including many more chromatic notes. Many new harps were bigger and the number of strings increased to about two dozen. The earlier 4-course lutes could be seen in the pictures up to the 1470s, but 5-course lutes appeared around 1430, spreading rapidly, and 6-course lutes appeared around 1475 and largely replaced the 5-course type by 1500. In the second half of the century, many gitterns expanded to 5 courses. There were difficulties in expanding such small instruments to 6 courses because, according to the Table at the end of Chapter 1b, an open-string range of two octaves with octave-paired lowest course gets to the edge of acceptability when the string length gets to as small as 41 cm, Some gitterns were made bigger, and were made like small lutes. When 6-course lutes became standard around 1500, the gittern of original size couldn't keep up its role as miniature lute and mostly went out of fashion.

The 15th century also saw the beginning of professional instrument making and string making. Increased trade made it possible for them to have enough customers to work full-time in their specialisms. We can expect that with such specialisation, average quality increased.

Another major change was the growth of playing vocal polyphony on instruments. Previously, there was probably some improvised polyphony, perhaps between the melody on the instrument and the voice being accompanied, but there is no evidence before the 15th century that instruments imitated vocal polyphony in performance. In this century, keyboard instruments (including the new harpsichord and clavichord) played all parts of vocal polyphony on one instrument, while some other instruments formed pairs to play the popular vocal polyphony (mainly Burgundian chansons). Popular pairs were gittern or harp & lute in the first half of the century, and two lutes in the second half. The lead instrument played a florid version of the descant part while the accomplice (called *tenorista* in Italy) played the other parts. The tenorista's lute then tended to have frets and to have been played with the fingers rather than with the usual quill. By the end of the century, some lute players (particularly Germans) were playing 4-part polyphony with fingers on a single fretted lute.

New types of fiddles, including those influenced by the lute

The second half of the fifteenth century saw the lute replace the harp as the most respected plucked instrument, and replace the fiddle as the most respected stringed instrument. Many fiddles and crowds continued as before.   Other fiddles, particularly those with three and five strings, equipped themselves to play polyphony in groups by acquiring bridges high enough to be curved (with fingerboards wedged to bring them to the strings), so that when bowed near them, individual notes could be played without sounding others.[102] These could be called 'vocal' fiddles.   Tinctoris was particularly impressed by the playing of many songs by two Flemish brothers, one playing the treble part and the other the tenor.   The smaller rebec was similarly equipped.   An Italian poem of c. 1420 by Prudenzani mentioned the playing of a *ribecche,* a *rubechette* and a *rubecone* in part songs.[103] This is the earliest example I know of when different sizes of the same instrument played together this way. Some fiddles continued as before but took on superficial lute characteristics such as body shape[104], or a lute-like angled-back straight pegbox[105].

We occasionally see a new kind of construction method on some normal fiddles of the time, where (as before) the sides were carved from the same piece of wood as the neck and peghead, but the back, as well as the soundboard, was attached afterwards.   This was an intermediate body construction method between the usual medieval 'carved' one and the usual Renaissance 'built-up' one of having separate sides bent to shape, and a separate neck, all assembled with the soundboard and back with glue.   The 'built-up' method was probably originally derived from the lute, which was made with a separate pegbox and neck, with the body made of bent staves glued together.

Another 15th century multi-purpose fiddle innovation involved a body with a step on the top near the maximum width, with two soundboards and alternative bridges for playing on each.   One soundboard, below the step was arched, and on it could be a high curved bridge for single-string bowing.   The other soundboard was flat, a continuation of the fingerboard, and on it could be a low flat bridge near the step, for multiple-string bowing[106].   High bridges, both curved and flat, started appearing on other fiddles then.   Players before the baroque were much more flexible about bridges than in recent times, gladly moving bridges up and down the soundboards to play at different pitches, exchanging types of bridges for different types of bowing and removing them when the instrument was not being played.

Some fiddle-bodied instruments were strung and played like small lutes.   Italian ones were just called **viola**, and similar French instruments were called *demi-luth*.[107]   A Spanish version, called **vihuela** was a dual-purpose instrument, both plucked and bowed.   It had lute stringing (9 strings in 5

---

[102] J. Tinctoris, *De Inventione et Usu Musicae* (c. 1487), trans. A. Baines, 'Fifteenth-century Instruments in Tnctoris's *De Inventione et Usu Musicae', Galpin Soc. J.* III (1950), pp. 19-26.

[103] Cited in Baines, A, *The Oxford Companion to Musical Instruments* (OUP, 1992), p. 279.

[104] for example, see one of Augostino di Duccio's angel musician reliefs from the Tempio Malatestiano at Rimini. Reproduced in *The World of Musical Instruments* (Hamlyn, 1972), p. 32, by A. Kendall.

[105] for example, see the Psalter in the Arsenal Libr,. Paris; a drawing of which is in H. Panum, *The Stringed Instruments of the Middle Ages*, trans. by Pulver (Reeves, London 1940, repr. 1971), Fig. 336, p. 387.

[106] One of these survives in the Corpus Domini Convent, Bologna, as a relic of Saint Caterina de' Vigri (1413-1463). Described by M. Tiella, *Galpin Society Journal* XXVIII (1975), pp. 60-70 and XXXI (1975), p. 146. A larger example is on a carving on a corbel at All Saints church at Broad Chalke, Wiltshire, shown as Plate 60 of J.& G. Montagu, *Minstrels and Angels* (Fallen Leaf, 1998), p. 28, and as Plate 117 of M. Remnant, *English Bowed Instruments* (Oxford 1989).

[107] J. Tinctoris, op cit.

courses). Except for waist cutouts, it essentially had a normal shallow flat fiddle-shaped body. But it had an elongated neck to take about 10 tied frets (as can be estimated from the depictions, this resulted in a string stop of about half a metre). Such a long neck suggests that the melody was mostly played on the top string. The waist cut-out in the body had sharp corners. This characteristic was new on a musical instrument. It gave the vihuela the resonance of a wider instrument with the bowing advantage of a narrower one. If the waist cut-out (where the bow is located in the pictures) had been near the bridge, the end strings could have been bowed without sounding others, but the bridge was located low on the soundboard so that bowing was well into the second fifth of the distance between bridge and nut. Then the melody could be played only on the end strings (the first string and the octave string on the 5th course) if bowing was very light, but with stronger bowing, adjacent courses sounding as well.[108]

At the common lute tunings in fourths with a third somewhere in the middle and octave-pair 5th, the end strings would be tuned a fifth apart, like on the *rebab* (the Moorish rebec). A possible alternative tuning that might have been easier for bowers would be if the top string was tuned up a tone, the lowest course dropped a minor third, and the tuning of the others appropriately adjusted, giving alternating fourths and fifths over two octaves, and the end strings would be an octave apart. The end melody strings would sound more prominently if they had higher tensions that the others.

The vihuela was probably developed by Moorish musicians who played the *rebab*, who thus contributed the vertical (neck upwards) holding position when bowed. This position also facilitates playing in high positions since the left hand doesn't support the instrument. The bridge was like that of a lute, low and flat, and glued to the soundboard. Internally, it probably had cross-bars glued under the soundboard on each side of the rose, as was the case with its lute progenitor and its guitar descendants.[109] Henri Arnout von Zwolle wrote a thesis around 1440 giving construction diagrams of the lute and various keyboard instruments, and he consistently showed bars bracketing roses, as if there was a principle that bars had to compensate for the weakening of soundboards by roses.

None of the early vihuelas survive, so we can not be sure about their construction method, but it is very likely that the multi-purpose vihuela was amongst the earliest 'built-up' fiddle-bodied instruments. When the sides of an instrument are carved, to preserve strength, they need to be thicker wherever the outline shape is at a large angle to the grain direction of the wood it is carved from. This increased thickness adds to the weight, and such regions around the points of the waist cut-outs (which the vihuela pioneered) would add a considerable amount. This can be avoided by the 'built-up' construction method. Spanish instrument makers specified this method in their training. Their guild examination rules from 1502 onwards required the construction of a vihuela assembled from many pieces of wood glued together (often in decorative patterns).[110]

The built-up construction method and waist cutouts of this instrument[111] were the origin of these

---

[108] These deductions come from practical experience with a copy I had made.
[109] E. Segerman, 'Speculations on the Renaissance viol, the ubiquity of soundholes bracketed by bars, and the history of soundposts', *FoMRHI Quarterly* 12 (July 1978), Comm. 136, pp. 20-4.
[110] J. M. Ward, *The Vihuela de Mano and its Music* (1953), New York University PhD Dissertation, Music, p. 4.
[111] An excellent collection of information on and illustrations of this instrument is in I. Woodfield, *The Early History of the*

characteristics on most later bowed and plucked instruments.

The demise of the lute in Spain

Towards the end of the 15th century in Spain, the Inquisition went to great lengths to eliminate all non-Christian aspects of society (as they defined it, just like radical religious fundamentalists try to do today when they get political power). The lute was still mostly played by Moorish musicians and as it was a conspicuous remnant of Arab culture in the country, public performance on it was greatly discouraged. Banning of the lute was partially successful in the Italian dominions of Spain (Tinctoris wrote that the *viola* was played more than the lute in the Italy he knew, but that was only temporary since the lute had long lost its Arab associations there, with an ancient Greek origin claimed). Though Moorish musicians were involved in the development of the vihuela, it probably was played mainly by Christian nobles (who probably were the models for the surviving pictures), so the plucked vihuela was able, in the next century, to take over the role of the lute in the musical culture.

Trumpet marine (and harp brays)

The trumpet marine was another 15th century innovation, probably inspired by the monochord. It was a tapering long thin wooden box of three or 4 sides, one being the soundboard[112]. A single gut string was bowed near the nut, between the nut and the finger. The finger touched the string at whichever node of the harmonics of the string's vibration that the player wanted to sound. The purpose of the finger is to inhibit the vibrations of modes that don't have a node at the finger position while keeping absorption of the energy of the modes with nodes there to a minimum. This is best accomplished by keeping the amplitude of the vibration to a minimum by making the string tension high. Thus one should use a low-twist string as thick as one can get. Since it only played harmonics, its notes were only those of the natural trumpet. To get a sound similar to that of the trumpet, the string was balanced over one foot of the bridge in such a way that the other foot was suspended very close to, but not actually touching the soundboard. Then when the string vibrated, that second foot rattled against the soundboard. The rattling sound was enhanced by attaching surfaces of very hard materials (metal or ivory) to the bridge foot and to the soundboard where they hit. This harmonious rattling idea probably came from a development on the harp of the time, where each string almost touched a bray that stuck out from the soundboard near where it was attached, and the resulting rattling when the string was plucked enhanced its sound. On the trumpet marine, one or more added strings could be added on the same surface of the instrument as the melody string, sounding sympathetically. Versions of the marine trumpet were played in every century to the 18th. French 18th century ones were large, with a very thick gut melody string (over 4 mm diameter) and dozens of identically-tuned sympathetic metal strings stretched inside the body cavity.

Viol (CUP, 1984).

[112] A good description was given in H. Glarean, *Dodecachordum* (Basle 1547), I:xvii. Praetorius quoted it extensively.

Cetra

The cetra was a revival of the citole in Italy that appeared around 1425. As with the clavichord and harpsichord, it exploited the new availability of iron wire for strings. It was a rival to the lute for the mantle of the original ancient Greek stringed instrument, a conceit that it inherited from the citole which had long claimed the appropriate pedigree. According to Tinctoris (c. 1490)[113], it was played with a quill, had four courses and was tuned: tone, tone, fourth and back a tone. That tuning implies five courses, and most writers have assumed that an extra tone was given at the beginning as a mistake. That is possibly the cause for the discrepancy, but another possibility is that he was giving the tuning of the less common 5-course instrument, with some course (probably the first one mentioned) omitted on the 4-course instrument.

Having intervals of only a tone and a fourth between neighbouring courses relates this tuning to that of the citole. The overall open-string tuning range of a fifth or sixth is possible with iron stringing alone, and this option is a possible reason for the restricted range, though Tinctoris mentioned an option of stringing in brass as well.

Tinctoris was ambiguous about whether the stated intervals started upwards or downwards. This ambiguity could have been inadvertent (he knew what he meant) or perhaps deliberate, where both interpretations were valid. Making the usual medieval assumption that the lowest note was *G* (Gam ut), and assuming Tinctoris's first 'tone' was not relevant for the usual 4-course instrument, the tunings were *G A d c* if it was upwards, or *A G c d* if it was downwards. It can be described as two pairs of tone-apart courses, separated by a fourth in the centre, and in the first of these tunings the highest of each pair is inside, adjacent to the fourth interval, and in the second tuning, the lowest of each pair is inside. Another way of viewing this tuning is that there is an inside pair and an outside pair of courses. The courses within each pair are a fourth apart. In the first tuning, the outside pair is a tone lower than the inside pair, and in the second tuning, the outside pair is a tone higher than the inside pair.

The first of these tunings is the earlier citole tuning with the first course dropped a fifth. The second of these relates to later 16th century cittern tunings, since the tone between the first and second courses is the same way around. It is the tuning of the iron and copper pairs of strings in the French cittern tuning if we reversed treble to bass direction, i.e. *A G c d* is raised an octave and a tone to *b' a' d' e'* and reversed to *e' d' a' b'* and the courses doubled. Then the remaining two strings of the French cittern were an octave-lower twisted *e* to go with the *e'* pair and a twisted *d* to go with the *d'* pair, resulting in the early French renaissance tuning of *ee'e' dd'd' a'a' b'b'*.

The body depth of the cetra usually tapered, so it was noticeably deeper at the neck end than at the tail end. This feature was not uncommon amongst citoles (the sole surviving citole, from Warwick Castle and now in the British Museum, has this feature). The cetra had distinctive wooden blocks as frets (like the Chinese pipa), but they extended well beyond the neck on the 'bass' side, probably fitting into slots in the neck. There were usually small spaces between the fret blocks. When the wood was

---

[113] J. Tinctoris, op cit.

worn from pressing the metal strings on it, it is likely that a bit was sawn off the end and it was pushed that much further into the slot, providing unworn surfaces to press the strings against. There has been no other explanation offered for the arbitrarily uneven lengths of these blocks on the 'bass' side, as seen in many of the illustrations. Those blocks constrained the left thumb to remaining behind them, rather than sticking up on the bass side of the neck, as was usual with other stringed instruments with fingerboards at that time.

With about seven blocks per octave, the stopping positions appear to be diatonic. It is likely that the positioning of the tones and semitones for each course was created by how the tops of the blocks were shaped (the staircase arrangement reported by some modern writers[114] is an optical illusion that is easily disproved by laying a straight-edge along the treble edge of the fingerboard[115]). The surface acting as a fret would have been gently curved to spread the wearing forces as widely as possible, and the highest part of the curve was the effective fret position. It is possible that the sequence of blocks was changed when playing in different modes.

If the effective fret position was on a gentle curve, the vibrating string would most probably slap against the part of the curve past the effective position towards the bridge, causing a buzz. A buzzing sound was in fashion then since harps at that time usually had brays. It was still fashionable for lutes early in the 16th century since the Capirola lute book[116] said that one sets the action of the strings over the frets low enough to make the lute sound like a harp.

The depictions show small cetras with 4, 5, and 6 strings.[117] On one 6-string cetra, the string spacings were grouped with three strings together on the 2nd course, with the other courses single. A possible reason for this could be that the 2nd course had brass strings, and since brass strings break much more often than iron ones, there was safety in numbers. Another possibility is that the 2nd course involved octave stringing. There were large ones with 9 strings.[118] On one, there was a single first course with the rest doubled. On another, all strings were depicted with equal spacing.

By the end of the 15th century the cetra had ceased to be fashionable and was, according to Tinctoris, mainly 'played by rustics to accompany light songs and to lead dance music'. A few decades earlier, it had the highest of reputations. A few decades later, with modifications, it was back in fashion.

Psaltery and dulcimer

The pig-snout-shaped psaltery illustrated by Memling had shorter octave strings for many of the lower courses. These strings were attached to pins in the soundboard which probably extended into a

---

[114] e.g. Wright, 'Citole' entry, *The New Grove Dictionary of Musical Instruments* (1984), p. 379, and the drawing on p. 40 of Baines's *European and American Musical Instruments* (1966).

[115] E. Segerman, 'Cetra fret blocks', *FoMRHI Q* 11 (Apr. 1978), Comm. 125, pp. 55-6.

[116] Capirola Lute Book (c.1517).

[117] E. Winternitz, Musical Instruments and their Symbolism in Western Art (London, 1967), Plates 4, 5, 13b.

[118] E. Winternitz, ibid, Plates 13b, 53a.

curved bar attached under the soundboard. The apparent shape of the bar conforms to the principle of bars located to bracket sound holes. After the 15th century, this design of psaltery fell into disfavour, and psaltery playing continued mainly as an alternative way of playing the dulcimer.

The dulcimer was another development that exploited the new availability of strong iron wire for strings, which were hit by a beater or hammer in each hand. It started to appear in the pictures around 1440. In western Europe it was called by names related to dulcimer (derived from *dulce melos*, meaning 'sweet sound'), in Germanic lands it was called *hackbrett* (meaning chopping board), in eastern Europe it was called *timpanum* or *cimbalum*, and in some Latin areas it went by normal psaltery names (when the psaltery dropped out of serious use in the 16th century).

In the 15th century, there were not much more than a half-dozen strings, and bridges near each end of the soundboard were under each string. The usual shape was the trapezoidal psaltery one. The other shape was an elongated rectangular box with uniform string length, derived from the monochord. This instrument was used for other purposes. With thick gut strings hit with a beater, it became a type of string drum. With frets under some of the strings, it became a type of fretted psaltery or zither, subsequently popular as a folk instrument.

Early in the 16th century, a bridge system that subsequently became rather standard was developed for dulcimers with the trapezoidal shape. Half the strings went over the bass bridge on one side and went through holes in the other (treble) bridge on the other side, while the other half of the strings went through holes in the bass bridge and went over the treble bridge and then on to the other side. The treble bridge was usually placed so that each string could produce two notes, that on one side a fifth higher than the other. The number of strings that sounded in unison in a course became two or more (but it rarely went over a half-dozen), and the number of courses increased to over a dozen on each bridge.

The Development of Western European Stringed Instruments

Chapter 5:   The development of liras and sets of viols

Lira da braccio and lira da gamba

During the last decades of the 15th century, the Italians revived the fiddle with a bourdon and called it the *lira* (the 'da braccio' was not yet needed for specification) It was cultivated by an intellectual elite who mainly used it for accompaniment of solo singing or recitation of epic and other poetry, emulating the ancient Greeks. Playing probably included instrumental interludes. Initially it had 5 strings including the bourdon, but from around 1500 most new ones acquired octave strings for the 4th and 5th courses. Since seven was 'known' to be the number of strings on the classical lyre, this supported its claim, rivaling that of the lute, of being the embodiment of the ancient Greek instrument that was the ancestor of all stringed instruments.

The early 5-string liras differed from 14th century bourdon fiddles mainly by having a much higher bridge, allowing the 1st string to be played independently, and giving a greater volume of sound. The fingerboard was wedged and the bridge was flat or almost so (with a bowing clearance angle per string at the bridge of less than 2 degrees[119]). Some may have had an alternative round-topped bridge for playing a single line in polyphony when it was trying to be modern and vocal rather than antique. Body construction was often of the type intermediate between being carved and built-up, with both the soundboard and back conspicuously sticking out where they were glued onto the sides (that were carved from the same piece of wood as the neck and peghead). Fully carved construction was still common. One sometimes sees the peghead design that became a signature of liras, which had a rounded lower part and a pointed upper part. In most later cases, the top of the point was cut off square.

The tuning for the 7-string lira, as given by the Pesaro ms[120], was *dd'/gg' d' a' e"*, with the symbol / separating the off-fingerboard and on-fingerboard strings. We can deduce the possible range of vibrating lengths from the Table of gut string ranges in Chapter 1. The relevant factors are that the Italian corista pitch standard was essentially the same as Praetorius's Chorthon, the highest string was e", and the lowest string was a high-twist *d* of an octave pair. The Table gives us 37 cm as the maximum length of the highest string and 41 cm for the minimum length of the lowest string. These lengths actually are typical of what we measure from the pictures (the lowest string didn't go over the nut, and was longer), indicating that the full range available was used. Then, larger instruments would have to be tuned lower and smaller ones higher than these nominal pitches at that pitch standard. The lira information in the Pesaro ms was written late in the 16th century, when pitch standards were well

---

[119] measured from several pictures with slight curvature. The geometry is presented in E. Segerman, 'Round bridges: the geometry of clearance angles', *FoMRHI Quarterly* 43 (April 1986), pp. 101-4. Relevant here is Section I. One measures c: the straight-line distance between the tops of the end strings and a: the distance between that line and the top of the middle string. If we call the number of strings n, we calculate the clearance angle per string from the formula $[2/(n-1)]\{arccos[(c^2-4a^2)/(c^2+4a^2)]$, which can be approximated by $455a/[c(n-1)]$ in degrees.

[120] transcribed in H. M. Brown, *Sixteenth-Century Instrumentation: The Music for the Florentine Intermedii* (AIM, 1973), pp. 223-5.

established. Thus the oddity that the first string was omitted in the lira music in the ms can possibly be explained by the lira of the music scribe having been larger than usual, so the top string didn't last long enough to be useful. Another possible explanation is that since the music was that for a beginner, the 1st string could have been taken off to simplify fingering when learning.

In 1533, Lanfranco[121] indicated what the intervals between strings in the lira tuning were, and they were the same as given in the Pesaro ms. Lanfranco named the 7 strings: *canto, sottanella, tenore, bordone acuto, bordone grave, basso acuto* and *basso grave*. Apparently, the early medieval implications of the string name 'bordone' being an off-fingerboard string had been lost by the 16th century, by which time it only meant the course between the *basso* (lowest) and the higher *tenore*. The only other report of a tuning for the lira was that of Praetorius, when the lira was of little more than antiquarian interest. His tuning was the same as in the Pesaro ms except that the highest string was at *d"* instead of *e"*. His lira was of normal size, and this difference might be explained by his expecting to tune it to his usual Cammerthon pitch standard, at which an *e"* top string wouldn't last while a *d"* would. Since the instrument was apparently only one for simple improvisation without an independent repertoire, a *d"* could well have been a common alternative.

Initially, the body shapes of liras varied greatly, but as the 16th century progressed, the standard Italian fiddle shape became most usual. Other fiddle characteristics were also adopted, such as a fully built-up construction and arched soundboard and back. The 7-string lira usually had a slightly curved bridge with a bowing clearance angle per string of about 3 degrees at the bridge[122], so that when bowed near the bridge one could have selected any three courses to bow simultaneously. If a chord had more notes, one had either to bow farther from the bridge or increase bow pressure. Alternatively, one could have arpeggiated the rest of the chord. If the Pesaro music was typical, the melody was the highest note in the chord.

The lira appears not to have been exported to other countries, and had limited popularity in Italy. I guess that reasons for this are that the lira was developed at the same time as the viols, and though the music that each could play was similar, the viols were chosen because they were easier to play, were attractively played at lower pitches, were more versatile, and that most people were more interested in being modern than pretending to be antique.

In the 1589 *Intermedii*, we first encounter the *lira da gamba* , otherwise known as *lirone perfetto, lirone doppia, lira grande* or *arciviolata lira*. Then the lira had to be distinguished from it by being called *lira da braccio*. Early in the 17th century, we can tell that the lira da braccio was no more in use since the lira da gamba started to be called 'lira' without the need of 'da gamba' to distinguish it.

The lira da gamba didn't play any individual voice consistently, being essentially a continuo instrument. It was generally of the size of a small bass viol. It had about a dozen strings, mainly tuned in a repeating sequence (from lowest to highest) of a rising fifth and a falling fourth. The bridge had

---

[121] G. M. Lanfranco da Terenzo, *Scintille di musica* (Brescia, 1533), p. 136-7.
[122] measured on an intarsia in the Louve dating from about 1515 attributed to Fra Vincenzo da Verona, reproduced in M. Pincherle, *Histoire Illustree de la Musique*, (Paris, 1959), p. 45.

very shallow curvature, with five or six strings bowed at one time being usual. To establish its *lira* credentials, it usually had an individualistic body shape, a leaf-shaped peg disk and a few off-fingerboard strings that could be plucked by the left thumb. An advantage it had was that it could offer bowed chords in any key with equal facility. Disadvantages were that the fingering patterns were unique (with no transfer with other instruments), and continuing a melodic line (within the chords) to another string required skipping strings. This type of lira was used till the end of the 17th century. There is more evidence for its use outside Italy than in it.

From bowed vihuelas to viols and lironi in Italy

The Spanish bowed vihuela was a soloistic 9-string fiddle continuing the old medieval traditions in many ways. The bowing, at the waist cut-out, which was far from the bridge, gave it a humming kind of bowed sound with little dynamic range. The end strings could have been played without sounding others if played very quietly, but normally several courses played simultaneously with the bow angled into the waist cut-out, and all five courses sounded if the bow was parallel to the soundboard. If the end strings were at a higher tension than the other strings, the melody would be stronger and the other strings much weaker. The vihuela differed from the older fiddles in that its usual tuning was likely to have been in fourths (with probably a third in the middle), its frets and long neck allowed a variety of chords (chords with thirds in them were acceptable by then) in different inversions to follow the melody up and down the 10-fret fingerboard. This suggested left-hand technique was very similar to that for the strummed baroque guitar a century later.

It makes considerable sense to list the steps in transforming this instrument into the later viol roughly in chronological order:

1) Bigger sizes than the original (with a string length of about half a meter) were made, and they played in pairs.

2) The players were given the freedom to bow the end strings at a range of distances from the bridge, not just at the restricting waist cut-out. The Italian way to do this was by raising the bridge height, which would require the bridge to be moveable with string fixing at a tailpiece (a return to medieval fiddle practice). This usually was coupled with moving the bridge closer to the waist cut-out. To keep the action manageable, a fingerboard that extended over the soundboard was glued on the neck. The German way to vary where the strings were bowed was to elongate the waist cut-out.

3) Different sizes aggregated into sets for playing polyphony.

4) The number of strings was reduced to 6, usually in three courses.

5) The number of strings per course was reduced to one, leading to a total of five or six strings. This was made possible by making the bridge top curved enough to allow the top string of a chord to be on a string other than the first, like on the lira. This allowed a much greater range for the melody when

fingering in low positions.

6) The depth of the body was increased, usually leading to an upper-bout back fold that saves weight by keeping the original neck depth at the heel. This increased the resonance at low pitches.

7) Since the relatively long neck for high-position playing was no more needed, the body was made relatively larger at the expense of fingerboard length, reducing the number of frets tied on the neck from 10 to 6-8. This increased the soundboard resonance.

8) The soundboard was bent or carved into an arch. This could increase soundboard resonance since it could be thinner while being just as strong. It is likely that the cross-bars under the soundboard on both sides of the sound holes were still there, at least initially.

9) The curvature at the top of the bridge was increased to allow all strings to be bowed independently.

The evidence for these modifications mostly comes from Italy. Some Spanish influence there would be expected since the Kingdom of Aragon controlled southern Italy, including Naples and Sicily (as well as Sardinia), but a greater influence was in the Papal States. The patronage and nepotism of the Spanish Borgia Popes from 1455, especially in the time of the papacy of Alexander VI (Rodrego) from 1492 to 1503, created a large Catalan-speaking community in Rome.

The earliest evidence for larger vihuelas is from 1493, when there was a report of a pair of Spaniards from Rome playing vihuelas almost as large as people[123]. This is the first evidence for more than one vihuela playing together, and for vihuelas about double the size of the original ones, presumably tuned an octave lower. Performances by such pairs of bass-size vihuelas were popular in Rome for at least a decade.

Surviving pictures provide the earliest evidence for freeing the bowing from the waist cutouts and for the reduction to three courses. It appears that Ferrara, one of the Papal States, was at the forefront in experiments modifying the vihuela. An altarpiece dated 1497 by the Ferrarese artist Lorenzo Costa shows two normally proportioned vihuelas (with long necks) playing together, one of original string length of around 50 cm, and the other with a string length around 70 cm, intermediate between the original and double size ones.[124] The tail string fixing and a higher bridge allowed the bowing to be not at the waist cutout. This freed the body design to vary, and in this painting, the upper corner of the waist cutout was rounded away. The bridge was placed much higher on the soundboard than earlier vihuelas (the curvature of the bridge top is not visible). There were six strings grouped in three closely-placed double courses. The bow angle was far from being perpendicular to the strings, so the sound quality changed during a bow stroke.

A painting dated 1500 by Francesco Francia, a colleague of Costa, shows an intermediate-size

---

[123] I. Woodfield, *The Early History of the Viol* (C.U.P., 1984), p. 80.

[124] *Madonna and Child*, altarpiece by Lorenzo Costa in the Church of San Giovanni at Bologna, reproduced as Fig. 53 in Woodfield, op. cit., p. 88.

viol of similar proportions and stringing, playing with a lute.[125]   It had a very novel body shape, narrow on the bottom half between the knees, and wider above. Bowing was in the middle of the string. These three vihuelas were simplified versions of the original ones since they played chords with the melody on top of only three courses.

The earliest clear evidence for different sizes playing polyphony together involves Alfonso d'Este, son of the Duke of Ferrara[126], who in 1499 ordered the making of five *viole da archo*, and by 1502 he played in a group of six *viole* in the festivities celebrating his marriage to Lucrezia Borgia. Since these instruments were called viols then, we shall call them viols as well (from about 1503, the name often used was *violoni*, meaning large *viole*, to distinguish them from the small ones, the new set of fiddles that were similarly developed from the vihuela). The six viols presumably included some of the original vihuela size, some of the double size and some of intermediate sizes. We shall call these sizes soprano, bass and contralto/tenor, the English equivalents of the Italian names used subsequently. It is likely that the viols in this set were 3-course ones similar to those depicted by Costa and Francia. This is the earliest evidence of a set of more than two viols playing together.

The earliest evidence for single courses is from Urbino, another Papal State, where a painting by Timoteo Viti dated from before 1505, shows a soprano viol with the same proportions as before but a more traditional body shape.[127] It had the wider neck for six single strings. There were two bridges depicted, a higher wider one with a slightly curved top (with about 4 degrees per string bow-clearance angle) and a lower narrower one with a flat top, probably for playing the six strings in three pairs, as in the Costa painting (the nut would probably have had alternative sets of notches in it for the two arrangements). The bridge with slightly curved top allowed the player to use strings other than the 1st for the melody, with the accompanying chord on lower strings. This is the same as the bridge of the lira. There is no evidence as to whether the viols or the lira had it first.

A wall painting dated 1505-8 by Il Garofalo in Ferrara shows a bit of the upper part of the body and the neck and peg box of a viol with five single strings.[128] Subsequent Italian viols had either five or six single strings.

The earliest evidence for a deeper body is a wall painting dated c. 1510 in Ferrara,[129] which shows a group of musical angels playing two bass viols, a large fiddle with the new vihuela shape (a waist cut-out with sharp corners), a large plucked viola and a large rebec. Each bass viol had six single strings, a slightly curved bridge top, the usual long vihuela neck, and it was bowed at about a third of the distance from bridge to nut. What is new here is that the body depth was about double that

---

[125] Madonna and Child, painting by Francesco Francia, now at the Hermitage, Leningrad, reproduced as Fig. 54 in Woodfield, op. cit., p. 89.

[126] W. F. Prizer, 'Isabella d'Este and Lorenzo da Pavia', *Early Music History* Vol. 2 (1982), p. 110.

[127] Madonna and Child, painting by Timoteo Viti, now at Brera, Milan, reproduced as Fig. 52 in Woodfield, op. cit., p. 86.

[128] wall painting by Il Garofalo in the Sala del Testoro of the Palaazzio di Ludovico il Moro at Ferrara, reproduced as Fig. 16 in M. Remnant, *Musical Instruments of the West* (Batsford, London, 1978), p. 31.

[129] The Coronation of the Virgin, wall painting by either Ludovico Mazzolino or Michele Coltellini at the Church of Santa Maria della Consolazione, reproduced as Fig. 42 in M. Remnant, op. cit, p. 54.

previously seen, like on later viols.

The earliest evidence for a longer body with a shorter neck is an intarsia at the Vatican dated c. 1510-1515,[130] which shows such a viol. This is a return to the proportions of medieval fiddles.

According to the evidence looked at until now, the changes had been quick (all within about two decades), universal (in Italy), complete and irreversible, as if they were driven by fashion with no competition from other fashions. The final two changes, arching of the soundboard and curving the bridge enough for individual-string playing, started in this same period, but flat soundboards on some viols continued till about the middle of the century, and the slightly curved bridge survived on the lirone type of viol (see below) well into the 17th century.

Concerning evidence for soundboard arching, it is not easy to be sure about whether the soundboard of a viol in a picture is arched. If it is viewed from near sideways and one can see the sound hole on the near side, but not on the far side, it is likely that an arch obstructed the view. This seems to be the case with the contralto/tenor viol in the 1497 Costa altarpiece, and with one of the two bass viols in the c. 1510 Ferrara wall painting. There is no evidence about arching in the other paintings discussed.

Evidence for a highly curved bridge is on the broken viol at the feet of Saint Cecilia in the painting by Raphael dated c. 1514.[131] It had a bridge with top curvature of well over 10 degrees per string, obviously for playing individual strings. This picture is a good example of how the apparent size of an instrument cannot be scaled relative to a person near it because the artist probably changed the size for symbolic purposes. As Woodfield wrote, 'the saint stands gazing at her vision of the celestial choir, while at her feet lies a pile of broken terrestrial instruments including a viol'.

I suggest that the disrespect for the viol in this painting was deliberately enhanced by the conspicuous highly-curved bridge, surprisingly still standing. The choice between a slightly and highly curved bridge was between playing the melody with and without chords beneath. The repertoire was most probably vocal music, greatly enlarged by the new availability of printed music books. Just playing the notes as indicated by the music would be appropriate for a beginner who couldn't finger chords or would not know which chords to use, but it would be looked down on by more advanced musicians. Playing the melody with the chords had always been the way that viols were played. It seems that with the growth in the complexity of single-line embellishment (division), as illustrated for recorder playing in Ganassi's *Fontegara* (1535),[132] did playing mostly single-line on the viol become respectable, and Ganassi could then write a method for the viol featuring it.[133]

In his viol method, Ganassi indicated that if one wanted to play in the fashion of the lira, a

---

[130] intarsia by Giovanni da Verona on one of the doors of the Stanze della Segnatura, repr. as Fig. 49 in Woodfield, op. cit., p. 84.

[131] Saint Cecilia, painting by Raphael, now in Pinacteca, Bologna, reproduced as Fig. 50 in Woodfield, op.cit., p. 85.

[132] S. di Ganassi del Fontego, *Opera intitulata Fontegara* (Venice, 1535).

[133] S. di Ganassi del Fontego, *Regulo Rubertina* (Venice, 1542) & *Lettione seconda* (Venice, 1543).

longer bow with slacker hair would work on a normal viol. Otherwise one could use a viol with flatter curvature on the bridge and fingerboard. He didn't call such a viol by any distinguishing name. When discussing origins, he claimed that Orpheus used a lira, an instrument like a viol, not a lute. Therefore he wrote that it would be preferable to call the viol a 'lirone', though most called it 'violone'.

From 1530 on, documents from Venice refer to *sonadori di lironi* (lirone players) using instruments with size names *sopran, falsetto, contralltto, tenor, basseto* and *bason*.[134] *Sonadori di violoni* were also mentioned. It is possible that *lironi* and violoni were synonyms in Venice, as Ganassi implied. Another possibility is that **lirone** mostly referred to the type of viol (or approach to tension of bow hair) described by Ganassi that specialized in playing chords with the melody, as the name 'large lira' implies. Supporting the hypothesis that there was such a distinction is the use of a lirone (size unspecified) in addition to viols to play in the 1565 Florentine *Intermedii*. What is most unlikely is that it was the same instrument as the **lira da gamba**, an instrument called for in the 1589 *Intermedii*, because there is no evidence that an instrument with this name ever came in different sizes that played together. In the 1568 edition of Giorgio Vasari's book on the history of art[135], he described a painting by Paulo Veronese[136] which includes what appears as a typical Italian bass viol of that time (of modern double bass size), which he referred to as a 'large lirone da gamba'[137]. Banchieri[138] wrote that the lirone and viola bastarda were special types of viols that needed much judgement in playing part music. Modern organologists have unfortunately usually considered that the *lirone* was the same instrument as the *lira da gamba*, apparently because both names imply a large lira.

Tunings of Italian viols in sets

In his 1533 book, Lanfranco[139] gave the earliest tunings for a set of Italian viols. All sizes had six strings in the relative tuning of the lute (fourths with a third in the middle) with the 6th string being *D* on the bass (with *E* as an alternative), *A* on the middle sizes, and *d* on the treble. Let us call these *D-A-d* and *E-A-d* sets. From what Ganassi later wrote, the alternative *E* bass was probably chosen when the instrument was not large enough to sound well an octave below the treble. A manuscript note that has been dated to 1536, found in the back of a published cookbook by M. Savonarola[140] gave viol set tunings ascribed to Alfonso della Viola. These were the *E-A-d* set for keys with *b* naturals and the *D-G-c* set, a tone lower, for keys with *b* flats. Going from one set of tunings for one key to the other set did not involve touching the tuning pegs - it was a matter of changing the assumptions made by the

---

[134] R. Baroncini 'Contributo alla storia del violino nel sedicesimo secolo: i <sonadori di violino> della Scuola Grande di San Rocco a Venezia', *Recercare* VI (Rome, 1994), Appendix A, pp. 136-185. The records of *sonadori de lironi* occur often from 1530 to 1622.

[135] G. Vasari, *Le Vite de piu eccellenti Architetti, Pittori, et Scultori Italiani...* (1568), ed. Milanese (Florence, 1906), VI, p. 373.

[136] P. Veronese, *Allegory of Music*, Palazzo Ducale, Venice, reproduced as Plate 6b in E. Winternitz *Musical Instruments and their Symbolism in Western Art* (Faber & Faber, London, 1967)

[137] E. Winternitz, op. cit. p. 55.

[138] A. Banchieri, *Conclusiono nel suono dell' organo* (Bologna, 1609), p. 69.

[139] G. M. Lanfranco, op. cit. p. 142.

[140] M. Savonarola, *De tutte le cose che se manzano comunamente* (Venice, 1515).

players of what pitches the strings were tuned to. Players usually do that anyway when they switch from one size to another.

In 1542-3, Ganassi made it clear that his only concern with pitch level was that it worked for the combination of viols available. He suggested that Gombert's advice in setting the pitch level of a choir applied to a set of viols. First priority was to avoid strain at the top of the treble. It is better that the bottom of the bass was a tone too low and just audible than the top of the treble was a semitone too high. Six-string viols, with two octaves of open-string range, had a quite critical relationship between pitch level and string length for avoiding excessive 1st string breakage and too poor focus in the sound of the high-twist gut 6th. On consulting the range limits table from Praetorius in Chapter 1b, we can see that there is no leeway if the string length was less than 73 cm. Smaller viols would have had to use thinner 6th strings than would be preferred to keep its sound full, producing less output than the other strings. Ganassi remarked that when assembling a set of viols, one could adjust the string length by how high or low on the soundboard the bridge was placed. There were limitations in this adjustment, and Ganassi's 'Regulos' were different sets of tunings that catered for these limitations.

Regulo 3 was used when the treble and bass could still not stretch to be an octave apart, so the tunings were each a fourth apart. This was also the case with the tunings of Alfonso della Viola and the alternative one of Lanfranco. Regulo 2 was when the middle sizes worked better a fourth above the bass than a fifth above it (as it was in Regulo 1). Each Regulo had three Ordines. The Ordines were the sets of pitches one assumed the strings of the viols were tuned to when reading the music, with the 1st when the key had no flats, the 2nd when it had one flat and the 3rd when it had two flats. Generally, Ordines 1 and 2 had the same tunings. The tunings of the 3rd Ordine were a tone lower than those of Ordines 1 and 2, This made the left-hand fingering the same as for the 1st, presumably to make the patterns of chording, ornamentation and division more familiar and easier because of the use of open strings. Alfonso della Viola used essentially the same system. Ganassi's alternative Regulo 3 1st Ordine set of assumed string pitches were all a tone higher than the normal one to avoid a treble tuning including an open-string b^b when there were no flats in the key.

In summary, Ganassi's 6-string sets for Regulo 1 were *D-G-d* in Ordines 1&2 and *C-F-c* in Ordine 3, for Regulo 2 they were *D-A-d* in Ordines 1&2 and *C-G-c* in Ordine 3, and for Regulo 3 they were *D-G-c* in Ordines 1&2, *E-A-d* in alternative Ordine 1 and *C-F-B^b* in Ordine 3.

Ganassi's Regulo 4 was a set of tunings for 5-string viols that he said most viol players used. The treble tuning was that of an *A* viol without the 6th (*d g b e' a'*), the middle sizes that of a *D* viol without the 6th (*G c e a d'*) and the bass was an octave lower than the treble (*D G B e a*). As described below, identical tunings for sets of 5-string viols were given in German sources from 1523 and 1532. A later Italian source from c. 1600 (Virgiliano) also gave the same tunings.[141]

Why were 5 strings the most popular? It is most likely that the majority of viol players wanted

---

[141] A. Virgiliano, *Il Dolcimelo* (c.1600), ms in the Civico Museo Bibliografico Musicale in Bologna. For a summary of its contents, see E. Segerman, 'Virgiliano on instruments and transpositions', *FoMRHI Quarterly* 97 (Oct. 1999), Comm. 1672. pp. 26-8.

to play their viols with other kinds of instruments, and they needed tuning leeway to be able to tune to a pitch level that was an easy transposition to get to the pitch level of instruments with less pitch flexibility, such as the lute, recorder and keyboards. Virgiliano gave tablature tables for transpositions for the low-clef set of up a tone, and for the high-clef set of down a tone, a minor 3rd, a 4th, a 5th, a major 6th and a minor 7th. From the table in Chapter 1b, we can see that the tuning leeway gained by having only five strings was a range of from 4 semitones for the treble viol to 7 semitones for the bass.

Ganassi also offered emergency tunings when only four strings were left with no available replacements, with *F A d g* for the bass, *c e a d'* for the middle sizes and *g b e' a'* for the treble. When only three strings were left, the tunings would be in fifths like the fiddles (*viole da braccio*), with *F c g* for the bass, *c g d'* for the middle sizes and *g d' a'* for the treble.

Ortiz[142] wrote that viols had six strings, used the *D-A-d* set of tunings, and also that they were tuned to the harpsichord. If viol sizes were the same as before, and the pitch names were the same on the viol and harpsichord, the harpsichord must have then been either very small or very big, tuned a fourth lower or fifth higher than usual. Lanfranco also reported the *D-A-d* set of viol tunings, saying that the tenor was tuned like the lute. He could well have just recorded the nominal pitches that players called their strings when reading music, and was unconcerned about absolute pitches. So when he gave only relative pitches for the strings of the fiddles and the lira, this could have only meant that the players of these instruments all played by ear, and though they may have had a name for each string, these names did not include pitch names.

Afterwards, tunings of 6-string viols in sets as given by Marinati (1587)[143], Ceretto (1601)[144] and Mersenne's (1636) Italian informant[145] were the same *D-A-d* set as those of Ortiz. But Zacconi (1592)[146], Banchieri (1609)[147] and Cerone (1613)[148], gave tunings of a *GG-D-G* set, all a fifth lower (Banchieri also included a fourth tuning, *DD* for a contrabass viol). The shift to lower nominal pitches made playing music in normal vocal clefs up a fifth on each instrument. What was different from earlier in the 16th century that induced the new tunings? One factor was the new availability of catlin (roped) gut bass strings, which gave the more respectable 6-string viols a pitch-range leeway similar to that had by the 5-string ones, making tuning adjustments possible that eased playing with other instruments at the increasingly-used corista pitch standard.

Following is a summary table of Italian tunings of viols in sets:

---

[142] D. Ortiz, *Trattodode glosas* (Rome, 1553).

[143] A. Marinati, *Somma di tutte le scienze* (Rome, 1587).

[144] S. Cerreto, *Della prattica musica* (Naples, 1601).

[145] M. Mersenne, *Harmonie Universelle* (Paris, 1636), Bk. IV, Prop. V.

[146] L. Zacconi, *Prattica di musica* (Venice, 1592).

[147] A. Banchieri, *Conclusioni del suono dell' organo* (Bologna, 1609).

[148] D. P. Cerone, *El Melopeo y Maestro* (Naples, 1613).

Reported Tunings of Italian Viols Played in Sets

Date	Source	Basso	Tenore & Contralto	Soprano	for keys
1533	Lanfranco	*D G c e a d'*	*A d g b e' a'*	*d g c' e' a' d''*	
	alternative bass	*E A d f♯ b e'*			
1536	ms add Savanarola bk	*E A d f♯ b e'*	*A d g b e' a'*	*d g c' e' a' d''*	with 0 flats
	(Alfonso della Viola)	*D G c e a d'*	*G c f a d' g'*	*c f b♭ d' g' c''*	with flats
1542	Ganassi Reg 1 Ord 1, 2	*D G c e a d'*	*G c f a d' g'*	*d g c' e' a' d''*	0 & 1 flat
	Regulo 1, Ordine 3	*C F B♭ d g c'*	*F B♭ e♭ g c' f*	*c f b♭ d' g' c''*	2 flats
	Regulo 2, Ordine 1, 2	*D G c e a d'*	*A d g b e' a'*	*d g c' e' a' d''*	0 & 1 flat
	Regulo 2, Ordine 3	*C F B♭ d g c'*	*G c f a d' g'*	*c f b♭ d' g' c''*	2 flats
	Regulo 3, Ordine 1, 2	*D G c e a d'*	*G c f a d' g'*	*c f b♭ d' g' c''*	0 & 1 flat
	alternative Ordine 1	*E A d f♯ b e'*	*A d g b e' a'*	*d g c' e' a' d''*	0 flats
	Regulo 3, Ordine 3	*C F B♭ d g c'*	*F B♭ e♭ g c' f*	*B♭ e♭ a♭ c' f' b♭'*	2 flats
	Regulo 4 (5 strings)	*D G B e a*	*G c e a d'*	*d g b e' a'*	
	if only four strings left	*F A d g*	*c e a d'*	*g b e' a'*	
	if only three strings left	*F c g*	*c g d'*	*g d' a'*	
1553	Ortiz	*D G c e a d'*	*A d g b e' a'*	*d g c' e' a' d''*	
1587	Marinati	*D G c e a d'*	*A d g b e' a'*	*d g c' e' a' d''*	
1592	Zacconi	*GG C F A d g*	*D G c e a d'*	*G c f a d' g'*	
c1600	Virgiliano	*D G B e a*	*G c e a d'*	*d g b e' a'*	
1601	Ceretto	*D G c e a d'*	*A d g b e' a'*	*d g c e' a' d''*	
1609	Banchieri	*GG C F A d g*	*D G c e a d'*	*G c f a d' g'*	
	DD GG C E A d	violone contrabasso			
1613	Cerone	*GG C F A d g*	*D G c e a d'*	*G c f a d' g'*	
1635	Mersenne's informant	*D G c e a d'*	*A d g b e' a'*	*d g c' e' a' d''*	

The simplest way to avoid problems of different kinds of instruments being able to play together is to choose a size that either observes the appropriate pitch standard or is an easy transposition to it. From around the middle of the 16th century, we see reference to *corista* as a pitch standard for normal voices and whatever instruments could play at without transposition. These were usually stringed instruments, flutes and mute cornets. There were local variations, but the usual pitch was about the same as Praetorius's preferred Chorthon, which was at about a' = 383 Hz.

At this standard, with roped-gut bass strings, the string length ranges (from the table in Chapter 1b) for the *D-A-d* set would be 63-82, 46-55 and 36-41 cm, and for the *GG-D-G* set they would be 88-123, 63-82 and 50-62 cm. The original viol sizes (from the vihuela) fit into the ranges of the *GG-D-G* set, and not into the *D-A-d* set. It is quite possible that some sets of viols or lironi were made smaller to play at corista. There is evidence for this happening in England, and later in France, but we have no evidence for this happening in Italy. If viols of original sizes assumed the *D-A-d* tunings were to play at corista, they would have to transpose, while if they assuming the *GG-D-G* set of tunings, they would be in corista, but the vocal ranges would lie on the higher strings. The *D-A-d* tunings were more appropriate for playing vocal music in the usual clef combinations, but the actual pitches would then have been lower than at corista.

Banchieri called his new *DD* viol *violone in contrabasso*, his *GG* viol *violone da gamba,* his *D* viol *viola mezzano da gamba*, and his *G* viol *quarta viola in soprano.* This illustrates a change in terminology from the early use of *violone* as any viol. The qualifying term *da gamba* or just the unqualified term *viola* replaced it to specify a normal viol in a set. The new use of the 'violone' term seems to have referred to the viol of original bass size that played at corista, with the *DD* viol a new larger version of it. The calculated string length range in corista for the *violone in contrabasso* is 111-164 cm. The evidence from Praetorius and the few surviving instruments is that it typically was about 125 cm. Both of these types of violones were extensively used as the continuo basses of 17th and 18th century fiddle ensembles. An increase in string tension for the violone to perform the role of continuo seems to be the reason for the change in terminology.

When a *contrabasso violone* was specified in 17th century Italian baroque music, there was no ambiguity about a *DD* tuning, but there could have been an ambiguity in the intended tuning if the specification was *contrabasso* without *violone*. The contrabass of a *D-A-d* set of viols was the *GG* viol, while that of the *GG-D-G* set was the *DD* viol. That ambiguity could have been deliberate if either would do. The range of the written music is not evidence of an intended choice since bass-instrument players then readily transposed phrases by an octave either for musical function or expression, or because it lay better on their instruments[149]. As with modern double basses, these instruments could be played high in their ranges as well as low, and Monteverdi's specification of *viola contrabasso* for an alto part in 'Altri canti d'Amor' in *Combattimento* should be taken seriously before rejecting it as an error.

The development of viols in Germany and their tunings

The earliest evidence of the viol in Germany is the woodblock of a *Gross Geigen* in Virdung's *Musica Getutscht* printed in 1511.[150] It shows the shallow body, nine strings, central soundboard rose and low flat glued lute-like bridge of the original vihuela. It differed from that vihuela in having an elongated waist cutout that allowed bowing of the end strings from a sixth to almost a half of the

---

[149] A. Agazzari, *Del sonare sopra il basso* (Rome, 1607), transl. into German by Praetorius in *Syntagma Musicum* III, p. 149, and into English by O. Strunk, *Source Readings in Music History - The Baroque Era* (New York, 1965), p. 69.
[150] S. Virdung, *Musica Getutscht* (Basle, 1511), p. B ij.

distance from the bridge to the nut. Also, the relative length of the neck was reduced to allow only 7 frets. At the original 10-fret neck length, the maximum bowing distance from the bridge (with Virdung's elongated waist) would be reduced to 1/3 of the bridge-nut distance. It seems that an increased range of bowing positions was more important to the players than keeping the original pitch range fingered on the fingerboard, probably because of the style of bowing.

From slightly later pictures, we can see that it is likely that the elongated waist was necessary because the most popular bowing style was with the bow tilted at around 45° from the strings. Since to sound the strings, the bow hair has to move perpendicular to the strings, at this angle, the position of the hair moves along the string during the bow stroke, and that position moves by about the same amount as the hair moves over the string.

In the transformation from original vihuela to viol, this instrument only relatively shortened the neck, and allowed different bowing distances from the bridge (done in a different way from the Italians). The original vihuela must have diffused to southern Catholic Germany and established itself as a highly respectable instrument before many of the changes made by the Italians.

When the Germans explored the alternative way of allowing a wider range of bowing positions on the viol by having a raised moveable bridge, and using single strings, like the Italians, they experimented with the new freedom in body design. Dated at c.1515, the famous Isenheim Altarpiece by Grünewald was an example of novel design.[151] The three viols shown in this painting were bowed in the middle of the strings, which has the same playing effect irrespective of whatever the bridge curvature was. The use of the deep waist cutout by the bow in the viol in the foreground allowed the end strings to be bowed without sounding any other.

The set of woodcuts by Hans Burgkmair in *The Triumph of Maximilian the Great* (c.1518) show several viols with 5 single strings with tail fixing of the strings, a moveable bridge and seriously angled bowing. The bowing ignored the waist cutouts, so the bridge must have been high enough to allow this. It was likely to have a slightly curved top so the melody (at least at the beginning of the stroke) could be on strings other than the end ones. There were no viols the size of a man, i.e. like the Italian bass.

The woodcut of a viol played with a lute in Judenkünig on the title page of his instruction book (1523) shows a similar viol, with a slightly curved bridge top, bowed at a serious angle.[152] The Munich ms 718 (1523)[153] gave three 5-string tunings in fourths with a third between the 3rd and 4th string, with the lowest strings at *D*, *G* and *d*. If the music went too high for these tunings (above the frets), the player was advised to assume higher tunings, with the lowest strings at *G*, *c* and *g*, which in essence transposes the music down a fourth on the instrument. Gerle (1532 and 1546)[154] gave the same tunings and advice, and also suggested that the bass could have a 6th string, tuned a tone below the 5th.

---

[151] M. Grünewald, *Isenheim Alterpiece*, now at the Grünewald Museum, Colmar

[152] H. Judenkünig, *Ain schone kunstliche unterweisung* (Vienna, 1523).

[153] Munich University Library (4° Cod. ms. 718) compiled by Jorg Welzell in 1523-4.

[154] H. Gerle, *Musica Teusch* (Nuremberg, 1532) & *Musica und Tabulater* (Nuremberg, 1546).

In 1528, Agricola published his first book on instruments.[155] The tunings he first gave were for a set having a 6-string bass with mean lute tuning (fourths with a third in the middle, with a *G* lowest string), 5-string middle sizes with the tuning of the bass without the lowest string, and a 5-string smallest size with the tuning of the middle sizes without the lowest string and an added *c'* on top. He then gave tunings of a set of 4-string viols or fiddles, with the string pitches of the bass and middle sizes the same as the four lowest of the first set, and those of the smallest size an octave higher than the bass. For this second set, he provided drawings of the four sizes which show the same design as the Virdung instrument, with the only significant difference being in the number of strings. This shows that the German version of the technique of playing the original vihuela was still highly regarded.

In the 1545 second edition of Agricola's book, the same set of drawings of four 4-string instruments were included. The tunings given were for a 5-string bass and other sizes with 4-strings. They were based on that of a treble lute (with an *A* lowest string) and a bass lute (with a *D* as the lowest string). The tuning for the bass was the four lowest strings of the treble lute plus a low *F* as the 5th, with an alternative being the five lowest strings of the bass lute but with the *D* 5th up to *F*. The middle sizes were tuned to the top four strings of the bass lute. The smallest size tuning was that of the top four strings of the treble lute, with an alternative being an octave higher than the middle sizes. Because of this large interval, the alternative treble was probably not involved in playing the usual part music of vocal origin in sets of viols, and was likely a soloistic viol.

A woodblock after the title page of Agricola's 2nd edition, entitled *Fraw Musica,* shows a woman playing a tenor lute, and in the background is a harp and a 4-string viol with tail string fixing and a moveable bridge with a clearly curved top. His drawings in the text may well represent a design that was most respected in his circle, but *Fraw Musica*'s viol could have represented what was also very popular. All the publishing activity for amateurs at the time could suggest that single-line playing using round-topped bridges would have been common by then.

The tuning diagrams of the viols had notes next to some frets indicating common pitches with the highest and lowest strings of a lute (*testudo acuta* & *gravis*) and the middle string of a cittern (*cithara media*). From this, we can tell that the bass viol could not have been much bigger than the lute. Lutes came in various sizes, but referring to a lute without size specification meant a particularly common lute, which we would expect be smaller than a bass. Thus Agricola's set of mostly 4-string viols was probably about 60 or 70% of the sizes of the Italian viol sets.

The 1546 Gerle edition mentioned above (I haven't seen a copy of the 1532 edition) was intended for young beginners, and it says clearly that one should bow only one string at a time, so the bridge top would then have been curved enough to allow this. He wrote that one should 'draw the bow straight and level on the strings at a place not too far from or too near to the bridge on which the strings lie'. There was no angled bowing here, as that would lead to bowing more than one string as the hair got far enough from the bridge during a long stroke. Gerle included woodcuts of a 5- and a 6-string

---

[155] M. Agricola, *Musica instrumentalis deudsch* (Wittenberg, 1529).

viol on which were shown the string names and tablature symbols on the neck. No bridges were shown, possibly because there was no room after the string names were written, or possibly because it was common to take the bridge out when a viol is not being played.

We have no tuning information on German viols in the second half of the century, but inventories testify to their continued popularity. Some of the pictures show quite large 4-string bowed instruments playing in ensembles with winds and treble fiddles.[156] The bowing was strongly angled. To modern eyes, they look like viols. There had been no German 4-string bass viols mentioned since 1528 (Agricola), and none so large, so it is probable that the pitch intervals between strings were fifths, and these were bass fiddles, equivalent to the French *basse de violon*. The modern association of right-angled waist corners and C holes with viols and sharper waist corners and f holes with fiddles is a poor indicator of historical identity. It is likely that the Germans just called them by the conveniently ambiguous term *grosse geigen*.

By Praetorius's time (1619), the acceptable lower limit to the open-string range had expanded with roped-gut strings, so 6-string tunings conforming to the pitch standard became easy if the standard was the usual one in France, England, Italy and south Germany, where the vast majority of viols were made. At that standard, the very fashionable English small *D-G-d* set at about 80, 60 and 40 cm string lengths, and the large Italian *GG-D-G* set at about 100, 80 and 60 cm string lengths, were all near as high in their ranges as they could be. But the pitch standard in north Germany, where Praetorius wrote, was a tone higher. Those instruments could not tune up to these pitches at this standard. Praetorius solution was to use the fashionable small English set of viols and tune them at the bottoms of their ranges, getting as close to the tuning of the large Italian set as possible. The result was a *GG-D-A* set.

All of Praetorius's tunings for viols need to be explained. Tunings labeled 3 and 4 for each size in his table of tunings were just reports of Agricola's 1528 tunings, and those labeled 5 were reports of Ganassi's emergency 3-string tunings in fifths. Tunings 1 and 2 were for Praetorius's own sets. The usual bass of his set was called *klein bass*, and three tunings were given for his tuning 1. One was the basic *GG* tuning, another was a *GG* viol with the 4th string down a semitone (to *E),* and the other (for a smaller bass) was an *AA* viol. Tuning 2 was a *FF^#* viol all in fourths. The set of viols Praetorius illustrated had double purfling, a characteristic of the vast majority of English viols and rare amongst non-English viols (except for later French and German viols made to look like English viols). At that time, English viols, players and repertoire were considered to be the leaders in Europe. The illustrated bass, with a string stop of 75 cm, was more than a fret-length shorter than the optimum of 82 cm (it could have been made as a solo bass or the second bass of a set), and was probably tuned to the *AA* alternative by Praetorius. The string stop of the tenor was 58 cm, and that of the treble was 40 cm.

Praetorius also mentioned a *gross bass* or *violone*. The tunings given were of a 5-string *EE* viol all in fourths, a normal 6-string *DD* viol and a 6-string *EE* viol all in fourths. The example illustrated had 6 strings and a string stop of 103 cm, which fits either of the 6-string tunings. Finally, a 5-string

---

[156] e.g. woodcuts by Jost Amman in *Ehebrecherbrücke des Königs Artus,* reproduced in *A History of Music in Pictures* ed. G. Kinsky (1930) p. 81.

gar gross bass or *gross contrabass geige* was listed and illustrated. Its tuning was *DD EE AA D G* with a string stop of 128 cm.

In 1628, D. Hitzler[157] reported the bowed instruments used in mixed ensembles of viols and fiddles in his area of southern Germany. Included were 6-string *bass geigen* with standard *C* and *D* viol tunings, and one of five strings with tuning *C E A d g* (which could have been the Italian 5-string bass fiddle depicted by Praetorius, but restrung to be tuned like a viol).

Later in the same region, the A.S. ms (mid-17th century)[158] reported two different sets. The preferred set had a 6-string *GG* bass, a 6-string *D* middle size and a 5-string treble with *f b♭ d' g' c"* tuning. A statement that the bass was tuned as high as it could go indicates that it was larger than Praetorius's bass (apparently of Italian size). The alternative set had a 6-string *AA* bass, a 6-string *G* middle size and a 5-string *d* treble tuned like Gerle's treble. The *G* viol of the alternative set was identified as a solo viol, and it probably played a decorated version of both tenor and alto parts. It could also have had a 7th string tuned to *c"*, which would also allow playing a treble part. This instrument could well have been a precursor of the *viola d'amore*.

Following is a summary table of tunings of German viols in sets:

[157] D. Hitzler, *Newe Musica* (Tubingen, 1628).
[158] A. S., *Instrumentalischer Bettlermantle* (mid 17th century), manuscript in the Special Collections of Edinburgh University Library. See E. Segerman, 'Violins, citterns and viols in the Edinburgh 'A.S.' manuscript', *FoMRHI Quarterly* 91 (Apr. 1998), Comm.1576, pp. 38-44.

Date	Source	Bassus	Tenor & Altus	Discantus
1523	Welzell (Munich 718)	*D G B e a*	*G c e a d'*	*d g b e' a'*
	alternatives	*G c e a d'*	*c f a d' g'*	*g c' e' a' d"*
1528	Agricola	*G c f a d' g'*	*c f a d' g'*	*f a d' g' c"*
	alternatives	*G c f a*	*c f a d'*	*g c' f' a'*
1532	Gerle	*D G B e a*	*G c e a d'*	*d g b e' a'*
	alternatives	*G c e a d'*	*c f a d' g'*	*g c' e' a' d"*
	alternative 6-string bass	*F G c e a d'*		
1545	Agricola	*F A d g b*	*c e a d'*	*g b e' a'*
	alternatives	*F G c e a*		*c' e' a' d"*
1619	Praetorius	*GG C F A d g*	*D G c e a d'*	*A d g b e' a'*
	Klein bass alternatives	*GG C E A d g*		
		AA D G B e a		
		FF# BB E A d g		
	EE AA D G c	Gross bass		
	DD GG C E A d	alternatives		
	EE AA D G c f			
	DD EE AA D G	Gar gross Bass		
c.1650	A.S. ms Edinburgh U.	*GG C F A d g*	*D G c e a d'*	*f b♭ d' g' c"*
	alternative bass, alt, disc	*AA D G B e a*	*G c f a d' g' (c")*	*d g b e' a'*

Early viols in Spain

In the extensive collection of pictures of Spanish vihuelas in Woodfield's book, almost all of the bowed ones dated from c.1500 to c.1510 had tail string fixing and a higher moveable bridge. Otherwise, the instrument design and playing style were usually as before. That seems to have been when the bowed and plucked vihuelas went their separate ways, with the plucked ones retaining the fixed glued bridge but adopting the Italian viola body design of a larger size and a waist without sharp corners. There are no later pictures of Spanish viol activity readily available. One probable piece of evidence of such activity is in a 15th century picture, on which there are blotches all over where paint has peeled off, except for where the instrument is.[159] It appears to be a normal mid-16th century 6-string treble viol (a Spanish one because of the decorative tiles on the soundboard) with a high bridge having the top curved for single-line playing. It is very likely that the viol was repainted in a contemporary form then.

---

[159] Madonna and Child with angel musicians (c.1470-80) Maestrazgo school, in San Felfu, Játiva, reproduced as Fig. 38 in Woodfield, op.cit., p. 62.

Sets of viols in France

There is a record of a viol player in France in the first decade of the 16th century[160], but for decades after then, evidence of viol activity is lacking. Nevertheless, it is clear that viols were popular enough by around 1547 for Gervais to have published a method for it then (now lost), which used tablature notation[161]. There are two 16th century surviving sources giving the tunings of French viols. Jambe de Fer's (1556)[162] set of tunings were all in fourths, and for 5-string viols with lowest strings at *E, B* and *e*, and Mareschall's (1589)[163] set was the same except that the *dessus* (treble) was a tone higher, with the lowest string at *f*$^\sharp$.

If these viols observed the *ton de chapelle* pitch standard, the calculated acceptable ranges of string stops of Jambe de Fer's set would have been 74-94, 54-63 and 43-47 cm, and of Mareschall's treble, 39-42 cm. There is a question about whether these viols may have been bigger, and like the Italian *D-A-d* set, played at lower than the common pitch standard. Rousseau (1687)[164] wrote that the early viols were considerably larger than the viols of his own time. The string stops of the sets of his time were about 80, 60 and 40 cm (with an alto at about 45 cm between the tenor and treble). If the difference was just that the string stops of the early sets were at the maxima of their ranges, it would be about 20%. Is that enough to explain Rousseau's comment?

To explore this question, we look at the two surviving pictures of 16th century French viols being played that I've seen. One is a drawing dated 1584 of an outdoor performance by a quartet of professionals playing on three middle-size viols plus a bass.[165] We know that they were professionals because they didn't have enough social status to be able to sit while playing in public, so the bass player stooped and the others knelt (playing a treble this way would be more awkward, and this could be why there isn't one). These viol sizes were <u>not</u> too big to play at the pitch standard. The other is a 1611 drawing of a 5-string bass viol played, and the string length is clearly over 100 cm long.[166] This viol may be an example of the terms *basse contre de viole* and *double basse contre de viole* which started to appear from 1556. Mersenne wrote that there was a wide range of bass viol sizes.

Jambe de Fer's illustration of a viol (half of it is missing in the sole surviving copy, but it was reprinted in Mersenne's book)[167] showed a bridge rounded enough to play individual strings when bowed near it. Yet a c.1585 drawing of a 5-string French viol[168] shows quite a flat bridge, implying that the original playing style of melody plus chords could have still been used later. That particular viol also had a lower-back fold as well as the usual one in the upper back, a feature found on a good number

[160] I Woodfield, op. cit. p. 196.

[161] I Woodfield, op. cit. pp. 199-200.

[162] P. Jambe de Fer, *Epitome musical* (Lyons 1556).

[163] S. Mareschall, *Porta Musices* (Basle 1589).

[164] J. Rousseau, *Traité de la viole* (Paris 1687), p. 19.

[165] *Escole de Musique*, anonymous drawing in Bibliothèque Nationale (Paris), Département des Etampes, Pol. 30, pl. 11.

[166] Drawing of the funeral of Charles III of Lorraine in 1608 by Frederic Brentel in Bibliothèque Nationale (Paris), Département des Etampes, PE 52, fol. 7.

[167] M. Mersenne, *Harmonie Universelle* (Paris 1636), Bk. IV, Prop V.

[168] T. Dart, *Galpin Soc J.* X (1957), p.88, drawings by Jacques Cellier (c.1585) in plates between pp. 62-3.

of surviving English treble viols (usually 'restored' away in the 20th century), suggesting that it was played against the shoulder, with the thinning of the body there making it more comfortable to hold there.

Mersenne credited Jacques Maduit (1557-1627) with the addition of a 6th string to French viols[169]. 17th century French viols, as reported by Mersenne and Rousseau, were tuned like the Renaissance lute in *D G c d* sets. The calculated ranges of string stops at the expected *ton de chapelle* standard for these tunings are 65-84, 51-63, 41-47 and 37-42 cm. But Mersenne stated that the English tuned their viols a tone lower than the French to 'render the harmony softer and more charming', while from the nominal pitches and pitch standards, we would expect little difference. This perhaps echoes Praetorius's statement that when playing alone the English viols played at the same pitches as his viols, which would be a minor third lower than how they were normally tuned. If the two observations were of the same practice, this would imply that Mersenne's viols were tuned to a standard a semitone lower than *ton de chapelle*. This standard was called 'opera' or 'theatrical' pitch[170] later in the century. Mersenne wrote that the bass viol he illustrated was about 4 1/2 feet (148 cm) long, and measurement of it leads to a string length of about 86 cm. This figure lends some credibility to the suggestion that French viols in his time tended to be tuned a bit lower than *ton de chapelle*.

The earliest evidence for the use of a soundpost on viols is given by Mersenne. He called it the 'soul' of the instrument, and wrote that it was directly under the treble foot of the bridge, and can be lifted up again through the sound hole when it has fallen down. The sound post was not mentioned in his discussion of fiddles, which might indicate that in a fiddle it was still permanently fixed when the instrument was opened up, as was the bass bar in both types of instrument. It is likely that the soundpost spread amongst viols after about 1600, as it did with fiddles of all sizes, when its combination with the bass bar led to the great success of the violin in Italy.

Following is a summary table of the tunings of French viols that played in sets:

Date	Source	Bas	Taille	Hautecontre	Dessus
1556	Jambe de Fer	*E A d g c'*	*B e a d' g'*	*B e a d' g'*	*e a d' g' c''*
1589	Mareschall	*E A d g c'*	*B e a d' g'*	*B e a d' g'*	*f# b e' a' d''*
1635	Mersenne	*D G c e a d'*	*G c f a d' g'*	*c f b♭ d' g' c''*	*d g c' e' a' d''*
1687	Rousseau	*D G c e a d'*	*G c f a d' g'*	*c f b♭ d' g' c''*	*d g c' e' a' d''*

---

[169] M. Mersenne, op. cit., 'Premiere Preface Generale au Lecteur'. His eulogy of Maduit is in Bk. VII, Prop. XXXI.

[170] G. Muffat, *Florilegium secundom* (Passau 1698)

Sets of viols in England

In the 16th century, there is much English evidence of viol playing, but none of tunings. A sculpture from the first few decades of the century decorating a church shows a treble viol bowed higher than the waist cutout, suggesting a melody-plus-chords playing style.[171] The neck was relatively short. A drawing by H. Holbein of the family of Thomas More dated c. 1527 shows the outline of another short-necked viol hanging with a bow on the wall.[172] It had a rose between the waist cutouts, which suggests that the soundboard was flat. A painting of the same family probably by R. Lockey (presumably after a Holbein original) shows a viol on a table with one of their heads obscuring the waist and bridge.[173] It had six strings and a relatively long neck, though it seems to be of later design. We can expect a strong Italian influence after 1540 when a few families of Sephardic Jewish musicians and instrument makers from Italy joined Henry VIII's musical establishment and dominated royal bowed-string playing for the rest of the century. Playing viols had become part of the education of choirboys, and in the middle of the century, professional choirboy ensembles of viols were commonly playing as entertainment for functions in London[174].

Why did the English reduce the sizes of their viols, as Rousseau stated?[175] It is possible that the choirboys used smaller viols than the usual Italian sizes both because their fingers were smaller than adults, and because at those sizes they could play at the easy transposition of a fourth lower than the 10 ft *FF* organ pitch that they sang in. With these smaller sizes, there was no reason for having less than six strings on each. These viol sizes were the only ones used in public viol performances around then, and these performances helped spread the popularity of viol playing outside the households of the nobility. This could well have been crucial in establishing the smaller sizes as the norm in England.

The 17th century sources that gave the tunings of the English set of viols indicated that they were a *D G d* set[176] at what Mace called 'Consort pitch' (the same as south German *chorthon* and Italian *corista*, and about the same as French *ton de chapelle*). The calculated possible string-length ranges for these pitches are 67-82, 53-62 and 38-41 cm. Talbot's (c.1694) measurements lead to string lengths of the consort bass and tenor viols of 81 and 61 cm respectively. This is consistent with Playford's statement that the highest string should be tuned as high as it could go. We can expect that the string length of the treble was about 40 cm. Talbot didn't measure a treble viol probably because he couldn't find one. The playing of viols in sets had faded by then, and many treble viols had been converted to tenor violins (violas)[177]. It is likely that many of his alternative tunings for the consort bass were for

---

[171] Wooden figure on a roof boss in St Andrew church in Buckland Monachorum Devon, photo as plate 33 in J & G Montagu, *Minstrels & Angels* (Fallen Leaf, Berkeley, 1998), p. 15.

[172] *The Family of Sir Thomas More* by Hans Holbein II, in Kupferstichkabinett, Basel

[173] *The More Family Group*, in Nostell Priory, Yorkshire

[174] I Woodfield, op. cit. p. 212-8.

[175] J. Rousseau, op. cit. p. 22.

[176] T. Robinson, *Schoole of Musicke* (London 1603); J. Playford, *An introduction to the skill of musick* (London 1674); T. Mace, *Musick's Monument* (London 1676); J. Talbot, Christ Church (Oxford) MS 1187 (c. 1694) - see E. Segerman 'The Sizes of English Viols and Talbot's Measurements', *Galpin Soc. J.* XLVIII (1995), pp. 33-45.

[177] E. Segerman, 'Viol-bodied Fiddles', *Galpin Soc. J.* XLIX (1996), pp. 204-6.

vocal accompaniment. He only mentioned a tenor viol tuning in a passage paraphrasing Mersenne's writings on the viol, and the tuning with an *A* lowest string was apparently from the Italian tunings mentioned by Mersenne. This was the only English source that reported a tenor tuning other than with a *G* lowest string. Supporting the point that this mention was not relevant to English tenor viols, is that the range of string lengths for a *A* viol is 46-55 cm, and Talbot's string length of 61 cm is outside this range.

For the string lengths of 81, 61 and 40 cm and roped-gut bass strings, the set could be tuned several semitones lower than the standard pitches. A common retuning for the bass was for the 6th string to be tuned a tone lower, to 'double *C* fa ut'. According to Praetorius, the English tuned their viol sets (with the lowest strings nominally at *D*, *A* and *e)* a fifth lower to his pitches of *GG*, *D* and *A* when playing alone (without voices, lute or organ) because they preferred the sound that produced. He apparently misunderstood what the nominal pitch of the lowest string of the English treble and tenor viols were. My scenario for his error is that he observed that the bass lowest string was tuned to his pitch, was told that its nominal pitch usually was *D* while it actually was tuned to its tone-lower alternative, and he just assumed that the relative tuning of the other viols relative to the bass was the same as with his viols. Since the English pitch standard was a tone lower than his and the English viols were normally tuned a tone lower than he thought they were, the drop of pitch was two tones less than the fifth he mentioned, which was a minor third. Thus the lowest strings of English viols when playing alone at English (consort) pitch were at *BB*, *E* and *B*.

During the 18th century, interest in viols decreased. Often with re-necking, original small solo basses were used as cellos, original tenor viols were used as small cellos, and original treble viols were used as violas. Consort basses were replaced by smaller basses with a wound 6th string. Barak Norman was apparently a leader in this development. The original ones could have been used as double bass viols (the English name for the violone) with a wound 6th string (as the German ones were), but English interest in using contrabass instruments was low, and they disappeared. The old wood of discarded instruments was valued to use as parts of new instruments and for repairs on currently-used instruments.

The playing of sets of viols were revived at the end of the 19th century, with Arnold Dolmetsch as a leader. Surviving small solo bass viols of cello size (with string stops around 68 cm) were what the new sizes were based on. They played well with a *D* lowest string at modern pitch or modern early-music pitch a semitone lower, and new tenors were developed at 3/4 of this bass's size, and trebles at half its size. Evidence for larger original sizes was disbelieved (and often still is). Surviving original tenor sizes were thought to have originally been small solo basses, and surviving original treble viols were thought to have originally been alto viols tuned a tone below the trebles (as 17th century French ones were tuned). Such alto viols work well in playing many parts in the music, and documentary evidence for their original use in England was sought, but not found. Getting an old instrument to work well musically in modern conditions does not help to discover its history.

Following is a summary table of the evidence on tunings of English viols in sets:

Date	Source	Bass	Tenor	Treble
1603	Robinson (viol tablature pitching singing)	*D G c e a d'*	*- - - - d' g'*	*- - c' e' a' -*
1619	Praetorius: English viols-nominal	*D 6th*	*A 6th* (an error)	*e 6th* (an error)
	when playing 'alone'	*BB 6th*	*E 6th*	*B 6th*
1674	Playford alternative bass	*D G c e a d'* *C G c e a d'*	*G c f a d' g'*	*d g c' e' a' d"*
1676	Mace	*D G c e a d'*	*G c f a d' g'*	*d g c' e' a' d"*
c.1694	Talbot ms alternatives for Consort bass	*D G c e a d'* *C G c e a d'* *E G B e a d'* *D A d♯ a d'* *F B♭ d f b♭ d'* *C F c f a c'* *C G c e g c'*	*A d g b e' a'* (an error copied from Mersenne)	*d g c' e' a' d"*
	FF AA D F♯ A *GG AA D F♯ A* *GG C F A d g*	Double bass: 5 string alternative: Mr Finger Double bass: 6 string (violone)		

The construction and design of viols

No surviving viols have flat soundboards like the original 15th century vihuelas had, but some paintings from the first half of the 16th century seem to imply this by showing a highish bridge with flat feet. When the soundboard was flat, there most probably were cross bars on each side of the sound holes, as on the original vihuela. An apparently transitional situation seen on some surviving viols was cross bars on each side of the sound holes combined with an arched soundboard. The cross bars followed the arching, and deficient treble response was corrected by a bass bar. Viol soundboards made late in the 16th century tended to be arched without any barring.[178]

In the mid 1530s, some German makers of thin viols decided to increase resonance in the bass not by following the Italian practice of deepening the body, but by using a combined treble bridge foot and soundpost that went through a rectangular hole in the soundboard.[179] There is no subsequent evidence for a soundpost on a viol till the 17th century when the combination of soundpost and bass bar

---

[178] A few had a bar similar to a bass bar but along the center. This could have been to get the ring mode in free-plate tuning, which may be associated with a warmer tone colour.
[179] Seen in woodcuts of viols in the Basel University copy of C. Egenolf *Reutterlein* (Frankfurt am Meyn, 1536).

was so successful on the violin that it was copied on all other bowed instruments.

The modern tradition of constructing arched soundboard or back plates is to carve the arched shape from two wedges of wood glued together. This inefficient use of soundboard wood derives from the Cremonese tradition that gained dominance in violin-making during the baroque period. It was used on some viols, but evidence is mounting that a more common method was to construct the arch from bent thin strips assembled somewhat like a lute's back. Earlier 16th century arched soundboards tended to be made from two strips of little more than twice the final thickness, each bent into a shallow arc with the joint surface planed at an angle to the curvature radii so that when assembled the plate had a compound arch. After assembly, the point at the joint was rounded off and the plate was fairly evenly thicknessed to shape. There is evidence of 3-piece bent soundboards later in that century. By the 17th century, English viols usually had 5-piece bent soundboards. They gained the status amongst viols that Cremona violins had, and French viols tended to copy them. By late in that century, 3-piece soundboards became fashionable again, sometimes with only the central part bent and the other parts carved. German 18th century viols revived the bent 2-part soundboard as well as having all-bent 3-part ones, single-bent 3-part ones and all-carved ones.

The backs of most surviving viols were flat with a fold in the upper bouts which lowers the weight by reducing the depth of the neck where it meets the body. The number of pieces of wood glued together to form the back tended to be larger for larger viols. When the back was arched, a way of accomplishing this in 16th century Italy was to make the part below the fold like a 2-part bent soundboard, and the part above the fold was a third piece of wood bent to fit the edges presented by the assembled first two pieces. Such construction was occasionally revived in 18th century Germany. In the second half of the 17th century, the violoncino, which apparently had a bass-violin body and a bass viol neck, and was tuned like a bass viol, became popular in Italy, and was used as a type of bass viol in France and England (as a division viol). These backs were probably all carved.

The body designs of viols were highly variable. Most had the sides flow to the side of the neck, but some had them come in perpendicularly, like on the violin. Most had right-angle corners on both sides of the waist cutout, but some had more pointy corners, like on the violin. Some had corners only for the upper bouts, and some had no corners at all, like on the guitar. There were other shapes as well. Within each design type, the variation appears to be so great that it gives the impression that no two viols were made on the same mould - that is if a mould was used. Very late in the viol's use, there are drawings of a mould in Diderot's Encyclopédie[180], involving a board with the back's shape, with a wedge for the part above the back fold. After the back was shaped and bent to fit, the neck and tail blocks were shaped and glued to it. Then a false plate with the shape of the soundboard was temporarily attached to the end blocks, after which the sides were fitted and glued to the end blocks. The false plate was then removed and the neck and soundboard fitted and glued.[181] What about earlier? The soundboard outlines of many surviving English viols are less symmetric than of their backs,

---

[180] Diderot & d'Alembert, *l'Encyclopédie Méthodique* (1762-77). The engravings were by Robert Benard.

[181] Miller, 'Diderot, viols and false tables', *FoMRHI Quarterly* 16 (July 1979), Comm. 214

implying that the design shape was applied to the back only, with the shape of the soundboard subject to variations introduced by the bending of the sides. With the body built up from the back, there may be no need to invest work into making any moulds. Perhaps there were not even templates at times, with sides bent by eye, and parts used in symmetric pairs if they were close enough in shape.

Chapter 6: Independent viols

Viols for vocal accompaniment

A major use of a stringed instrument has always been for simple accompaniment of the player's singing. More accomplished players would play instrumental interludes. Any viol (or lirone) of a set could be used this way. The sensitivity of human hearing is greatest at the pitch of crying babies (2-3 kHz), and falls off steadily as pitch gets lower. So if the voice is to stand out, it helps if its pitch, or strong harmonics of its pitch (modern vocal training strengthens these harmonics), would be higher than the pitches of the accompaniment. High male voices were strongly preferred in medieval times presumably because that evoked a stronger response than lower male voices (we see a parallel nowadays in pop music). Instruments then were conveniently small because of the need for portability and ready replacement. For accompaniment, they provided drones and perhaps other background sounds and interludes that did not compete with the voice. In the 15th century, playing vocal polyphony on instruments grew, so instruments could play the tenor and contratenor parts to the voice's descant in polyphonic songs (perhaps in addition, an instrument played the descant as well for heterophony with the voice). The increased respectability of lower voices set the scene for the development of larger instruments that played at lower pitches. Bass and tenor viols were such instruments, and they were excellent for accompanying singing of the male voice in its natural range.

Italian 16th century examples of self-accompaniment by a single viol were in the 1539 Florentine *Intermedii*[182] and in Ganassi[183]. A large fraction of the extensive 'lute song' repertoire published in England early in the 17th century specified a 'viola da gamba' as an alternative (not in addition) to the lute in accompanying the voice. With only the need of balancing with the voice, there was no need to conform to any pitch standard. And with fingering easier on smaller viols, such a bass was usually considerably smaller than the optimal size of the bass of a set. Almost all of the surviving 17th century English bass viols are of the smaller sizes made for this purpose (they survived because they could be used as cellos after the demise of viol playing). In the last decade of the century, using a metal-wound 6th string became acceptable, so small basses became suitable for any bass-viol function. Makers such as Barak Norman started to make new ones to be used this way. Such small sizes, with a wound 6th string, were also characteristic of 18th century bass viols elsewhere.

Viola bastarda and lyra viol

In the 1570's, when roped-gut strings became affordable and generally available, a specialist viol called *viola bastarda* appeared in Italy. The size was between tenor and bass, and the bridge was curved to play single lines. Its purpose was to give solo interpretations of well known part songs.

---

[182] *O begli anni del oro, o secol divo* by F. Corteccia.
[183] *Io vorei Dio d'amore* in *Lettione seconda* (1543) Chapter 16.

Sometimes it skipped amongst the parts played in a highly decorated way, and sometimes it did what the lute did, involving arpeggiated chords. It was a style of playing, often in different (especially extended) tunings, and not a special instrument recognizable by any criterion other than size when seeing it. The extended tunings included fourths (a viol characteristic) and fifths (a fiddle characteristic). The name could have come from considering it to be an offspring from a union of these two families of instruments, or that its playing included bits from each size in the family.

The five *viola bastarda* tunings listed by Praetorius were *D G c e a d'*, *C G c e a d'*, *AA E A e a d'*, *AA D A d a d'* and *AA D G d g d'*. The first four of these were used in English viol tablatures before 1610, the last two of these called 'Alfonsoe' and 'eights'. A different one used in England, *C F c f a d'*, was sometimes called 'bandora set' or 'Leero way'. We also find that tuning used on a particularly small viol of tenor size (it had to be that small because of the large stretches required in the tablature), called 'lyra viol'. From about 1610, new lyra viols were fitted with metal sympathetic strings. Praetorius indicated there were eight sympathetic strings, of steel, brass and twisted brass, tuned accurately to the bowed gut strings.[184] Within a few decades, the sympathetic strings were largely discarded[185], and the lyra viol continued as just a viol to accompany singing and played solos from tablature in an enormous variety of different tunings. Later in the century, fingering demands were more relaxed, and larger lyra viols were preferred, a string length of about 72 cm, two frets shorter than a consort bass, being typical late in the century.

When a bowed instrument has sympathetic strings, the vibrations of each bowed note will induce vibrations in non-bowed strings well tuned to the fundamental or a strong harmonic of the bowed note. The musical contribution of the sympathetic strings is that when the bowed note stops sounding, one can still hear the sympathetic strings sounding softly. This effect is the same as reverberation, which sound engineers often add artificially to recordings to make the sound more attractive.

Barytone viol

By about 1640, the English player Walter Rowe working in Germany, played a viol called 'barretone', which essentially was a lyra viol (having sympathetic strings) with a modified neck so that the thumb of the stopping hand could pluck the metal strings running underneath the widened

---

[184] In March 1609, Edney and Gill applied for a court privilege (that was not successful) for 'the sole making of viols, violins and lutes with the addition of wire strings beside the ordinary strings for bettering of the sound, being an invention of theirs not formerly practiced or known.' - quoted in D. Lasocki, *Galpin Soc. J.* XXXVIII (1985), pp. 130-1, fn. 59. Playford (1661) attributed the invention of metal sympathetic strings to Daniel Farrant, and Kircher (1650) gave the credit to the Duke of Somerset.

[185] The specially strong ferrous wire made by Meuler in Nuremberg became no longer available, so the tuning of the sympathetic strings could no more cover the full range of the bowed strings. The full range is not necessary, so there must have been other important factors involved.

fingerboard.[186] When mentioned in the Talbot ms,[187] two tunings for the bowed strings were given, a 'lyra' one of *C c e g c' e'* and an 'ordinary' one 'as bass viol only 3 notes higher'. There were 18 'wire strings for the thumb' tuned *GG AA* and chromatic from *BB* to *d*. Talbot's informant was G. Finger, an Austrian musician working in London. The instrument was popular mostly in Austria, where the aristocracy cultivated it throughout the 18th century. The tuning of the bowed strings then was usually the same as a standard 6- or 7- string bass viol. One aristocrat had Haydn write much music for it.

Around 1650, the principle of adding metal sympathetic strings to a bowed gut-strung instrument was picked up by the Norwegian *Hardanger fiddle*, a local version of the violin. The sympathetic strings were tuned to the tonic chord of the key played in.

Viola d'amore

In 1679, John Evelyn recorded hearing a German playing a *viol d'amore*, which had 5 wire strings played Lyra way (i.e. with chords and a special tuning), but otherwise was an ordinary violin. Rousseau (1687) mentioned that the *viole d'amour* was a treble viol with brass bowed strings. Daniel Speer (1687) wrote that the *viola di lamor* was a viol with iron or silver strings, with special tunings. In early 18th century Germany, the name *viola d'amore* applied to a soloistic treble viol in a variety of tunings with two types of stringings. The first had only six bowed strings, with the 1st gut, the next three of iron or brass, and the last two metal-wound. Majer gave the tuning *f a c' f' a' c"* and 15 others.[188] The other type had six or seven bowed strings of gut with metal-covered gut basses, and about the same number of iron or brass sympathetic strings.

By the second half of the 18th century, the design with metal sympathetic strings prevailed. The usual tuning was *(A) d a d' f#' a' d"*, with the *f#'* retuned to *f'* in appropriate keys. In this design, the sympathetic stings were usually held in place on one end by a small pins going through a thin hardwood bridge glued onto the soundboard under the tailpiece used for the bowed strings. They then went over a bar carved in the bridge, and then through a tunnel between the fingerboard and the neck to a nut on the neck just below the nut for the bowed strings on the fingerboard. From there they went through a slot in the back of the pegbox, and along that back on the outside until past the pegs for the bowed strings, and back through another slot to the inside of the pegbox and on to their tuning pegs, which continued past the pegs for the bowed strings. If the number of sympathetic strings was double that of the bowed strings, the instrument was called 'English violette'. An Italian book by A. Sgargi (1747)[189] described an amateur's shoulder viol (*viola da spalla*) called *viol d'amour* or *viola angelica* with six or seven bowed strings of gut (with the basses copper-wound) and brass sympathetic strings

---

[186] There was an all-plucked instrument that similarly had the left thumb plucking strings, while the other fingers of the left hand stopped other strings on a fingerboard that were sounded by the right hand. It was the polyphont, which was probably invented at about the same time.

[187] *James Talbot Manuscript*, Christ Church Library Music MS 1187, Oxford, c. 1694; discussed in R. Donington, 'James Talbot's Manuscript', *Galpin Soc. J.* III (1950).

[188] J. F. B. C. Majer, *Museum Musicum* (Schwäbisch Hall, 1732), p. 83-4.

[189] M. Tiella, 'On Francesco Antonio Sgargi's book [...] La viola da sei, o sette corde, in Bologna 1747 per Tommaso Colli a S. Tommaso d'Acquino', *FoMRHI Quarterly* 100 (July 2000), Comm. 1719, pp. 36-9.

tuned chromatically. The tuning was *(G) c e a d' g' c"* for the bowed strings, and the metal sympathetic strings were tuned chromatically from *f* to *e'*, with no particular order in their placement.

These instruments were popular in the 18th century, and were occasionally written for in the 19th and first half of the 20th century. Its body usually was essentially that of a treble viol but of less depth, appropriate for being held against the shoulder or neck. Players like to be able to watch their fingering viewed over the bridge.

Division viol and violoncino

Around the middle of the 17th century, a new kind of soloistic bass viol appeared in England, called 'division viol'. Its string length was about 76 cm, one fret shorter than on a consort bass. In his method for playing this instrument, Simpson[190] indicated that he preferred the design that had the shape of a violin, with 'the Bellyes digged out of the Plank' By contrast, other English viols then had their bellies (soundboards) made of bent staves glued together (with 4 joints). The division viol that Talbot measured (c. 1694) was of this violinistic type (with an arched back as well) and the body dimensions were very close to those he gave for the bass violin. That was the usual bass violin in England (except for the royal music establishment, which used the French *basse de violon*), and apparently came from the Italian *basso da braccio*. It is likely that the division viol had an Italian origin, with the Italian model having a *basso da braccio* body on which was a longer and wider viol neck. The Talbot division viol seems to have been of this type, while the example Simpson illustrated had a longer body and shorter neck, giving the same 30 inch string length.

The division viol was tuned the same as the bass viol of a set, and its playing style was like that of the *viola bastarda* without extended tunings and most of the chords. The Italian instrument popular at the same time as the division viol, and with the same playing style, was the *violoncino*. The first we hear of the *violoncino* is around 1640, and it seems to have been a revival of the *viola bastarda* (which we last hear of in the 1630's), but without extended tunings and apparently with a *basso da braccio* body. The name means 'small *violone*', which was appropriate since it was tuned like a viol and was smaller than the *violone*, which was the only popular viol in Italy at the time. When there was a small resurgence of interest in other viols in Italy later in the 17th century, violinistic exaggeratedly pointed corners were as likely to be in the design as the right-angle corners of the usual English and French viol shapes. This was not new in Italy, since the bodies of viols shown in Virgiliano's drawings (c.1600) were also of this violinistic shape.

In the middle of the 17th century, a school of soloist bass viol players developed in France. Rousseau credited one of them, Sainte Colombe, with introducing to the bass viol both a 7th string tuned a fourth lower (*AA*) than the sixth, and strings wound with silver. In the 18th century, we hear of *violes voutées*, which were viols with violin-shaped bodies (having arched backs). They could well have been the French equivalents of the division viol and the *violoncino*. Some of their ordinary viols then, with flat backs, also had the violinistic sharpened waist corners.

---

[190] C. Simpson, *The Division-Viol* (London 1665).

Miniature soloistic viols

At various times, we find viols smaller than any that were normally used in sets. In a Portuguese painting from early in the 16th century, a small 5-string viol was playing with a string drum and a tiny rebec[191]. In another, the famous painting *St. Cecilia* by Raphael, a very small broken 6-string viol lies at her feet[192]. In the latter case, there is reason to suspect that the relative sizes of the viol and Cecilia had been altered for symbolic reasons (the apparent size is also inconsistent with a 6-string 2-octave open-string range). The 4-string alternative treble viol mentioned in the 1545 edition of Agricola's book was probably also a miniature soloistic viol.[193]

A later example was the *sopranino di viola* called for in the 1589 Florentine *Intermedii*, played to acclaim by Alessandro Striggio. The name implies that it was smaller than a *soprano* (treble). This seems to have been the *violetta picciola* that Zacconi called a particularly small viol. When reading this in Zacconi, it seems that Praetorius couldn't imagine what this double-diminutive *viola* could be, so he listed the name both as a fiddle and a viol. The fashion for this soloistic viol was short lived (one was listed in a German inventory at that time[194]). One by Juan Maria da Brescia survives in the Hill Collection in Oxford. Its string length of 30 cm implies that in *corista,* it was a viol with a *g* catlin lowest string that just filled the range.

Late in the 17th century the *dessus de viole*, (a normal 6-string treble with a *d* lowest string), became quite active in playing the generally available violin repertoire in France. (Similarly, earlier in the century, most of the English string music that was not exclusively for viols had the 'treble' part deliberately ambiguous as to whether a treble viol or violin was intended). Because of the way it was usually held between the knees, the treble viol could be played more easily in higher positions than the violin. By the end of the century, a smaller *dessus de viole* (with a string stop of about 33 cm, about 4 frets smaller) with a metal-wound 6th was developed to play at the higher ensemble pitch standards popular then[195]. This instrument could also be used to play the violin repertoire in first position if the nominal pitches of its strings was assumed to be a minor third lower (this pitch standard was called the 'very low French chamber pitch' by Quantz, about 3 1/2 semitones below modern). The instrument was then called a *pardessus de viole.* To minimize relearning of fingering, it was tuned like the normal treble without its lowest string, with an added *g"* string on top (*g c'e'a'd" g"*). This shifted the third from between the 3rd and 4th strings to between the 4th and 5th, and only involved tuning the 4th string down a semitone to change from a *dessus* at a high pitch standard to a *pardessus* at the low pitch standard.

Around 1725, a new 5-string *pardessus* tuning (at the same low pinch standard) became popular, particularly amongst ladies. The palindromic tuning, *g d' a' d" g"*, had the higher three

---

[191] illustrated in Plate 86 in Woodfield op. cit.

[192] illustrated in Plate 50 in Woodfield op. cit.

[193]appears in *The Three Graces* by Hans Baldung Grien, Prado

[194] 'viole de gamba oder die grosz geigen ... 2 pasz, 4 tenor, 2 discant und ain clainer discant' in the 1596 inventory of Archduke Ferdinand's instruments in Ambras Castle - quoted in Woodfield op. cit., p. 193.

[195] E. Segerman, 'The anomalous size of the pardessus de viole', *FoMRHI Quarterly* 105 (Oct. 2001), Comm. 1779, p. 18.

strings like the *pardessus de viole* and the lower three strings like the violin. Holding and bowing was like a viol, and frets were used. To conform to this new fashion, many earlier *pardessus* viols dropped a string and were played with the new tuning. Violins were converted by replacing the neck, peg box, bridge and tailpiece. New instruments were made with either traditional viol bodies or with bodies that were various compromises between a viol and a violin. This new instrument was called either *pardessus de viole à cinq cordes* or *quinton*[196]. Either name was sometimes used for any instrument with that tuning, but the *pardessus* name appears to have mostly been used when the body design was like a viol, and the *quinton* name was mostly used when the design had obvious violinistic aspects. The popularity of this instrument peaked around 1750 and it was waning when the French Revolution terminated it.

Baroque and later double-bass viols

It has been mentioned that viols with a string length of about a meter were normal bass viols that were played in sets in the 16th century. They were called 'double bass viols' in England when the sizes of all viols in sets was reduced (the 'double' apparently referred to its going down to pitches like *GG* which were named with double letters). In Italy, all viols were called violones until late in the century when the bass was particularly in demand for mixed ensembles. The name then focused on this size, and smaller viols had to do with names like *viola* or *viola da gamba*. An even larger contrabass violone was developed to satisfy the desire for a deeper bass sound.

In Germany, later in the 17th century, Prinner[197] mentioned a new 5-string violone tuning of *FF AA D F# B (*as well as the usual 6-string *GG* one). With the top string down a tone to *A,* this 5-string tuning was mentioned in the Talbot ms (c. 1694), and remained particularly popular around Vienna till well into the 19th century (it was the type of violone usually used when Mozart and Haydn was played there). A new 4-string version of the violone was also developed[198]. It was tuned an octave below the highest four strings of the ordinary one (*FF AA D G*), with the 4th string more often either a semitone lower at *EE* (resulting in the tuning that later became standard on the double bass), or a tone higher at *GG*.

In the 18th century, the function of the bass viol was taken over by smaller ones with a wound 6th string, and the cello rapidly gained ground as the small bass of string ensembles. Early in the century, 6-string violones still predominated as the large basses. The usual *GG* tuning was used on surviving consort-size bass viols with a wound 6th and on full-size violones with all-gut stringing. Some large violones (probably originally contrabass types) had a low *CC* string (probably metal-wound). The use of reduced-range violones with 4 and 5 strings grew steadily, and these replaced the 6-string violones by the second half of the century. The term *violone* (or *violon* in German) was gradually replaced by *contrabasso* during the century. The Italians had been using the term *contrabasso* from the 17th century.

---

[196] M. Herzog, 'Is the *quinton* a viol? A puzzle unraveled', *Early Music* (Feb. 2000), pp. 8-31.

[197] J. J. Prinner, *Musicalischer Schlissl* (1677), ms. in Music Division, Library of Congress, Washington, D.C., U.S.A.

[198] B. Bismantova, *Regule per Violoncello e Violone* (Ferrara, 1694).

Late in the 18th century, a 3-string violone (called *contrabasso* by then) became an alternative to the 4-string variety. It didn't become prominent until the 19th century, when the two leading virtuosos (Dragonetti and Bottesini) used it. Tunings usually were *GG D A* (called 'French', an octave below the top three strings of the cello) or *AA D G* (called 'Italian', an octave below the top three strings of the original violone). It was an instrument of ordinary size and used octave transposition to play in such a constricted range. One advantage was to allow higher string tensions. This made the instrument louder and allowed the bow to dig into notes without touching other strings while bowing not necessarily close to the bridge. Another advantage was of not needing any metal-wound string, so it consistently provided the fundamental-rich foundation note for an orchestra that a thick all-gut string provides. It was common for orchestras to have both 3-string and 4-string instruments. The 4th string of 4-string double basses had very thin metal winding on a very thick gut core. Late Romantic composers demanded lower notes in their music, and that led to the abandonment of 3-string double basses in the 20th century[199].

---

[199] A. Planyavsky, *The Baroque Double Bass Violone* (Scarecrow Press 1998), translated by J. Barket; see review by E. Segerman in *Early Music* XXVII/4 (Nov. 1999), pp. 660-1.

The Development of Western European Stringed Instruments

Chapter 7: Renaissance and baroque fiddles

Ensemble fiddles in 16th century Italy

As mentioned before, around 1500, Italian instrument makers adapted the vihuela to become *viole da arco* (bowed violas or viols in English) in different sizes to play together in sets. The sizes had three tunings with the string length of the smallest about the same as the original vihuela (about half a metre), that of the largest double that, and that of the intermediate ones intermediate. At about the same time, the Italians also made fiddles with many vihuela design features, and called them small bowed violas. There were also three tunings with the string lengths about half that of the corresponding viols. This set of small bowed violas apparently replaced the similar set of rebecs popular in the 15th century in playing part music, with the middle size of rebec surviving as a soloistic fiddle until it was replaced by the violin. The fiddles that played part music in the 15th century were soon replaced by these small violas, while the fiddles that played on multiple strings were replaced by the lira. The new fiddles retained the tuning in fifths.

The earliest Italian picture of a new fiddle I know of is from 1505-8.[200] It had 3 strings with a string length of about 36 cm, making it of an intermediate size. It had all the features of a viol at that time except that it didn't have frets or the 10-fret-equivalent long neck that viols still had for a few years more. It is possible that the new fiddles never went through the long-neck vihuela-like phase, and the viols eventually followed the fiddles in this respect. This fiddle had *f* or S holes between the waist cut outs on both sides of the strings. I know of no earlier instrument that had such holes. The earliest picture of French fiddles, from 1516[201], shows a set playing together, and each one had a rose in the soundboard (like the original vihuela), and a moveable bridge. The earliest depiction of German fiddles, from 1528[202] , shows woodcuts of a set, and each had not only the rose but also the glued fixed bridge of the original vihuela. Either the original vihuela spread to France and Germany before the Italians developed it into sets of fiddles and viols, and they independently developed sets, or they copied (and kept using) earlier Italian designs of which we have no surviving evidence.

The earliest name I am aware of for the set of Italian fiddles is *violette da braccio & da arco senza tasti*, meaning 'small bowed unfretted arm violas', used by Lanfranco (1533)[203]. By contrast, his name for viols was *violoni da tasti & da arco*, meaning 'large bowed fretted violas'. With all tunings in fifths, Lanfranco's *soprano*, *contralto* and *tenore* fiddles had three strings, and his *basso* had four. The third string of the *soprano* was in unison with the second of the *contralto* and *tenore* and with the first

---

[200] Wall painting by Garofalo in the Palazzo di Ludovico, Sala del Tesoro in Ferrara; photo as Fig. 45 in M. Remnant, *Musical Instruments of the West* (Batsford, London, 1978), p .58.

[201] Paris woodcut depicting four musical philosophers; reproduced as Fig. 1 in D. D. Boyden, *The History of Violin Playing* (OUP, 1965), p. 13.

[202] M. Agricola, *Musica instrumentalis deudsch* (Wittemberg, 1528).

[203] G. M. Lanfranco, *Scintille di musica* (Brescia, 1533).

string of the *basso*. He gave no nominal string pitches, probably because the players didn't use pitch names for their strings.

This set of fiddles, usually called *viole da braccio* or *violini* (the latter always in the plural, and meaning, as *violette* did, small violas), seems to have continued essentially unaltered until early in the 17th century. The same relative tunings were given by Zacconi (1592)[204] and Cerone (1613)[205], except that these late sources indicated that a fourth string was usually (Zacconi) or occasionally (Cerone) added at the bottom of the middle sizes, and was occasionally (Zacconi) added at the bottom of the *soprano*.

Zacconi provided nominal pitches as well, which gave the lowest string of the basso as BB^b, which requires the string length to have been at least 96 cm long at the usual Italian *corista* pitch standard (equivalent to Praetorius's chorthon). There is no evidence for such a large 4-string bass fiddle in Italy in the 16th century. We should then consider the possibility that fiddle strings sounded an octave higher than written when reading the generally available (mostly vocal) music in the usual clefs. Then the actual pitches of the strings at corista would have been: *basso*: $B^b f c' g'$, *contralto & tenore*: *(f) c' g' d"* and *soprano*: *(c') g' d" a"*. We can calculate the ranges of string lengths for these tunings assuming corista (most probably consistently followed by Zacconi's time) and high-twist lowest strings (the type used when the sizes and tunings were established). Reading off the string lengths from the table in Chapter 1b, the ranges would be 55-62, 29-41 and 21-27 cm respectively for the 4-string *basso*, 3-string middle sizes and 3-string *soprano*. The range for a 4-string middle size would be 40-41cm, and for a 4-string *soprano* would be 29-27 cm. With the calculated minimum greater than the maximum for the *soprano*, either the 4-string *soprano* adopted catlin 4th strings, or those strings were thinner than would be optimum for balance.

Now let us measure the string lengths of the fiddles in the set depicted in the famous fresco by Gaudenzio Ferrari dated 1535-6.[206] There are plenty of faces to scale to (with no apparent variation in size with placement relative to the viewer). The string length of the bass appears to have been about 62 cm, and that of the 3-string middle size about 42 cm. We cannot see the bridges on the other two fiddles (smaller and each with three pegs) since one (of fairly normal appearance) is seen from the side and back, while the other (of fantastic shape and a lira-like peg plate) is seen from the back. Guessing where each bridge might have been from its position relative to the waist leads to string lengths in the region of about 27 to 29 cm on both. These fiddles could have been two *soprani*, or one *soprano* at its maximum string length and one *contralto* at its minimum. These measured string lengths agree very well (to the accuracy expected) with the theoretical deductions assuming the hypothesis that the fiddles sounded an octave higher than Zacconi's tuning pitches imply, and are inconsistent with the hypothesis that they played at pitch.

---

[204] L. Zacconi, *Prattica di musica* (Venice, 1592).

[205] D. P. Cerone, *El Melopeo y Maestro* (Naples, 1613).

[206] Fresco painted by G. Ferrari in the cupola of the Church of Santa Maria dei Miracoli in Saronno.

The above conclusions about sizes and tunings of the *viole da braccio* in the 16th century differ from those given by David Boyden in his famous book, where he claimed that there was no distinction between the *soprano viola da braccio* and the *violino*, that the *soprano* and middle fiddle tunings in the 16th century were the same as later, and that the *basso* tuning was the same as the French bass, i.e. Bb^b $F\ c\ g$.[207] In the over 40 years since its publication, no-one has critically examined his analysis of 16th century Italian fiddle tunings. Boyden ignored the tuning given by Lanfranco, arbitrarily added an extra highest string to the *soprano* given by Cerone and presented a set of 4 tunings based on an interpretation of Zacconi, an author whose writings he stated were confusing and inconsistent. Boyden wrote 'To understand Zacconi, we must keep in mind and accept that 1. *Viole da braccio* is a general term that includes *violino*... 2. Through an oversight Zacconi does not include the alto-register instrument among the *viole da braccio* but only among the *violini*... 3. Zacconi actually admits four tuning registers for the violin family, not the usual three...'.

Zacconi's Venetian Italian is difficult to read, but there is only one instance (the tuning of the *violino*, about which there is no doubt) where he seems to have been inconsistent. Boyden's three points are inconsistent with what Zacconi wrote. Boyden's point 1. is only true in the sense that the *violino* belonged to the category of a bowed viola held by the arm, but this should not be confused with the fact that *viole da braccio* was a term also applied to a specific set of fiddles. The *violino* was treated separately as a different category of instrument from the *viole da braccio* family by Zacconi, Cerone and Virgiliano.[208] The tuning information was given separately within each category. Concerning Boyden's related points 2 and 3, as he admits, Zacconi clearly indicated that there were but three tunings in his section on the fiddle family. Boyden wrote that detailed arguments supporting his case could be found in an article he had previously written.[209] The problems with his analysis in that article were discussed in a review of it by me.[210]

There is no justification for Boyden's conflation of Zacconi's *violino* and *viole da braccio* information into one combined set when there was no evidence for them ever playing together in Italy before the 17th century. Boyden's assumption that Zacconi's *soprano viola da braccio* had four strings is also highly questionable. Zacconi wrote that the *viole da braccio* were tuned in fifths, like the *violino*. He was concerned with communicating the playing range in first position, which was *F-a'* for the *tenore* and 'other violas of the middle' (resulting in the tuning *F c g d'*), and BB^b-d' for the bass (resulting in the tuning $BB^b F\ c\ g$). It is significant that he gave no playing range for the *soprano*. That is most probably because there was an ambiguity about whether it was the 'ordinary' one or the other one. Zacconi wrote that the highest string of the *basso* was in unison with the lowest string of the 'ordinary' *soprano* (implying that this was not true for a different *soprano* that was not the ordinary one). The obvious choice is between whether the ordinary *soprano* had three or four strings.

[207] D. D. Boyden, *The History of violin Playing from its Origins to 1761* (O.U.P. 1965), pp. 42-3.

[208] A. Virgiliano *Il Dolcimelo* (c.1600) manuscript in the Civico Museo Bibliografico Musicale, Bologna. A description of the contents of this manuscript by is in E. Segerman, *FoMRHI Quarterly* 97 (Oct. 1999), Comm. 1672, pp. 26-8.

[209] D. D. Boyden, 'Monteverdi's *Violini piccoli alla Francese* and *Viole da brazzo*', *Annales Musicologiques* VI (Paris, 1958-63), pp. 377-402.

[210] E. Segerman, 'Review: "Monteverdi's *Violini piccoli alla Francese* and *Viole da brazzo*" by D. D. Boyden', *FoMRHI Quarterly* 101 (Oct. 2000), Comm. 1738, pp. 28-32.

Boyden assumed that the ordinary *soprano* had four strings, which would give it the violin tuning. In support of this choice is Zacconi's statement elsewhere that viols had six strings and *viole da braccio* had four. This must have been intended as a general statistical statement, implying 'most' before each instrument's name, because Zacconi must have known of 5-string Italian viols since Ganassi wrote of their prevalence, and Virgiliano considered only them. So <u>most</u> viols had six strings and <u>most</u> fiddles four. What makes this 4-string assumption for the *soprano* quite unacceptable is that it makes it more than an octave higher than the *tenore* and 'other violas of the middle'. This gap is too big for any sensible Renaissance set of instruments. Boyden realized this and introduced a baroque viola tuning to fill it. But this is inconsistent with Zacconi's giving only one tuning for the *tenore* and other 'violas of the middle'. If the usual *soprano* had three strings (and the unusual one four), this problem is resolved, and Zacconi's tunings would be consistent with those given by Lanfranco and Cerone.

Soloistic fiddles in 16th century Italy

Throughout the history of European musical instruments, there have been many innovations that were intended to be improvements over what was previously available. These have been readily accepted if they allowed musicians to do things they felt were useful that they couldn't do before, or they made it easier or more convenient for them to do what they had been doing before. These innovations have not readily been accepted if it changed the sound quality that their instruments produced, no matter how 'improved' the sound might appear to later ears. This is because musicians and their audiences grew up with, and thoroughly enjoyed, the sounds their instruments produced previously, and any change in that sound would not be immediately perceived as any improvement.

This is amply illustrated in the adoption of new types of low bass gut strings that produced more harmonics in the sound, making it more focused and richer. Musicians quickly adopted these strings to extend downwards the ranges of their instruments so that the new lowest string sounded just as dull as the old lowest string did, and were reluctant to change the type of string whenever it was acceptable previously. So when metal winding was invented around 1660, some *violone* players would have quickly used them to tune down to the pitches of the *contrabasso violone*, and some *basso viola da braccio* players used them to tune a fifth lower, allowing them to play *violone* parts with more agility (thus acquiring the name *violoncello*, meaning 'little violone'). Yet it took almost a century for a metal-wound violin 4th string to be commonly used in Italy, and then probably because the quicker response and more variety in tone colors it offered was very useful in the current style of playing.

When roped-gut (catlin) bass strings became generally available in the 1570's, we can understand that the *viola da braccio* family did not immediately adopt them and did so only when they had to lower the tunings of their lower members early in the 17th century. The viols adopted them to allow 6-string viols to play with other instruments at the *corista* pitch standard. These strings also led to the development of the *viola bastarda*, a new soloistic instrument with variable (including extended) tunings that played, besides arpeggiated chords, highly divided versions of all parts, especially the bass. *Il violino* (in the singular) was a new soloistic fiddle that developed then, and it is likely to have performed a musical function similar to the viola bastarda.

Zacconi, Virgiliano and Cerone dealt with *il violino* and the family of *viole da braccio*, and clearly treated them as completely separate entities. The tuning information given by Zacconi and Cerone shows that *il violino* did not correspond with any member of that family. Earlier 16th century sources occasionally mentioned *violini* (always in the plural), obviously referring to small bowed violas, an alternative name for *viole da braccio*. Sources in the final quarter of the century mentioned *il violino,* referring either to a solitary fiddle or one that played with other instruments that were not members of the *viola da braccio* family. It appears that there was a class divide, with the *viole da braccio* and/or its players considered dance-band inferiors, while the *violino* played with the more respectable instruments like lutes, viols, winds and keyboards. Outside of Italy, Italian *viole da braccio* apparently were given more respect. They played with fully respectable instruments in Munich under Lassus in 1568 and worked for the French Court.

The only 16th century evidence on *violino* tuning was given by Zacconi. He wrote that it had a first-position fingered range of 17 diatonic notes, and when he specified the limits of that range in the usual hexachord pitch names, it was from *c* to either *a'* or *a''* (ambiguous in that notation). The latter represents either 13 or 20 diatonic notes, and is different from the 17 stated. He followed this with a diagram showing a range of 17 notes from *g* to *b''*. From another statement, that the *violino* was, as the *viole da braccio* were, generally tuned in fifths, we arrive at the tuning of *g d' a' e''*. It appears that this was the usual type of *violino*.

The anomalous range of *c* to *a'* or *a''* has been interpreted as referring to a specific larger size of *violino* that coexisted with the usual one. But Zacconi wrote as if he was referring to a single instrument, not a family of instruments of varying sizes, so an explanation that assumes this would be preferred. Assuming an *a'* highest note implies a 3-string tuning of *c g d'*, but rather more likely it is an *a''* highest note, implying a *d''* highest string. With that 20 note range, four strings could be tuned in three sixths,[211] or five strings could be tuned in three fifths and a fourth (combinations of fourths and fifths were particularly common in tunings of the *viola bastarda)*. This range would cover almost all the range of the usual *violino* plus an added fifth in the bass. Zacconi did not mention how many strings the *violino* had, and that could be because there was some ambiguity about it.

The violin appears to have originated as an Italian adaptation of the French *dessus de violon*, which was the size of a modern viola, at about 37 cm string length[212]. The adaptation involved using the newly generally-available roped-gut bass strings to enhance bass sound and to tune in different ways: The usual tuning was the same as the French original, *g d' a' e''*. A second way would be either to shift the bridge or use a thinner 4th, and then tune upwards in some way from *c*. A third would be not to move the bridge nor use a thinner 4th, but tune upwards in some way from *d*. Either of the latter two ways could have been used to play the *violino* part in Giovanni Gabrielli's *Sonata Pian e Forte* (1597), that goes below *g*.

---

[211] His statement that the tuning of *violini* was in fifths could easily have been statistical (omitting 'most'), since he stated that viols had six strings, while actually many at the time had five.

[212] see p. 109.

When a *violino* was to be played only in the usual tuning, it could have been somewhat smaller. With this tuning and a catlin 4th, the string-length limits would be 30-37 cm. Three-string *viole da braccio* with the middle tuning (*c' g' d''*) had a string length range of 29-41 cm, with the *contralto* being small in that range. These small ones could easily have been converted to small violins.

Before the appearance of the *violino*, the soloistic fiddles played in Italy were the *lira da braccio* and the rebec. Such rebecs are often seen in Italian pictures earlier in the 16th century (mostly of *contralto* size, while French rebecs were of *soprano* fiddle size). A rebec is probably what the *ribechino* was when it was called for in the 1539, 1568 and 1586 Florentine *Intermedii*. It was quite eclipsed when the *violino* appeared, and when Monteverdi apparently wanted to revive it's sound in Orfeo (1607), he had to use the French version, played by the only soloistic fiddlers then available, the *violino* players. He thus specified the *violino piccolo alla Francese*. After the rebec was replaced by the *violino*, there was a lingering use of rebec words to refer to any soloistic fiddle in Italian and Iberian terminology. This usage has survived to modern times in what the Portuguese have called the violin.

Italian fiddles in the 17th century

The 1600 publication *Rappresentatione di animo* by Cavalieri [213] specified that a solo *violino* played the soprano part in an ensemble. This appears to represent a change of its musical function from musical-line promiscuity strong in the lower range to a commitment to express the treble line. This change of musical function could be due to the appearance of new *violino* players with a different technique (perhaps *viole da braccio* players) or a physical change enhancing the treble response of the instrument (such as the introduction of the bass bar). Since later, when the *violino* and *viole da braccio* joined forces, they still kept their separate identities, it is more likely that this change was associated with a physical change in the instrument.

The amount of sound we hear depends crucially on how strongly the soundboard is pumped by the feet of the bridge. A bar or post under one foot inhibits its pumping motion and, by geometry, enhances the pumping motion of the other foot when bowing strings that went over that other end of the bridge top (see Appendix 2). Around the middle of the 16th century, a bar under the bass foot had been used on viols with cross-bars under the arched soundboard, which would have had an unbalanced poor treble response without it.[214] Also, it was known that enhancing the bass could be achieved by a sound post under the treble foot. Some German viols in the 1530's had an integral sound post and treble bridge foot going through a hole in the soundboard (like the Welsh crwth and the Greek and Cretan *lyra*). Having a sound post was probably what made it possible to have a useful low fourth string on the smaller members of the French family of fiddles when such fiddles elsewhere only had three strings. The *violino* probably inherited a sound post with its French-fiddle origins. It wouldn't make any sense to inhibit the motion of both feet of the bridge at the same time, and this would be demonstrated if one tested the same kind of inhibitor under both feet. This may explain why it took

---

[213] E. Cavalieri, *Rappresentatione di anima, et di corpo* (1600).

[214] We discovered this by once mistakenly gluing the bass bar on the wrong side while making one of these viols. The bass response was glorious but the treble response was very poor.

half a century to discover that the particular combination of a sound post under the treble foot plus a bar under the bass foot creates a balanced instrument with both the treble and the bass response enhanced. This combination works because the sound post inhibits low frequency vibrations much more than high frequency vibrations, and the bass bar does the reverse.

The improvisation and elaborate musical decoration in its soloistic background gave the *violino* a special musical dimension to offer to its new role as a strong treble ensemble instrument. It had a full dynamic range (as well as pitch range) that could imitate the voice more accurately than previous stringed instruments, and that conformed with the philosophy of the time that voice imitation was particularly virtuous. Demand for it grew dramatically. Violin players often worked in pairs, and if one was playing in the usual tuning, and the other in a tuning extended downwards, they could form a set like that of the *viole da braccio* by adding a bass. That could be a *basso viola da braccio*, with added bass bar, sound post and roped-gut thick strings, which would then tune comfortably an octave lower than the *violino*. Such a *violino* family did appear briefly, performing the functions of a *viole da braccio* set. Banchieri (1605, 1609)[215] mentioned such a set of *violini da braccio*, with the *primo violino per il basso* tuned: *G d a e'*, the *secondo violino accordi* tuned: *d g d' a'*, and the *ultimo violino per il canto* tuned: *g d' a' e"*. The low *d* in the tuning of the middle member is as low as a *violino* of original size could go without moving the bridge or using a thinner weaker 4th string, and is most unlikely to have been a mistake. This ensemble of *violini da braccio* played at normal vocal pitches, an octave lower than the *viole da braccio*, and it was acceptable for 'serious' music as well as for dance music.

Within a decade, we find the establishment of the standard early baroque fiddle ensemble with the *violino* playing the soprano part and *viole da braccio* playing the other parts, with the middle parts tuned to *c g d' a'*, and the *basso* tuned to *G d a e'*. The problem is to form a theory for how the transition to this situation occurred, with the only evidence being the ranges of the *viole da braccio* parts (when they still played separately from the *violini*) in Monteverdi's *Orfeo*. My suggestion follows:

The success of the sets of *violini da braccio* would have been both a problem and an opportunity for the players of the *viole da braccio*. The problem would be that this set could replace them, leading to unemployment. The opportunity would be that by successfully emulating this new violini set, they could achieve higher status. So it appears that they replaced the *soprano* by the *contralto*, started to play at written pitch, to use roped-gut lower strings, and to adopt the sound post. They also dropped the pitch of the *tenore* by a fourth, and of the *basso* by a minor third. This mimicking would be more complete if the contralto also tuned up a tone to violin tuning (it often was small enough to do that). The resulting *viole da braccio* set was tuned *basso*: *G d a e"*, *tenore*: *c g d' a'* and *soprano* (formerly *contralto*): *f c g' d"* or *g d a' e"*. With these changes in the *viole da braccio*, the only remaining difference between the new *soprano* (originally *contralto*) member and the *violino* was in the style of playing and perhaps the installation of a bass bar.

With these changes, the *viole da braccio* became acceptable for respectable music in Italy, and

---

[215] A. Banchieri, *L'organo suonarino* (Venice, 1605) and *Conclusioni nel suono dell' organo* (Bologna, 1609).

two sets (totaling ten instruments), apparently with these tunings (deduced from the ranges of the parts), were used in Monteverdi's *Orfeo* (1607). A pair of *violini*, with their players doubling on *violini piccolo alla Francese*, were also called for, but they did not play together with the *viole da braccio* (though a *basso da braccio* was included with other instruments in the continuo accompaniment). Within a few years, the *violini* and *viole da braccio* agreed to play together, as in Monteverdi's *Vespers* (1610). This would have involved the original *contralto* ceding the *soprano* role to the *violino* (or becoming one if it was small enough), and tuning down to rejoin the *tenore* if it was large enough.

With the *violino* and the modified *viole da braccio* working together, we hear no more of a *violino* with extended or lower ranges than the usual one. After a while, we also hear no more of a *soprano viola da braccio*, since this new set of *da braccio* instruments (with the *violino* playing the soprano parts and *viole da braccio* playing the others) became standard. The original *soprano viola da braccio* was not abandoned in Germany, where later in the 17th century it was called *violino piccolo*.

The 16th century habit of using both the terms *violini* and *viole da braccio* for this set of *da braccio* instruments continued with no ambiguity, but when specifying individual parts, the distinction between the *violino* as the soprano of the set and a *viola da braccio* as any other member was still usually observed. This implies that the players wanted to maintain that distinction even though the *viole da braccio* had adopted the physical *violino* characteristics (of roped-gut basses, sound posts and bass bars) that previously distinguished them. The *violino* was still different: in its florid flamboyant non-democratic style of playing. Bach's solo violin music recalled some of its original style of playing.

One important factor that led to the respectability of the *viole da braccio* in the first decade of the 17th century was that the gentleman amateurs acquired and learned to play them. They had been playing viols and still valued the deep bass sounds that the large viols produced. So they had made two unusually large bass fiddles that mostly filled their possible ranges with roped-gut basses, each with five strings tuned in fifths. We don't know of any special early Italian names for them. The large *basso*, with a 72 cm string length, had the top four strings tuned an octave below the *violino: C G d a e'* at the Italian *corista* standard. This was the *bas-geig de bracio* illustrated by Praetorius, but not listed in his tunings. A famous painting by Pieter Claesz[216] in the Louvre apparently depicted this instrument.

Praetorius did not illustrate the contrabass fiddle, but gave its tuning as *FF C G d a* in the tuning tables, a fourth lower than the large bass. He called it *gross quint-bass*. At the *corista* Italian pitch standard, this tuning would be *GG D A e b*, with the lowest 4 strings two octaves below the violin. It would probably have had a string length of over 90 cm (the calculated range is 88-98 cm). The set of five *violini* illustrated by Virgiliano (c. 1600) had relative sizes that are appropriate for them being this instrument (with frets) plus two each of 4-string *soprano* and *contralto viole da braccio*. The tuning of this largest bass fiddle without its top *b* string (an octave below the usual *basso da braccio*) was given for Kircher's (1650)[217] '*violone*'.

---

[216] *Still-life with Musical Instruments*, reproduced in A. Kendall, *The World of Musical Instruments* (Hamlyn, 1972).

[217] A. Kircher, *Musurgia Universalis* (Rome, 1650). His tuning diagrams for all other bowed instruments gave string pitches an octave higher than the actual tuning, and it is assumed that this also applied to his 'violone'.

Large bass fiddles

Around the middle of the 17th century, there is evidence for another large fiddle tuned in fifths being called *'violone'*. It was sometimes more specifically called *violone da braccio*. In northern Italy, a large 4-string bass fiddle was used tuned to: $BB^b F c g^{218}$. This was the French *basse de violon* that was made for export there, with a string length of at least 78 cm. It is likely that it was played mostly by amateur gentlemen, since professional fiddlers (being of servant class, had to stand while playing and often had to play while walking) usually preferred smaller more portable instruments. This instrument was considered to be equivalent to the usual *violone* (a double bass viol) in fulfilling its usual role as the ambiguous low bass/contrabass of string ensembles. This tuning lacks only the lowest three semitones of the usual *violone* viol tuning.

The invention of gut strings wound with metal around 1660 allowed shorter string lengths while still having the lowest string sounding acceptably. So, while previously, to have a *C* low string, the string length had to be at least 72 cm long, it could then be much shorter. This allowed the small *basso da braccio*, with a string length of about 62 cm, to acquire a low *C* string. Some added a fifth string and tuned like the earlier large 5-string bass: *C G d a e'*, while many did not change Others just tuned down a fifth to *C G d a*, and concentrated on playing bass lines that were usually expected to be played on the *violone*. Since these versions of the original *basso da braccio* were smaller than a *violone* but performed its musical role, they assumed the name *violoncello*. At the end of the 17th century, larger *violoncelli* (of modern size, with string stop about 68 cm) began to be made. This gave the instrument the power to perform adequately the role of the *violone* in large halls or churches. Some players, preferring the sound of an all-gut *C* string to one wound with metal, opted for a string stop of 72 cm, or a bit more, reviving the early gentleman's instrument in a 4-string version. Modern early-music players have often mistakenly assumed that surviving examples of these large cellos had been French basses.

As the 18th century progressed, both sizes of larger cellos gained in popularity, but the original smaller size, in 5-string and 4-string high- and low-tuning versions, continued to be used, and they were sometimes then called *violoncello piccolo*[219]. If suspended diagonally, with the lower back against the right shoulder, the neck held downwards to the left, and bowed along the other diagonal, it was sometimes called *viola da spalla*. Also, tenor viols played that way became 6-string *viole da spalla*. After the middle of that century, it seems that the quicker response of metal-wound basses became more important than the groggy masculine sound of all-gut basses. So the *violino* acquired a metal-wound 4th string, and the larger cello with an all-gut 4th went out of fashion.

---

[218] G. Zannetti, *Il Scolaro* (Milan, 1645). Also, G. M. Bononcini, *Della Sonate da Camera, e da Ballo, Opera Secondo* (Venice, 1667), No 37 and 38. Here the 'violone' part was given with a scordatura tuning of *C G d g* (i.e. with the lower three strings tuned up a tone) .

[219] The bass line in some Bach cantatas was written in treble clef, apparently for a violinist to play on a bass tuned an octave down from written.

Fiddles in France and England

A Paris woodcut showing the date MD.XVI.XIIII (presumably 1516) depicted four sitting philosophers playing small bowed instruments, the smallest held against the neck, and the others vertically between the knees.[220] The downwards way of holding the larger ones, the waist cutouts and soundboard roses (probably with a flat soundboard), show a close connection between these instruments and the original *vihuela*. Yet the sizes seem progressively to decrease from that of the *vihuela*, to half its dimensions, implying that they were fiddles of the same sizes and general pitch levels as the Italian ones.

The later French 16th century name for an ensemble fiddle was *violon* (plural *violons*). The ending of '*on*' in a name implied 'largeness' in French as well as Italian, and indeed, when the earliest surviving French tuning information on fiddles appeared in 1556[221], the tunings imply larger sizes than the Italian (and original French) ones. They were a fourth lower, except for the bass, which was an octave lower. If we can associate the earliest use of the name *violons* with the development of the larger fiddle sizes, that development happened very early, around 1520[222]. The name for the original set of sizes was not used for very long, so it is not surprising that there is no surviving record of it. The size change was early enough for the derivation to be forgotten by 1556, when Jambe de Fer mistakenly stated that the Italian name for a fiddle was *violon da braccio*.

Since the English names for ensemble fiddles in the 16th century were variants of *violon* (with an 'an' or 'en' ending, as well as 'on'), it is very likely that the English instruments were similar to the French ones.

All of the fiddles mentioned by Jambe de Fer had four strings. The tunings were *basse*: $BB^b F c g$, *taille* (tenor) and *hautcontre* (alto): $c g d' a'$, and *dessus:(treble)* $g d' a' e''$. Assuming that roped-gut strings were initially not used, and that the *ton de chapelle* pitch standard was relevant, the calculated string-length ranges would be 101-126, 53-56 and 37-37 cm respectively. The *La Volta* painting of the Valois court c.1580[223] shows three *dessus de violons* of this size and one *basse* of about 100 cm string length in the fiddle band. Roped-gut strings could allow smaller instruments more convenient to handle, with string lengths down to about 78 cm on the *basse* and 42 cm on the *hautcontre*. The similar *La Volta* painting (from around the same time), suggested to be showing Queen Elizabeth dancing with the Earl of Leicester, also with three trebles and a bass (and four strings on each), had a bass with about 80 cm string length[224], appropriate for a roped-gut BB^b 4th. It is possible that one of the trebles used a roped-gut *c* to tune like a *hautcontre*.

---

[220] reproduced in D. D. Boyden (1965) op. cit. Figure 1, p. 13.

[221] P. Jambe de Fer, *Epitome musical* (Lyons 1556).

[222] 'Pour le trompettes et vjollons de Verceil' is mentioned in Torino, Archivio di Stato, *Tesoreria generale Savoia*, reg. 181, c. 194 (1523), cited in R. Baroncini, 'Contributo alla storia del violino nel sedicesimo secolo', *Recercare* VI (1994), pp. 61-190.

[223] reproduced in D. D. Boyden (1965), Plate 13.

[224] reproduced in D. D. Boyden (1965), Plate 14.

We can make a good guess about the motivation of French fiddlers to opt for larger instruments. Jambe de Fer wrote that 'we call viols those with which gentlemen, merchants and other men of virtue pass their time', while there are 'few people who play ... [the *violons*] except those that make their living from it'. The higher social status of the viol could have made the fiddlers want their instruments to be more like viols. This can explain both larger sizes (and lower pitches) and the increased overall pitch range of the set created by the bass dropping a fifth more than the other two tunings. The gap created by this increased overall pitch range is the obvious motivation for increasing the number of strings on the middle sizes to four. The extension of the bass range of the smaller sizes could well have been facilitated by the insertion of a sound post. Some German viols in the 1530's had the treble feet of their bridges going through holes in the soundboard acting largely as sound posts, so it was probably known that sound posts can enhance the bass.

The surviving Andrea Amati instruments decorated with the arms of Charles IX of France (who died in 1574) need to be discussed. They have been updated since, but what we know most about their original sizes is their body lengths. In all of the 16th century Italian and French fiddles in pictures I've seen, the string lengths were greater than the body lengths. Compared to the baroque, the neck lengths were usually a bit longer and the bridge position was usually lower on the soundboard. According to Witten,[225] the body length of Amati's 'small violins' is 34.2 cm, and of the 'large violins' is 35.4 cm. They could have originally been made to be 4-string French *dessus de violons* tuned to $g \, d' \, a' \, e''$, which had string lengths of 37 cm (with no leeway). We don't know whether they were made to be played by the king's French fiddle band or by the Italian fiddle band he also employed. If these instruments were for the Italian fiddle band, they originally were *contralto viole da braccio*, probably with 3 strings tuned to $c' \, g' \, d''$. The range of string lengths for this tuning is 29 to 41 cm.

The only uncut Amati Charles IX 'viola' has a body length of 47 cm. If it was originally for the French fiddle band, it would have been a middle-size *violon* tuned to $c \, g \, d' \, a'$, which had a range of string lengths of 51 to 56 cm. If it was originally for the Italian fiddle band, it would have been a *basso viola da braccio* tuned to $B^b \, f \, c' \, g'$, which had a string-length range of 55 to 62 cm.

There are no uncut 'cellos' in the Amati set, but Witten estimated the original body length to be 79.5 cm. If they were originally made for the French royal band, they could have originally been examples of the *basse de violon* with the tuning $BB^b \, F \, c \, g$ that was of the later size that had a roped gut 4th. That instrument had a string-length range of 78 to 126 cm. The roped-gut 4th had limited availability at high expense from Barcelona before the 3rd quarter of the 16th century, and there is evidence that French kings were willing to buy the most expensive strings.[226] The only way that this could have been made for the Italian fiddle band would have been if the preference of the French for large basses led the band to use an octave bass tuned like the *basse de violon*. It is possible that for that band, Amati invented the 5-string large *basso* (that Praetorius illustrated, but with a longer neck) by using the roped-gut strings that the king could afford. There is evidence on at least one of the surviving

---

[225] L. C. Witten II, 'The surviving instruments of Andrea Amati', *Early Music* 10/4 (Oct. 1982), pp. 487-94.

[226] L. Wright (private communication) noticed that in the financial records of the French court, 4 viols were bought for Henry II in 1543 for 180 Livre tournoise at the same time that a set of strings for one viol was bought for 9 Livre tournoise. A set of 5 gut strings costing 1/5 the price of an average viol fit for a king is indeed expensive.

'cellos' that it had 5 strings some time in its history.

Around 1600, the English started to change the name of their set of fiddles from variants of *violons* to 'violins'. The singular term *violin* occurred in Venetian documents from 1576 onwards when referring to the soloistic *violino*[227]. The change of English terminology apparently reflected a growing interest in the fancy new style of soloistic bowed-instrument performance emerging from Italy. The *viola bastarda* was emulated on a small bass viol (probably originally made for vocal accompaniment) played 'leero way', and the *violino* was also emulated on the treble vyollen (apparently often rather unsuccessfully if we believe the scathing comments about attempts at playing it in plays of the period). The 17th century Italian fiddle band including the *violino* performed more dramatically and vocally than the French fiddle band, and it must have fascinated the English. Yet the English often played violins with viols, calling it a 'four-string treble' while the treble viol was called a 'six-string treble'.[228] There was a fashion in the 1630s to make some violins with bodies that looked like viols.[229]

By then, the only difference in sizes and tunings between the French and Italian sets of fiddles was in the basses. The English, at least outside the royal music establishment, apparently tended to use the handier Italian bass. The French themselves could have occasionally used the Italian bass. A French drawing of c. 1650, showed boy angels playing three fiddles of *dessus* size plus a considerably larger instrument played in the *viola da spalla* position, apparently performing the role of a bass[230]. From it's size, it could have been a large *taille,* tuned *c g d' a'* with a string length of about 56 cm, or a *basso viola da braccio* tuned, perhaps more appropriately, a fifth lower, with a string length of about 62 cm.

From late in the 17th century, complications developed in distinguishing between what a bass viol and a bass violin were in England. The Talbot ms discussed Lewis's bass violin made for Lord Abergenny that had six strings tuned like a bass viol, and was particularly loud. He also wrote 'Some for Vocal Accompaniment will tune Viol (B[ass]) by 5ths as Violin'. Thus tuning was not a distinguishing factor. Simpson mentioned the type of division viol that he preferred that had a body built like a violin, so the type of body was not a distinguishing factor. Talbot wrote 'Bass viols of all sizes, least large the Bass violin', which indicates that bass violins could belong to the category of bass viols. This would all make sense if we assume that 'bass viol' was a generic term for bass bowed instrument, and when there was a distinction, violins played louder for lighter music while viols played softer for more serious music. The name used related to musical function, like the 'violone' in Italy. Bass violins could use lighter stringing, which made playing softer, and would functionally be viols. In later centuries, cellos were sometimes called bass viols.

By the last decade of the 17th century in England, metal-wound strings were not yet used on violins, but they could be used on the 4th string of a bass violin[231], probably on the usual one with the small Italian size to tune like the large French one (used by the royal fiddle band) for playing French

---

[227] R. Baroncini, 'Contributo alla storia del violino nel sedicesimo secolo', *Recercare* VI (1994).

[228] E. Segerman, 'A 1656 Tabley ms: on viol players, cittern and gittern', *FoMRHI Q,* 46 (Jan. 1987), Comm. 773, pp. 34-5.

[229] E. Segerman, 'Viol-bodied Fiddles', *Galpin Soc. J.* XLIX (1996), pp. 204-6.

[230] reproduced in D. D. Boyden (1965), Plate 32.

[231] mentioned in the Talbot ms (c. 1694).

fiddle-band music. Early in the next century, most French violins had close-wound 4th's and half-wound 3rd's (a stringing popular for most of the century), though others still used all-gut stringing. At least till the 1740's, the *basse de violon* still used all-gut stringing[232]. After the modern-size violoncello was developed in Italy around 1700, it was adopted soon in England, replacing previously-used bass violins[233]. It was used to some extent in France, but the *basse de violon* still dominated for much of the century. The *Encyclopédie* table of tunings (c. 1770) has a note mentioning a *Contre Bass* tuned a fifth or an octave below the *Basse*.

Fiddles in Germany

Early in the 16th century, the Germans developed two types of sets of fiddles, with three strings on each size. One was the Spanish design of a *vihuela* with a cut-out waist and a rose between the cut-outs, but with a short neck. It also had frets and a glued bridge. The other was a club or pear shaped carved fiddle with a fretless flat fingerboard continuous with the top surface of the body and a step downwards (near the body's widest point) to the curved proper soundboard that had a clearly rounded bridge on it. This instrument was a descendant of the 15th century dual-purpose fiddle of this design, but there is no 16th century evidence of the use of a low flat bridge above the step. A relation to the 15th century Italian set of rebecs is likely.

Virdung (1511) illustrated one of those with the club shape. He called them *clein Geigen*. Agricola (1528), calling them *klein Geigen*, illustrated four sizes of each of both types. The tunings given were *Bassus: F c g, Tenor & Altus: c g d'* and *Discantus: g d' a'*. These, as with the Italian fiddles, were most probably pitches for reading, with sounding pitches an octave higher.

The three tunings in Gerle's (1533) *kleynen Geyglen* were relative only, and differed from Agricola's only that the bass was an octave below the treble, and that it had a fourth string a fifth below the third. The bass was illustrated, and it was club shaped, the bridge was curved, the soundboard extended all the way to the neck narrowing and the fingerboard was overhanging.

Agricola's second edition (1545) discussed two kinds of fiddles, the *Polischen Geigen* (from Poland) and *kleinen handgeigen*. The tunings of the two types were the same, differing from the first edition only in the bass, which was an octave below the treble, with an added 4th string tuned a tone below the 3rd (*F G d a, c g d'* and *g d' a'*, sounding an octave higher). The calculated string length ranges for these tunings, assuming a pitch standard of Catholic chorthon, would be 40-55, 29-41 and 21-27 cm. The *kleinen handgeigen* were illustrated by the same drawings of club-shaped fiddles as in the first edition. The *Polischen Geigen* were not illustrated. They replaced the fretted fiddles (with glued bridges) of the first edition. We can conclude that the strings were bowed individually because they were stopped not by being pressed against a fingerboard but by being pressed sideways by left-hand fingernails (like the Indian *sarangi* is fingered today).

---

[232] E. Segerman, 'Strings through the ages III: viola, bass violin and 'cello stringings', *The Strad* 99/1176 (April 1988), pp. 295-9: the evidence relates to Prin's thick string for the trumpet marine.

[233] R. North, *Roger North on Music … Essays … c.1695 - c.1728* (London, 1969), ed. J. Wilson, p. 304; North commented on the great improvement in the quality of bass violins since his youth, which is likely due to the introduction of the violoncello of modern size.

No more evidence on tunings of fiddles has been reported in Germany for the rest of the 16th century. As mentioned in the chapter on German viols, there were large bass and contrabass fiddles that played in mixed ensembles[234]. There was increasing Italian influence. Italian *viola da braccio* players were employed in the Bavarian court in the 1560s[235]. The set of four real fiddles 'played' by cherubs standing on the capitals in Freiberg cathedral (installed in 1588) were made in Germany but were of largely Italianate design[236].

A collection of fiddle tunings and scaled illustrations was given by Praetorius (1619, 1620). The tunings were at the Cammerthon pitch standard, which was a tone higher than that assumed for the fiddle tunings previously considered here. Drawing 8 of plate XVI shows a *Klein Geig/ Posche genant* and drawings 1 and 2 of plate XXI show *Kleine Poschen/ Geigen ein Octav höher*. These were soloistic fiddles of the type that would have been called a rebec in Italy, France and England, with the first two having three strings, and the third four. The string lengths were 18, 23 and 27 cm respectively, with the third narrower and more elongated than the others. The first two can be associated with the *a' e" b"* and *g' d" a"* tunings in the tuning tables. The third only fits the *violino* tuning in the table, *g d' a' e"*, and appears to have been a dancing-master's violin. The text associates at least the first of these as the *pochette* played in France. I know of no evidence of another type of French fiddle at this high pitch at this time, which is also the pitch of the *violino piccolo alla Francese* in Monteverdi's *Orfeo,* and so this instrument appears to have been such a rebec.

The table includes tunings for the *Klein Discant Geige*: *c' g' d" a"*, the *Discant Viol[a], Violino*: *g d' a' e"* and *Tenor Viol[a]*: *c g d' a'*. The string lengths on the illustrations were 23 cm (called *Discant Geig ein Quart höher*), 30 cm (called *Rechte Discant-Geig*) and 35 cm (called *Tenor-Geig*). The *Klein Discant Geige* was the original treble fiddle of the 16th century Italian and later German fiddle sets (later called *violino piccolo*), and the *Rechte Discant Viol[a]* or *Violino* and the *Tenor Viol[a]* were the current treble and alto/tenor fiddles in such sets. These string lengths were smaller than Italian ones, appropriate for the higher pitch standard.

The table includes two 4-string tunings for the *Bass Viol[a] de Braccio*, neither of which was illustrated. The first was *F c g d'* (*G d a e'* at the Italian pitch standard), and appears to have been the normal Italian *basso viola da braccio*. The second was *C G d a*, which has a calculated possible string-length range of 63-98 cm. This range includes the over 78 cm range of the French *basse de violon*. We know that Praetorius was trying to be comprehensive. He surely knew about this French instrument, and this seems to be the only place that he could have included it. His tuning for it was two tones higher than the pitches the French tuned it to.

The *Bas-Geig de bracio* that Praetorius illustrated had five strings and a string length of 72 cm.

[234] e.g. woodcuts by Jost Amman in G. Kinsky, *A History of Music in Pictures* (Dent 1929), p. 81.

[235] M. Troiano, *Discorsi della trionfi, giostre, apparati* (Munich 1568), mentioned in D. D. Boyden (1965), op.cit. pp. 62.

[236] T. Flemming, 'Die Akte Freiberg', *Concerto* 53 (May 1990). See also G. Lyndon-Jones. 'Real Instruments and Fake Putti', *FoMRHI Quarterly 73* (Oct. 1993), Comm. 1186, p. 21.

It almost filled the possible range for gut stringing, so its tuning at his pitch standard could only be *BB^b f c g d'*. It seems to have been the Italian gentleman's bass fiddle tuned *C G d a e'* at the Italian pitch standard. This 5-string bass was not listed in the table, but a 5-string contrabass called *Gross Quint-Bass* was listed (and not illustrated). The tuning given was *FF C G d a*, and it had a calculated string-length range of 88-98 cm. This contrabass fiddle also seems to have been an Italian gentleman's instrument (apparently illustrated by Virgiliano). At the Italian pitch standard, the tuning would have been *GG D A e b*.

The other pieces of 17th century German evidence come from southern German areas, where the pitch standard could be either Cammerthon or the Chorthon a tone lower. The tunings of Hitzler's (1628) fiddles were *Discant: g d' a' e''*, *Alt: c g d' a'*, *Tenor: F c g d'* and *Bass: C F c g*. The first two were the standard instruments played throughout Europe. The *Tenor* was apparently the Italian *basso da braccio*. This is the only early instance when this instrument was called a 'tenor'. The *Bass* was apparently the French *basse de violon* with the lowest string tuned up a tone. The A. S. manuscript from the middle of the century gave the same first two tunings (the second serving for *Alt* and *Tenor*) as Praetorius and Hitzler, and the *Bass* tuning was *C G d a*, as in Praetorius's higher tuning of the *basse de violon*.

In 1687, Steer[237] described a *Fagott-geige* (bassoon fiddle), which was a tour de force of metal-overspun (wound) strings. It was tuned like a bass *C G d a*, but was the size of a *tenor geige*. The bassoon in the name seems to have referred to the buzzing sound that it was reported to produce from its overspun strings. From about 1725 a 5-string version of this instrument appeared, called *viola pomposa*, tuned like the 5-string *violoncello piccolo* (with a high *e'*). This inspired the invention of a *violino pomposa* of violin size tuned an octave higher than the *viola pomposa* (combining the violin and viola tunings). It was not widely used. The octave of the pitches notated in the *viola pomposa* repertoire seem to imply *violino pomposa* tuning, but that probably only means that the *viola pomposa* was mainly played by violinists.

Leopold Mozart (1756)[238] listed the dozen bowed stringed instruments he knew. He numbered them as 1:- the almost obsolete little pochette or Kit, 2:- a practice violin with a board instead of a body, 3:- a small violin (half or quarter size) played by children, and no more used (as the *Violino Piccolo*) to play concertos because ordinary violins could play the music in higher positions, 4:- the violin, 5:- the *Bratsch* (from *braccio*) or *Viola*, that plays alto and tenor, 6:- the *Fagott-geige*, 7:- the violoncello, 8:- the *Violon* (violone) in different sizes with appropriately different tunings, tuned (to play?) an octave below the violoncello, usually with 4 strings, sometimes 3 strings, larger ones 5 strings (these used frets), 9:- the *Viola di Gamba* with 6 or 7 strings, 10:- the *Viola di Bordone* (Barytone), 11:- the *Viola d'Amore* with 6 bowed gut strings (the lower ones covered with metal) and 'steel' sympathetic strings, and 12:- the *English Violette* which differed from the viola d'amore by having 7 bowed strings and 14 sympathetic strings. He also mentioned the trumpet marine with one thick gut string and a 3-cornered body.

---

[237] D. Steer, *Grund-richter... Unterricht* (Ulm 1687)
[238] L. Mozart, *Versuch einer gründlichen Violinschule* (Augsburg 1756).

When discussing the violin, Mozart advocated strict equal tension between the strings, that could be confirmed by hanging the same weight from each. He also mentioned that the 4th string was thicker than the 3rd, which was thicker than the 2nd, which was thicker than the 1st. With equal tension, these thickness relations are met by all-gut strings, and can only possibly be met with metal wound strings if the windings were open wound, i.e. spaced so the gut core can be seen between them. Either just the 4th or both 4th and 3rd could be overspun this way. If metal winding was generally used, he would probably have mentioned it, as he did with the *viola d'amore*. It is likely that he deliberately avoided the issue.

Previously, Majer (1732)[239] wrote that the biggest violin string was gut, most often overspun with silver. It is unlikely that his violin was strung in far from equal tension, so this implies that in his experience, the 4th was usually open wound. It appears that both an all-gut and an open-wound overspun 4th had strong adherents in the 18th century. Some Germans still preferred an all-gut 4th in the 19th century. A writer from as late as 1855 stated that an all-gut violin 4th was preferred to a metal-wound one by discerning players[240].

---

[239] J. F. B. C. Majer, *Museum Musicum* (Nürnberg 1732).
[240] H. W. von Gontershausen, *Neu-eröffnetes Magazin musikalischer Tonwerkzeuge* (Frankfurt, 1855), p. 241. Quoted in C. Sachs, *The History of Musical Instruments* (Norton 1940), p. 361

The Development of Western European Stringed Instruments

Chapter 8: Renaissance and baroque plucked fingerboard instruments
usually strung with gut

Lutes with a single neck

By the beginning of the 16th century, the 6-course lute had almost completely replaced the 5-course lute. There were some experiments with 7-course lutes at that time, but they didn't last.[241] The 1st course was usually single, the 2nd and 3rd unison pairs, and the 4th, 5th and 6th courses were octave pairs. The number of courses was stable at six till the last quarter of the century, when the use of 7-course lutes grew.[242] The 7th course was tuned either a tone lower than the 6th or a fourth lower. Tuning the 6th course down a tone had always been an occasional practice, but a fourth down from the normal 6th pitch was new, and can be associated with the new availability of catlin roped-gut low strings. By 1598, there was a publication for an 8-course lute that added another tone to the range, fully exploiting these strings.[243] John Dowland was being up-to-date in 1603 when he wrote for a 9-course lute in his *Third Booke of Ayres*.[244] The 10-course lute appeared in the second decade of the 17th century.[245] This lute filled the extra fifth of range with a diatonic scale of basses, while those with fewer courses had gaps in the range.

Players (such as John Dowland), willing and able to be fussy about string quality, tended to have doubled first courses. If, like him, they were also fussy about avoiding the change of sound when a melody moves from an octaved to a unison course, they had all courses down to the 6th in unison pairs. If the lowest course was a fifth lower than the 6th, it almost certainly would have had to be an octave pair. The bass course at which the change from unison to octave pair occurred probably depended on the quality of the catlin strings available. Players who were either less fussy or didn't have the opportunity to select the best strings (like the French) had single 1st courses, and the course number where it changed from unison to octave stringing was lower.

Lutes with six courses can rarely be seen in pictures after 1600, while those with 7-courses can still be seen well into the 17th century. From around 1620, an outrider holding a single peg on top of the treble side of the peg box appears in the pictures. It was probably used to convert most 8-course lutes to 9-course ones, and 9-course lutes to 10-course ones. That outrider and a single first course became standard on lutes after then.

---

[241] S. Virdung, Musica getutscht (Basle, 1511), p. Jiii, mentioned that some lutes had 14 strings in 7 courses. The manuscript 596. HH. 24 in the Bologna University Library specified a 7-course (plucked) *viola*.

[242] G. C. Barbetta, Libro primo (Venice, 1562) was for a lute with the 7th course a tone below the 6th, while his *Novae tabulae musicae testudinariae hexachordae et heptachordae* (Strassburg, 1582) had the 7th course a fourth below. J. Kingston's English translation (London, 1574) of A. Le Roy's *A Brief and Plain Instruction* lute tutor (lost) mentioned that a few Italian lutenists were playing on lutes with a 7th course a fourth lower than the 6th.

[243] M. Reymann, *Noctes musicae, studio et industria* (Heidelberg, 1598).

[244] J. Dowland, *The third and last booke of songs or ayres* (London, 1603).

[245] e.g. John Sturt ms.

There is virtue in defining 'Renaissance lute' as 'a lute without a treble peg box outrider'. That outrider can be associated with the start of the explosion of the various baroque tunings. The Renaissance tuning itself is not a good criterion since it was an alternate to the baroque tunings on all of the types of lutes for much of the 17th century.

There was a usual medium size of Renaissance lute with the highest string called *g'*. It was called 'mean' in England, 'mezzano' in Italy and 'alto' in places like Germany where the name indicated the main clef that would be read from when playing a vocal part. A smaller standard size was tuned a tone higher than the mean and was called 'picciolo' in Italy, 'discant' in Germany, and 'treble' in England. The English treble was also often tuned down a tone (to the same pitches as the mean lute) to play highly divided high parts at consort pitch. A large standard lute, which was called 'bass' in most languages and 'grande' in Italian, was tuned a fourth below the mean. There were less popular sizes, with a 'contrabass' or 'octave bass' considerably larger than the bass, a 'tenor' between the mean and bass sizes, a 'small treble' somewhat smaller than the treble, and an 'octave' lute smaller than the small treble.

Most lutes were made in countries that had a stringed-instrument pitch standard about a tone below modern (i.e. everywhere in Europe except for Protestant Germany and Scandinavia). This is the probable explanation for the apparent degree of consistency in the association of size names with sizes and pitch levels. At that standard the size names were associated with first courses tuned to *g* (or *a*) on the contrabass, *d'* on the bass, *e'* (or *f'*) on the tenor, *g'* on the mean, *a'* on the treble, *b'* (or *b♭'*) on the small treble and *c"* or *d"* on the octave lute. These are the nominal pitches given by Praetorius plus a few alternatives (in parenthesis) that were probably also used.

The following Table gives the calculated longest and shortest string lengths for these sizes taken from the range Table in Chapter 1b. When the calculated shortest length is longer than the longest length (which is impossible), that range would not work well on that size of lute. In these cases, the shortest length is shown in smaller numbers in italics.

Maximum and Minimum Lute String Lengths
at German Catholic chorthon, Italian corista and English consort pitch

Size name	great bass		bass	tenor		mean or alto	treble or descant	small treble		small octave	
Pitch of 1st course	*g*	*(a)*	*d'*	*e'*	*(f')*	*g'*	*a'*	*(bb')*	*b'*	*c"*	*d"*
Longest string length (lengths in cm)	123	110	82	73	69	62	55	52	49	46	41
Shortest string length <0>	108	98	78	71	68	62	*56*	*54*	*51*	*49*	*45*
<semitones less than <1>	103	94	74	68	65	59	54	51	49	*47*	*43*
2 octaves and a 5th <2>	98	89	71	65	62	56	51	49	47	45	41
in the total open- <3>	94	85	68	62	59	54	49	47	45	43	39
string range with <4>	89	82	65	59	56	51	47	45	43	41	37
catlin basses> <5>	85	78	62	56	54	49	45	43	41	39	35
2-octave range with high-twist basses	98	89	71	65	62	56	51	49	47	45	41
Typical string length	98	89	77	69	65	59	53	50	48	45	41

The numbers such as <2> in the second column refer to the number of semitones less than 2 octaves and a fifth in the total range, as indicated under 'Shortest string length' in the first column. This refers to the later lutes (using catlin bass strings), but the two rows on the bottom refer to the original 16th century 6-course lutes for which the standard sizes were developed. The last row, considered typical, is the average between the longest and shortest string lengths for these lutes, except for the great bass lutes, for which the shortest is given (because of large finger stretch). It is expected that this average represents a preference for backing away an equal amount from each limit. These theoretically-derived string lengths correspond well with the distribution of string lengths of surviving lutes.

For each size, the tuning intervals between the top six courses will be indicated by the tablature letter indicating the fingered fret that gives a unison with the next-highest course. So **h** is a fifth, **f** is a fourth, **e** a major third, **d** a minor third, **c** a tone and **b** a semitone. Then the Renaissance tuning in fourths with a third in the middle is **ffeff**, and when the lowest course was tuned down a tone, the notation used is **hfeff**.

An occasional variant in the first few years of the 17th century, called 'cordes avalées', had the intervals of **hfef** for the top five courses. The top three intervals had the guitar or bandora **fef** sequence, and Praetorius used the term 'corda valle' for such a 4-string tuning for a cittern. There was a brief peripheral fashion then for an 8- or 9-course lute in such a tuning, with the extraordinary open-string range of 2 octaves and a sixth[246]. In paintings of that time, we occasionally see lutes that had two bent-

---

[246] A. Francisque, *Le trésor d'Orphée* (Paris, 1600) with the bass intervals **fccd**, J-B Besard, *Thesaurus harmonicus* (Köln, 1603) with the bass intervals **fcf**, and J. Danyel, *Songs for the Lute Viol and Voice* (London, 1606) with the bass intervals **fcdc**.

back peg boxes with the bass one (at the end of a small extension of the neck and fingerboard) holding two courses.[247] This is an obvious way to get that extra range. In the music tablatures, the lowest two courses were never stopped, and it is suggested that these tunings were intended to be played on this type of lute.

Before the middle of the 17th century, new tunings for the top six courses of the 10-course lute were developed and spread, which we now call 'baroque' tunings. They each had a total open-string range that was reduced relative to the original range of 2 octaves. With the number of semitones of reduction added in parenthesis, tunings developed then included those with intervals:
ffdef (2), called 'harp-way flat' or 'Lawrence'
ffedf (2), called 'harp way'
ffede (3), called 'English Gaultier', 'B sharp' or 'new tuning' by Mersenne, used by Dufaut
ffedd (4), used by MeZangeau (Mersenne), and in the duet by William Lawes
ffded (4), called 'B flat' by Mersenne, used by Chancy and Dufaut
fdefd (4), used by Dufaut
edefd (5), used by Dufaut and Mercure

The above tunings that survived after the first half of the century were:
ffded (4), called 'Flat French' by Mace
fdefd (4), called 'B flatt', 'Goate' or 'Mercure' by Burwell (depending on chromatic alterations in the basses) and 'new' by Mace - ubiquitous in the late baroque (called 'D-minor' nowadays).

New tunings in the second half of the century were:
edfed (5), called 'Trumpet' or 'Jenkins' by Burwell (depending on chromatic alterations in the basses), used by Jacques de Saint Luc
fedfe (3), called 'B-sharp' by Burwell, used by Lauffensteiner, called D-major nowadays
fdede (4), used by Reusner.

On the Table, some combinations of a large pitch range and short string length will not work properly when the longest calculated length is shorter than the shortest length (shown with the shortest length in italics). These combinations are avoided in all baroque tunings in all of the standard sizes. These tunings were mostly developed in France. There is evidence for the popularity of particularly small French lutes late in the Renaissance[248]. It is then quite possible that the French initially developed these tunings to play on 10-course lutes that were smaller than mean size.

Mersenne (1636) called the **ffede** tuning 'B sharp', and the **ffded** one 'B flat'. Over a generation later, the Burwell ms (c.1670) called a new tuning with intervals **fedfe** 'B sharp', and the

---

[247] e.g. Anon painting *St. Cecilia and the Angel* (c.1610) in the Galleria Nazionale, Rome, illustrated in M. Pincherle, *An Illustrated History of Music* (London, 1962), p. 84.
[248] E. Segerman, 'A late 16th century French picture with instruments', *FoMRHI Quarterly* 101 (Oct. 2000), Comm. 1736, p. 25.

fdefd one 'B flat'. From its use in ensemble music[249], it is clear that in the Burwell case (and most probably is true in the Mersenne case as well) the name of the tuning was the pitch of the first course on a lute of small treble size. We have to seriously consider the possibility that the music from much of the 17th century in baroque tunings was often played on quite small lutes. The Burwell ms lute had 11 courses, but the range was no more than that for 10 courses, since she wrote that the 'good masters' used only the high octave string of the 11th, as an alternative to a fingered note on the 6th course.

With the reduced-range baroque tunings, the innate larger range of larger lutes would allow the adding of an 11th course. By the end of the century, the tuning with intervals **fdefd** on larger lutes (mainly of normal tenor size and 11 courses) became dominant.

The 12-course two-headed lute, probably invented in the 1620s, was another solution to the problem of gut strings allowing a smaller open-string range on smaller lutes of normal design. It had two peg boxes, both with a shallow S shape. The bent-back one, tuning the 8 stopped courses, was attached to most of the neck width. To the remaining neck width was attached a second peg box, near parallel to the neck, tuning the 4 courses (with individual nuts for each) of unstopped bass strings. Of small-treble size with a stopped string length of about 50 cm and with Renaissance tuning, the strings ranged from *C* to *b'*.[250] As the other tunings became popular, it adopted them too, with some of the range contraction not only in the bass but in the treble as well (so the first course was not tuned as high as it could go). It had a short vogue in France where it was soon rejected because the basses were considered to be too strong. It nevertheless remained popular in England and northern Europe for about half a century. Mace's famous 'Musick's Monument' (1676) was mostly about this instrument with the **ffded** tuning.[251] With the contracted-range baroque tunings, it could be larger. Some pictures from the 17th century show larger 12-course lutes of this design (one of small tenor size is seen a famous painting by Sorgh[252]), and late in the century, the Talbot ms gave measurements of a 12-course two-headed lute of mean size.

Around 1700, the Germans converted the 11-course lute into a 13-course one by adding an outrider on top of the bass side of the peg box which included four pegs and a nut which added about 5 cm to the string length.

An analysis of the string holes in the bridges of surviving lutes with one nut and Renaissance tuning suggests that the tension of a top single string was about 3 Kg, that of the next five or six courses was fairly constant at about 2.2 Kg, and then that of the lower courses steadily dropped to

---

[249] T. Crawford, 'An Unusual Consort Revealed in an Oxford Manuscript', *Chelys* 6 (1975-6), pp. 61-8; discussed in D.& E. Segerman, 'On baroque lute stringing and tunings', *FoMRHI Quarterly* 16 (July 1979), Comm. 215, pp. 26-33.

[250] One made by Raphael Mëst in 1633 has survived in the Linhöping Library; see O. Vang & E. Segerman, 'Two-headed lute news', *FoMRHI Quarterly* 13 (Oct. 1978), Comm. 156, pp. 30-2, 37-8.

[251] E. Segerman, 'The size of the English 12-course lute', *FoMRHI Quarterly* 92 (July 1998), Comm. 1592, pp. 31-2.

[252] e.g. painting by H. M. Sorgh reproduced as Fig 10 in the 'Lute' entry in *The New Dictionary of Musical Instruments* 2 (MacMillan, 1984), ed. S. Sadie, p. 558.

about 1.5 Kg at two octaves and a fifth below the first.[253] This is mostly consistent with the equal-tension string diameters given by Mersenne.[254] This study indicates that the tensions of the strings of the 11-course baroque lute were similar, but that of the lowest string was at about 1.7 Kg tension.

Lutes with two necks (or with extended necks)

We have seen above how reduced open-string range tunings were developed to back away from the pitch-string length limits of gut stringing. Another way to back away from these limits is to make the string lengths of the bass strings (tuned diatonically so it can played like a harp) considerable longer than the fingered higher strings. Such instruments are now often called 'extended-neck' lutes.

In Italy, Piccinini invented the two-necked lute (as Mersenne called it) around 1595, and called it an *arciliuto* (archlute).[255] After that, as he reported, others applied its principle to the chitarrone. The chitarrone had been invented around 1585 by Naldi, who strung an octave bass or bass lute with the upper one or two courses usually tuned somewhat lower than normal, while the lower courses were tuned almost an octave higher (to appropriate pitches for a mean or treble single-necked lute). This was a re-entrant version of a normal Renaissance lute tuning, with the 1st or both the 1st and 2nd courses an octave lower than expected from the other strings. Strumming was probably a large component of the use of Naldi's instrument since the name 'chitarrone' means large guitar, and guitars were then mainly strummed. More than a decade later, the chitarrone copied the long second neck of the archlute, while retaining its name. The name *tiorba* (theorbo) was also used for that version of it. *Tiorba* was the name of a hurdy gurdy that beggars played, and this name could well have been adopted initially as a humorous nickname for the large two-necked chitarrone, perhaps because the long strings sounded on and on, like hurdy gurdy drones. By about 1650 the theorbo name completely replaced the chitarrone name in Italy. It had always been the name for it when it diffused outside of Italy. The theorbo had a longer first neck than the archlute (then also called 'theorboed lute'), and always had re-entrant tuning of the fingered strings, while the archlute always had the fingered strings in normal lute tuning.

Piccinini's account of the origin of two-necked lutes has been disputed by D. A. Smith[256], who has insisted that the chitarrone that Naldi invented must have already had a long second neck. He has researched the details of Piccinini's story, but found no evidence that is inconsistent with it. When Piccinini published it, there must have quite a few influential people still alive who would have remembered whether two-necked lutes were played between 1585 and 1595, and it would have been foolish for him to have tried to rewrite the history, as Smith has suggested. A refutation of Smith's theory was published by Christoforetti[257], but Smith is adamant in trusting his belief more than a

---

[253] E. Segerman, 'An analysis of the bridge hole data on lutes in Comms, 1288 and 1350', *FoMRHI Quarterly* 107-8 (April-July 1998), Comm.1807, pp. 26-31.

[254] M. Mersenne, *Harmonie universelle* (Paris, 1636), Book 2, Prop. II, discussed in E. Segerman, 'String tension on Mersenne's lute', *FoMRHI Quarterly* 11 (April 1978), Comm. 129, p. 65.

[255] A. Piccinini, *Intavolatura di liuto et di chitarrone, libro primo* (Bologna, 1623), pp. 5,8.

[256] D. A. Smith, 'On the Origin of the Chitarrone', *JAMIS* 32 (1979), pp. 440-62, and *A History of the Lute from Antiquity to the Renaissance* (Lute Society of America, 2002), pp. 83-4.

[257] O. Cristoforetti, introduction to a reprint of Piccinini's book (Florence, 1983), Franch translation in *Musique Ancienne* 19

straightforward acceptance of the historical evidence.

Piccinini mentioned that before inventing the second neck, his previous attempt to give longer lengths to low strings was an instrument with the extra length going over a very long body. Though it was not a success, the prototype instrument survives.[258] Low on the soundboard is a bridge for 3 single bass strings, and well up on the soundboard is another bridge for 7 double courses of length appropriate for a tenor lute, 3/5 the length of the bass strings. The idea was not really new, since an unlabelled instrument with many bridges that varied string length on a long flat body[259] had already existed in Archduke Ferdinand's collection in Ambras (the nucleus of the current collection in Vienna K. M.) and was called 'a large strange lute with two peg boxes and three roses' in a 1596 inventory.

Two-necked lutes had a somewhat wider-than-normal lute neck under the fingerboard. On the end of this neck was the nut for the fingered strings. Inserted into the end of this neck, instead of the bent-back peg box of a normal lute, was a second neck angled slightly backwards and sideways from being parallel to it. There was a scoop carved out of the near end of the second neck, which served as a peg box for the fingered strings. These were tuned from pegs inserted through the sides of this neck. On the far end of the second neck was the peg box for tuning the longer unfingered strings (diapasons). The Italian swan-neck design for the second peg box had it glued to the end of the second neck, rising above it and extending back towards the bridge, with its nut on the bridge end. The French design had the second nut near the end of the second neck, with the peg box extending further away from the bridge, with its curved design often ending with a scroll on its back (the opposite direction from that on a violin). The design that appears in many Dutch paintings of archlutes had the second nut on the end of the second neck, with the strings going over it around to the back of that neck, and they were tuned from a second peg box scooped out of the far end of that neck. The English design had most of the diapasons tuned from a slot in the second neck that was continuous with the peg box for the fingered strings, with a series of nuts for them attached to that neck, plus another nut and French-style curved peg box for the lowest diapasons attached to the end of the second neck.

The names for two-necked lutes fall into two basic categories, with 'chitarrone' equivalent to 'theorbo', and 'theorboed lute' equivalent to 'archlute'. In the 17th century, archlutes were tuned with the first six courses in Renaissance-lute intervals, with the lower courses tuned in a diatonic scale (in the key of the music) down from the sixth (the last course was sometimes tuned to an additional useful chromatic bass note). In the 18th century outside Italy, the tuning tended progressively to become that of the usual French baroque lute. Theorbos had the same relative tuning as the archlutes except that the top one or two courses were reentrant, tuned an octave lower than they would otherwise be. The other

---

(March, 1985), pp. 4-19.

[258] Wendelin Venere (Padua 1595), in Vienna K. M. (Schlosser Cat. No. A. 46).

[259] Vienna K. M. (Schlosser Cat. No. A. 60). The body of this instrument has an asymmetric shape, flat back and a succession of single-course bridges from lower left to upper right. The lowest 4 of these are doubled and are tuned from a bent-back peg box attached to a very short neck coming from the top of the body. The next 6 courses are doubled and tuned from a normal lute pegbox on the end of a neck that has 5 individual fixed frets for each course on the fingerboard. Finally, there are 3 single courses tuned from the right shoulder of the body. The string length ranges for the three sets are 107-127, 70-90 and 32-37 cm. Some of the design features used in the polyphont and other instruments first appeared in this one.

courses were tuned to normal lute pitches, but with string lengths much longer than an archlute at the same pitch level.

At the usual 17th century lute pitch standard of between 2 and 3 semitones lower than modern, we can calculate that for a theorbo *g, a* or *d'* first course and with two reentrant courses, the string length of the stopped strings had to be less than 110, 98 or 73 cm, and with one reentrant course, 82, 73 or 55 cm. For an archlute *d', g'* or *a'* top string, the string length had to be less than 82, 62 or 55 cm. The tone of the lowest diapason course would be just acceptable when it was tuned to *EE, GG, AA, C* or *D*, if it was an octave pair and the string length was greater than 89, 78, 71, 62 or 56 cm, and if it was a single string and the string length was greater than 101, 88, 80, 70 or 63 cm. All of these limits were generally avoided.

Praetorius illustrated Roman and Paduan types of theorbos, each with two reentrant courses. The Roman one had 6 stopped single courses at 89 cm string length with tuning *G c f a d g* and 8 single diapasons with double that string length tuned diatonically from *FF* to *F*. The Paduan type had 8 stopped single courses at 97 cm string length tuned *E F G c f a d g* and 8 single diapasons with 4/3 that string length tuned diatonically from *DD* to *D*. On the Paduan type, the lowest stopped and diapason strings were much closer to the lowest limit for acceptable tone than on the Roman type. The reason why that type did not survive and the Roman type prevailed (sometimes with doubled stopped courses) may be that a bright focused bass tone was needed for continuo work in the larger acoustics that theorbos usually played in, and getting near to the inharmonicity limits on the lowest strings was less acceptable. The Roman one did not need thick roped-gut strings and sounded better.

The archlute that Praetorius illustrated had a string length of 72 cm for the 6 doubled courses of stopped strings and 3/2 that for the 8 single diapasons. With a gut first course, the highest pitch would be *d'* at Praetorius's standard or *e'* at the Italian standard, but Praetorius reported the pitch to be *g'*. This discrepancy is resolved with Praetorius's comment that some two-necked lutes (and even some ordinary lutes) were strung with brass and steel instead of gut. An indication that the stringing was metal in this case is in the illustration, where the strings go over a free bridge rather than tied to a fixed glued bridge, as was usual in other gut-strung plucked instruments. There was a period from about 1580 to 1620 when the wire maker Jobst Meuler of Nuremberg, using a secret process, produced steel that could be tuned as high as gut and even higher, and he eventually perfected it to be as strong as modern piano-wire steel. After 1620, he was effectively stopped from selling it with the secret unrevealed, so such strong steel became unavailable (and remained so till the 19th century). Instruments that were developed to use this steel (such as the orpharion and various citterns) had to lower their tunings and lost popularity. Instruments developed for gut that alternatively used metal stringing (like the violin and some lutes like this archlute) reverted to gut stringing.

Gut-strung archlutes were made in a variety of sizes (bass, tenor, mean and treble), with 6 or 7 doubled stopped courses and from 4 to 8 either single or doubled diapason courses. The string-length ratio of diapason to stopped courses was between 1.4 to 1.6 before the 1660s, and then became more than 2 after then. A possible explanation for this change is that metal-wound gut strings were invented then, and the added brightness when they were used on the lowest of the stopped (fingered) courses allowed longer diapasons to give the same difference in sound quality between that lowest stopped course and the highest diapason as before, while making the sound of the lower diapasons more like theorbos.

From later in the 17th century, theorbos and archlutes were extensively used throughout Europe until late in the 18th century. Playing with nails was more common on these kinds of lute than on any other type. Large theorbos were mainly used for continuo in large ensembles in churches and opera houses. Nominal pitch for the first course was usually *g* or *a*. Smaller theorbos were used for continuo in smaller halls, and for the solo music that was written for the instrument. Archlutes were mainly used for vocal accompaniment, solo music and continuo in small ensembles.

In 18th century Germany, a 13-course archlute that was an alternative to the 13-course lute was developed and became quite popular. It had a French design second peg box and a crank-shaped second neck (probably copied from the angelique) that made the string length of the five unstopped diapason courses usually less than 1.4 times that of the eight stopped courses.

An analysis of the hole diameters in the bridges of surviving Renaissance-tuning archlutes suggests that the tension of the lowest of the stopped strings was about 1.7 Kg, and of the lowest of the diapasons 2 Kg or more. Of the surviving German 13-course archlutes, the tensions of the lowest string of each set was about 2 Kg.[260]

Vihuela and viola

As mentioned in Chapter 4, the Inquisition in Spain effectively banned the lute, considering it to be a Moorish instrument that was non-Christian. The multi-purpose 15th century vihuela (with a waist cut-out having sharp corners) was politically acceptable as a substitute for the lute, but even with a 10-fret neck, it was small-treble size, smaller than most lutes. There was much cultural interchange between Spain and the Spanish-held regions of southern Italy and the Spanish-led papacy. The Italian plucked viola (with no corners in the waist) was in normal lute sizes with an 8-fret neck length. To perform the functions of the lute, associated with the switch from 5 to 6 or 7 courses (and the bowed vihuela pursuing a different course), the Spanish adopted the Italian body design and string lengths, but had relatively smaller bodies to retain the original vihuela's 10-fret neck. By the second quarter of the century, the new vihuela distanced itself further from the lute by replacing the peg box with a peg plate with the pegs coming in from the back.

As stated above, lutes in the 16th century had size names, with the most popular one, called 'mean' in English and *mezzano* in Italian, tuned with the top string called *g'*, with the string length about 59 cm. The 'treble' or *picciolo* or *discant* was usually tuned a tone higher (with the top string nominally at *a'*) and had a string length of about 53 cm. The bass was tuned a 4th below the most popular one (having the top string at *d'*), and had a string length of about 77 cm. There was another one, sometimes called 'tenor', tuned a tone above the bass (with a top string at *e'*) with a string length of

---

[260] E. Segerman, 'An analysis of the bridge hole data...' op. cit.

about 69 cm. The pitch standard was more than a tone below modern, which was usual in most Catholic countries and in England. The viola (da mano) had these sizes for some time, and the new vihuela adopted them.

Valderrabano mentioned a *vihuela mayor* and a *vihuela menor* when writing for two vihuelas tuned a fourth apart.[261] We can associate the *vihuela mayor* with the bass or tenor sizes, which would then associate the *vihuela menor* with the mean or the treble sizes respectively. He also wrote duets for two vihuelas a minor third apart (probably a tenor and a mean) and a fifth apart (a bass and a treble). In Bermudo's terminology,[262] it is linguistically likely that his *vihuela comun* was equivalent to the mean, and his *discante* was equivalent to the treble. He mentioned a trio that played together. That trio had a *discante*, a 4-course guitar with the top string a tone higher than the *discante* and a vihuela tuned a fourth lower than the *discante*. This vihuela would then be tenor size, and the guitar string length would be less than 50 cm.

Bermudo also wrote that a *vihuela de siete ordines* was particularly large and was played by famous soloists. It was most probably of bass size. The common tuning he gave for it was **fffeff**. He suggested a new tuning of **hfhfhf**, but fearing that strings the requisite size would be difficult to obtain, he suggested **hfehfe** as an alternative. The open-string ranges for these tunings are 2 octaves and a fourth, 3 octaves and 2 octaves and a minor sixth respectively. The common tuning covers the range of a 7-string lute with roped-gut low basses. His first suggested new tuning is anomalously large, and would be impractical because of poor bass string sound. His alternative tuning just fits into the range for catlin strings and an octave-pair 7th course on a full-size bass with 82 cm string length.

This is not the only indication then that the Spanish had catlin bass strings when they were not affordably and reliably available enough elsewhere in Europe to allow instruments that relied on them to be designed, such as the 7-course lute. Another indication is that the vihuela had all six courses in unison pairs, implying that the string qualities that Dowland insisted on were generally available in Spain earlier in the century. Another is that there was a thriving string-making industry in Barcelona, and the most credible origin for the English string-type name 'catlin' is 'Catalan', implying that when the name originated, such strings were imported from Barcelona. Also, while the lute grew in popularity elsewhere in the second half of the century, the vihuela declined, and this could be associated with the probable decline in the string-making industry when the South German merchants who ran the Spanish economy were ruined when the Spanish court became massively bankrupt in 1557.[263] Munich was previously where expensive high quality strings (more elastic and uniform) had come from, and it is likely that Munich string makers set up the Barcelona industry. Gold and silver from America made the Spanish aristocracy very affluent, and they could afford the most expensive strings.

---

[261] E. de Valderrábano, *Libro de musica de vihuela, intitulado Silva de sirenas* (Valladolid, 1554).

[262] J. Bermudo, *Declaración de instrumentos musicales* (Osuna, 1555).

[263] F. Braudel, The Mediterranean and the Mediterranian World in the Age of Philip II, 2nd ed. (1966), English transl. by Reynolds (1972), p. 511.

When the vihuela declined in popularity, so did the Italian viola. This is probably because the conversion of vihuelas to 5-course guitars (see below) became so popular that violas converted as well.

Milan's music[264] includes a barre on the first fret while simultaneously fingering the 5th fret, which from the finger-stretch discussion in Chapter 1, calculates to a string length of less than 59 cm. This is inconclusive about whether it was of mean or *discante* size. The latter is supported by his tendency to consider that his 1st course was tuned to *a'*. Mudarra's guitar music[265] has a stretch including the 3rd and 8th frets, which calculates to a string length of less than 54 cm.

Bermudo mentioned a 5-course guitar, and Fuenllana published music[266] for a 5-course vihuela (with guitar tuning, i.e. the third was between the 2nd and 3rd courses), which appeared in his book before music for a 4-course guitar. It is possible that Bermudo didn't call the *discante* a vihuela because with 6 courses it would be a vihuela, while with 5 courses (tuned like Fuenllana's), he considered it to be a guitar, so to him the name had to be deliberately ambiguous. The Dias guitar at the Royal College of Music[267] was probably such a 5-course *discante*.

Estimation from facial dimension of string lengths of vihuelas from drawings of the time of high popularity results in a few of tenor size and most of the mean size. The only surviving vihuela from this period is the one in Paris, and it is of full bass size.[268] That instrument has a neck that is so narrow that the strings would have to be so thin that it could only be sounded very delicately, and not fit to be the bass of an ensemble. Except for the soundboard, bridge and pegs, all visible parts of the instrument were made of small pieces of wood glued together in decorative patterns, and so it was probably an instrument that was part of a maker's examination.

Four-course guitar (gittern)

Late in the 15th century, Tinctoris[269] wrote that the medieval gittern (a miniature lute usually with four courses) was used rarely 'because of the thinness of its sound', and when he heard it in Catalonia, it was played more by women to accompany love songs than by men. A few years after this, those who bowed vihuelas modified or replaced them to have moveable bridges, and those who plucked vihuelas replaced them with 10-fret violas to fill the ecological niches of the lute. It is likely that some of the original vihuelas that had become redundant got into the hands of gittern players, who just took off a course (two strings) and played them as gitterns. It was the right size (small treble, from a lute prospective) and was probably more resonant than the old gittern. It would have been appropriate then for any instrument that gittern-players played, and played like a gittern, to have been called a gittern (*guitarra* in Spanish), regardless of its shape. With the new design of gittern, gittern-

[264] L. de Milán, *Libro de música de vihuela de mano ... intitulado El maestro* (Valencia, 1536).

[265] A. Mudarra, *Tres libros de musica en cifras para vihuela* (Seville, 1546).

[266] M. de Fuenllana, *Libro de música para vihuela, intituldo Orphenica lyra* (Valladolid, 1554)

[267] Guitar by Belchior Dias (1581) at the Royal College of Music, No. 171, London

[268] Vihuela in the Musée Jacquemart-André, Paris

[269] J. Tinctoris, *De Inventione et Usu Musicae* (c. 1487), trans. A. Baines, 'Fifteenth-century Instruments in Tnctoris's *De Inventione et Usu Musicae*', Galpin Soc. J. III (1950), pp. 19-26.

playing began to prosper again in Spain.[270]   Within a few decades, gitterns copied the body design (without the sharp corners on the waist) and the peg plate (for holding the tuning pegs) of the current vihuela, and then looked like a miniature version of it.

By the middle of the 16th century, such gitterns had spread to the rest of Europe and the overseas colonies of European countries, as the vihuelas played then didn't. Gitterns were played (at least in Spain and Italy) through the 17th and 18th centuries. We now call this instrument the 'Renaissance guitar'.   The adjective 'Renaissance' is modern and the noun 'guitar' is 17th century English. In the 16th century the instrument was called 'gittern' in England, *guitarra* in Spain, *guiterne* in France, *chitarra* in Italy and *quinterne* in Germany. Some baroque names for it were 'Italian guitar' and *chitarrino*. In most countries other than Spain, the relative neck length was reduced to limit the number of frets tied on it to only eight, like on the lute, and the peg plate often reverted to a curved pegbox.

In most of the surviving music, this instrument was plucked pseudo-polyphonically (like the lute), but another important component of playing style was strumming.

Tunings given by Bermudo had the intervals **fef**, called *temple nuevos* (new tuning) and **hef**, called *temple viejos* (old tuning), with the 4th course an octave pair, the 3rd and 2nd courses unison pairs, and a single 1st nominally tuned to *a'*. The French called his old tuning *à corde avalée*, sometimes tuned the 3rd course down a semitone to give the intervals **eff**, and sometimes had that course as an octave pair.[271] The low string of the octave pair of the 4th course was called *bordón* by the Spanish and *bourdon* by the French. Sometimes, especially for strumming, that course was described as having no bordon when the 4th course was a unison pair at the high octave.

With a much smaller open-string pitch range than the lute, the lower limit to the string length (dictated by inharmonicity in the sound of the lowest string) allowed much smaller string lengths than on the lute, viola or vihuela for a particular pitch of the first string. So the top string could be tuned to *a'* with the string length considerably less than the lute minimum of 51 cm. String lengths could be as small as 38 cm.[272] With shorter string lengths, tuning to higher pitches was quite possible. Some higher pitches reported had the 1st string tuned to *b'*[273] and *d"*[274].

Five-course baroque or Spanish guitar

A new large five-course Spanish guitar was developed late in the 16th century. In publications from the 17th century and later, Vicente Espinel (1550-1624) was credited with adding the 5th course

---

[270] An early 16th century illustration of the original vihuela probably used as a gittern is given as Fig. 21 in I. Woodfield, *The Early History of the Viol* (Cambridge, 1984), p. 44.

[271] C. Dobson, E. Segerman & J. Tyler, 'The tuning of the four-course French cittern and of the four-course guitar in the 16th century', *Lute Society J.* XVI (1974), pp. 17-23.

[272] E. Segerman & D. Abbott, 'Stringed instruments on the Eglantine table', *Early Music* 4/4 (Oct. 1976), p. 485.

[273] S. Cerreto, *Della prattica musica vocale et strumentale* (Naples, 1601)

[274] J. Rowbotham, *The Breffe and Playne Instruction to Lerne to Play on the Gyttron and also the Cetterne* (London, 1568).

to the guitar. This cannot be true since 5-course guitars already existed when he was a child, but he probably contributed to the instrument's history in some other way. This new instrument was called 'Spanish Guitar' to distinguish it from the smaller four-course guitar which, though originally Spanish, had become universal, with local variations. This name was first mentioned in print in 1604 and in a manuscript source tentatively dated to be from the 1590's. A *chitarrino alla Spagnola* was specified in the 1589 *Intermedii*. The diminutive probably implies both that the guitar was of the old small size (probably a 5-course *discante*), and that the more usual one was by then bigger. Strumming was the primary playing style on guitars at this time, so the 5-course guitar repertoire could be played on the 4-course guitar as well.

Seventeenth century Italian manuals indicated that there were three sizes. The usual one, being the middle size, was called *chitarra mezzano*. Its string length was around 69 cm, the tenor size for lutes, violas and vihuelas, and the nominal pitch of the first course was stated to be *e'* in some sources and *d'* in others. No guitar methods indicated that the top string should be tuned as high as it can go, as some lute ones did. The *chitarra grande* was tuned a tone lower than the *chitarra mezzano*, the bass size for lutes, violas and vihuelas. The *chitarra piccola* was tuned a fourth higher than the *chitarra mezzano* (a fifth higher than the *chitarra grande*), the treble size for lutes, violas and the earlier Spanish 5-course *discante*. The *chitarrino* was a new name for the 4-course Renaissance guitar, and was treated like a *chitarra piccola* without its 5th course. The *chitarriglia* was mentioned as a smaller than usual guitar in several 17th century books, and one gave tunings with the top string in *g'* or *f'*. It is likely that its size was of the mean lute, viola and vihuela.

All of the standard sizes of the Spanish guitar and its design were those of previous standard vihuelas, and this suggests that the earliest Spanish guitars were previously vihuelas (which could no more be strung with the quality strings previously available). There is a 16th century painting of an angel in Barcelona Cathedral playing an instrument that from the tiles in the soundboard looks like a vihuela (tenor size) but had 5 courses (with a single 1st), like a *chitarra mezzano*. This appears to be a picture of such a converted vihuela. In 17th century Spain, guitars were often still called vihuelas.

We need to ask why the most popular guitar size was larger than the most popular size of the lute, vihuela and viola. It is likely that when guitarists restrung these vihuelas as guitars, and they strummed them, they noticed that the lower resonances of these larger instruments amplified the low-frequency components of the noises of hitting the strings during strumming, giving the percussion an attractive sound somewhat like a male-voice consonant. It is also possible that hearing this Spanish guitar influenced Naldi to restring large lutes and invent the chitarrone in the 1580s. In return, it is possible that the success of the chitarrone later encouraged the Spanish guitar to enhance its low resonance further by substantially increasing its body depth to have the body proportions of viols. Since the body resonances support the normal sounds of the lower-pitched strings much more than the higher ones, to achieve balance, there was a tendency for the lower strings to have lower tensions than the higher strings.

The Spanish guitar became very popular in Italy early in the first quarter of the 17th century, and in France late in the second quarter, when a mixture of single-note plucking (like on a lute) and strumming became popular. Praetorius (1619) mentioned with disdain the strummed 5-course guitar (*quinterna*) in his text, but listed two 4-course tunings in his tunings table, and showed a 6-course viola da mano of small-treble size in his illustration. It was probably played as a *chitarra piccola*, but he couldn't bear to draw fewer strings than there were pegs. England and German-speaking countries later followed French interest in the instrument, but these countries never adopted it as completely as Spain, Italy and France. This guitar remained popular till around 1800 when it was replaced by the 6-string guitar. In the 18th century, when the Neapolitans developed metal-strung mandoras with fixed frets and a bend in the soundboard at the bridge (see below), they did the same to the guitar. This instrument has since been called *chitarra battente*. There were also theorboed guitars, which involved a second neck, just like theorboed lutes. There are surviving design details for such a theorboed guitar by Stradivari.

The nominal tuning of 5-course guitars had the intervals **ffef**, with the 5th and 4th courses in octave pairs, the 3rd and 2nd courses in unison pairs and usually a single first (though the peg plate usually had ten pegs, with the spare 1st-course peg possibly used to tune a string that was broken at a farther peg). As with the 4-course guitar, the low string of an octave pair was called a 'bordon', and tuning variations were described by the number of bordons in the course, so having 'no bordons' meant that the course had both strings at the high octave, 'two bordons' meant that both strings were at the low octave. Two bordons was rare, reported only in Spain, where it was used mainly for strumming. Single bordons on both courses was always common in Spain, Italy and France. No bordons on both courses was similarly common, mainly for strumming. The tuning with one bordon on the 4th course and no bordons on the 5th course was common in the late 17th century 'golden' period, mainly in France, but used some elsewhere. The tuning in two 17th century Italian manuscripts had no bordons on the 4th and 5th courses and one bordon on the third. An attractive effect called 'campanella' happened when a melody danced amongst the high courses and the no-bordon 5th, with the sounds on each course ringing on and mingling with subsequent notes on other courses. This was another example (like sympathetic strings) of overlap of the sounding of notes being considered attractive.

There are indications of string diameters from Montesardo (1606),[275] Stradivari (c.1700), Castillion (1729), Corrette (1763)[276] and Baillon (1781).[277] All referred to guitars with one bordon on both courses. Opposite to lute octave pairs, the bordon was on the side of the next higher course. The bordons were gut in Montesardo's and Stradivari's sets, open-wound on gut in Castillion's set, open-wound 4th and close-wound 5th on silk in Corrette's set and close-would on silk in Baillon's set. String tensions were greatest on the higher strings and smallest on the lowest strings, becoming closer to uniform later in the 18th century, as in Baillon's set, when the guitar was increasingly played for arpeggiated accompaniment.[278]

---

[275] E. Segerman, 'A few notes on Montesardo's 5-course guitar tuning', *FoMRHI Quarterly* 106 (Jan. 2002), Comm. 1798, p. 44.

[276] M. Corrette, *Les dons d'Apollon. Méthode pour apprendre la guitarre* (Paris, 1763).

[277] E. Segerman, 'Stringings of the baroque guitar in the 18th century', *FoMRHI Quarterly* 97 (Oct. 1999), Comm. 1676, pp. 40-3.

[278] For more information, see M. Hall, *Baroque Guitar Stringing, a Survey of the Evidence*, Booklet 9, The Lute Society (2003).

Angel lute or angelique

The angel lute or angelique was a kind of archlute with single courses tuned diatonically like a harp, and was popular later in the 17th and early in the 18th centuries. Praetorius (1620)[279] drew a 23-stringed instrument that appears to be a lute body and neck converted to a harp by replacing the bridge by a very long one diagonally across the soundboard and having a straight arm for the pegs attached to the end of the lute neck at about $45°$ to it. The lute neck was not used for stopping strings. Mersenne (1636) mentioned a way of playing a normal lute like a harp or spinet by setting it up with 15 single strings.[280] All strings would be plucked open but the top three strings would sometimes be stopped to play higher pitches. It is not clear whether this was an instrument that was actually played or whether it was just a suggestion of what could be done. He wrote: 'This would impart new graces to the lute because the harmony of the open strings is greater and lasts a very long time'.

The main advantage such an instrument had over the ordinary lute (and the harp and spinet), is that one can use the fingerboard to play the lute's slurred graces on any note, not just whenever appropriate fingers are available. A particularly effective lute grace that is only poorly imitated on keyboards is the acciaccatura, which ends up with the same note sounding on different strings on the lute, and is much easier on the angel lute.[281]

The earliest appearance of the angelique name that I am aware of is the inclusion of two of them in an inventory of the contents of the shop of Jean Desmoulins on his death in 1648.[282] One was 'un [luth] acomodé à la mode d'Angleterre', as Mersenne suggested.

A surviving angelique from around 1680 is of tenor-lute size, has eight strings over the fingerboard and eight diapasons, with the latter string length about 5/3 that of the former.[283] A drawing of 1687 shows an angelique of treble or mean lute size with ten fingerboard strings and five diapasons, with the same relationship of string lengths.[284]

Pohlmann's survey of surviving lutes[285] lists 18th century German angel lutes of tenor size with ten strings on the fingerboard and six diapasons with 3/2 the string length, and some of treble size with nine strings on the fingerboard and eight diapasons with twice the string length. He also lists (p. 183) seven sources of music for the instrument from the middle to the end of the 17th century.

---

[279] M. Praetorius, *Theatrum Instrumentorum seu Sciagraphia* (Wolfenbüttel, 1620), Plate XXXVI, No. 2.

[280] M. Mersenne, op.cit. Bk. 2 Prop. XI.

[281] In *A treatise of good taste* (1749), Germiniani wrote of the player: 'In accompanying grave Movements, he should make use of Accaiccaturas, for these rightly placed, have a wonderful Effect. No performer ... should flatter himself that he is able to accompany well till he is Master of this delicate and admirable secret which has been in use above a hundred years.' Quoted in *New Grove DoMI* I p. 485. It was used in the c. 1600 lute solo repertoire.

[282] J. Dugot, 'La facture des instruments à cordes au temps de Jacque Dumesnil et Jean Desmoulins', *Instrumentalistes et Luthiers Parisiens,* (Alencon, 1988), ed. F. Gétreau, pp. 28,39.

[283] Paris, Musée Instrumental du C.N.S.M. E. 980.2.317, photo. *Instrumentalistes et Luthiers Parisiens*, op.cit. p. 42.

[284] N. Bonnart, *Damon, joüant de l'Angelique* (1687), repro. *Instrumentalistes et Luthiers Parisiens* op.cit. p. 47.

[285] E. Pohlmann, *Laute Theorbe Chitarrone* 2nd edition (1972), p. 416.

The angel lute measured in the Talbot ms (c.1694) had ten strings over the fingerboard with a short tenor string length of 66 cm (the highest still tuned to *e'*) and six 'bass' strings with a string length 3/2 that of the shorter ones.[286] The neck had nine frets of graded thicknesses. Both of Talbot's advisers on this instrument (Agutter and Crevecoeur) mentioned 'the long head is made twisting to carry the uppermost rank on its Nut', This describes a small dog's leg (or offset) in the design of the second neck that was unique with this instrument until it was copied by the late baroque German archlute that was an alternative to the 13-course single-neck lute. Crevecoeur indicated that it was 'more proper for slow and grave lessons than for quick and brisk [ones] by reason of the continuance of sound when touched which may breed discord'.

How much is too much discord bred by the 'continuance of sound' in this last comment is a judgment of taste that needs to be understood in the historical context, which includes its being the purpose of the campanella style on the Spanish guitar and the sympathetic strings on the viola d'amore, and the inefficient damping on many early stringed keyboard instruments after notes were played.

The dismissal by Prynne (1961)[287] of the angel lute as a 'rather unsatisfactory instrument [that] tried to take advantage of the more ringing tone of strings sounded open, but at the expense of compass' has no historical basis. The compass was no less than that of the 6-course Renaissance lute and the 18th century gallichon, which was adequate for all melodic and most harmonic purposes. For transfer of technique in finding the notes, the angel lute would have been more attractive for players with previous keyboard or harp experience than players with lute experience, but they would most probably have acquired it with the intention of adding the lutistic ornamentation that was so prized at the time.

Colascione, colachon and gallichon

Around 1497, Tinctoris[288] reported that Turkish prisoners (taken after their defeat about a decade earlier by the Neapolitans) played an instrument in the shape of a large spoon that they called *tambura*. He wrote that it had three strings tuned to octave, fifth and fourth. I know of no independent evidence to resolve the inconsistency between the number of strings and number of intervals. Tinctoris was being politically correct to condemn as barbarous the players, the instrument and the music played on it, but he was obviously impressed, as the Neapolitans apparently were. It was played in that region as a folk instrument up to the 20th century. The body was usually of small-treble lute size. Praetorius (1619) was not aware of it, but Mersenne (1636) called it a *colachon* and discussed and drew a picture of it.[289] He stated that it was about 4 or 5 feet (130-160 cm) long and had either two strings tuned a fifth apart or three strings tuned (from the lowest) an octave and then a fifth. It had the form of a lute with a very long fingerboard. The soundboard could be half wood and half parchment, but fir (like on other instruments) was best.

---

[286] M. Prynne, 'James Talbot's Manuscript: IV. Plucked strings - The Lute Family', *The Galpin Soc J.* XIV (1961), pp. 52-68.
[287] M. Prynne, op. cit.
[288] J. Tinctoris, *De Inventione et Usu Musicae* (c. 1487), trans. A. Baines, 'Fifteenth-century Instruments in Tnctoris's *De Inventione et Usu Musicæ'*, *Galpin Soc. J.* III (1950), pp. 19-26.
[289] M. Mersenne, op. cit., Bk. 2 Prop. XVI.

In one of three engravings of the coronation of Louis XIV is depicted the singers and string players of the Chapelle du Roy.[290] The lutes have remarkably long necks. They may have been colachons with large bodies, or archlutes with the second-peg box design not the usual one for French archlutes (the details that distinguish between archlute and colachon necks were not drawn). A clearer picture of an earlier 17th century larger-bodied colachon is a 1644 Nuremberg vignette.[291] Late in the 17th century, there was increasing use of large-bodied colachons in orchestral music as an alternative to the theorbo. Talbot (c.1694) measured a colachon that had 6 strings and a bass lute body, with a neck long enough for the string length to be that of a great bass lute, i.e. about a meter. The neck was long enough to have 12 tied frets on it, but Mr. Finger, Talbot's informant on this instrument, indicated that it had only 7 frets. The tuning given by Finger was *C D G c e a* (**cffef**), with *AA* an alternative for the 6th string (**fffef**). The first was the same tuning as the 6-course bandora, a wire-strung instrument discussed in the next chapter, while the second had the same intervals as the later 6-string guitar. Around the same time, Janovka[292] described the 'Galizona or Colachon' as having either 6 or 8 strings or doubled courses, the former in Finger's bandora tuning, and the latter in the same tuning with a *BB* 7th and *AA* 8th (**cbcffef**). It had 7 frets on the neck.

There are several drawings of public performances early in the 18th century showing continuo colachons being played.[293] In these pictures, we see that the peg box was straight and bent back, like on a lute. The original 3-string colascione had a violin-like curved peg box.

Janovka also wrote that there was a related smaller instrument tuned a fourth higher called *mandora*. There is much 18th century music for this smaller instrument, but it was often called by names like *gallichone* derived from *colachon*. It seems that the name became associated with the relative tunings of the strings, leaving the ambiguity between the name applying to the continuo colachon or the related type of mandora to be resolved by the musical context. The *gallichon* name for it suggests that the smaller instrument was originally a large lute that was adapted to perform the colachon function by using metal-wound basses to tune to the lower pitches of the continuo colachon.

In 18th century German lands (mainly in southern areas like Austria), the *mandore* or *gallichon* that was a shorter-necked version of the colachon flourished as a solo and ensemble instrument played with a full finger-plucking technique. There is much surviving repertoire in manuscript. It was usually tuned to *D G c f a d'* (**fffef**), with the 6th course sometimes tuned up to *F*. A 7-course version had both, *D F G c f a d'* (**dcffef**). The 1st course was single and the others double. With its bent-back peg box, the instrument looked like a Renaissance lute of tenor size except for the baroque single-string rider on

---

[290] *La Pompeuse et magnifique cæremonie du sacre du Roy Louis XIV fait a Rheims le 7. Juin 1654* (Paris, 1655), at Bibliothèque Nationale, Paris; reproduced ed. U. Sherrington & G. Oldham, *Music Libraries and Instruments* (Hinrichsen, 1961), plate 103.

[291] G. P. Harsdörffer, *Frauenzimmergesprächsspiele* IV (Nuremberg, 1644); reproduced ed. G. Kinsky, *A History of Music in Pictures* (Dent, 1930), p. 181.

[292] T. B. Janovka, *Clavis ad thesaurum* (Prague, 1701)

[293] Engraving by R. Trevitt, *A Prospect of the Choir*, St. Paul's Cathedral, London, at a general Thanksgiving for the successes of Marlborough's campaign against the French, 31 December 1706, reproduced in *Early Music* 8/2 (April 1980), pp. 178-80, 183; drawings in the Kupferstichkabinett, Dresden (1719) reproduced in *Early Music* 8/1 (Jan. 1980), pp. 48-9.

the treble side of the peg box. Many survive in museums today, and their identification as mandores or gallichons happened in 1979, too late for most of the classic books on instrument history.[294] This instrument was a strong influence on the late 18th century development of the 6-course guitar and the German folk guitar (laute) with a lute body.

Mandora and mandolin

The medieval gittern as a miniature lute was well out of fashion in Latin countries by 1500, but it lasted for a few decades more in southern Germany. The only small round-backed stringed instrument that was still extensively used was the rebec. By the middle of the century, a 3-string plucked instrument like the rebec *(*that was smaller than all other plucked instruments, and may have just been a plucked rebec) was played in Spain, where it was called *bandurria*.[295] Bermudo reported the tuning intervals to be **hh**, **hf** or **fh** (**h** is a fifth and **f** is a fourth), with **fh** the oldest and most common. Fretting was diatonic, chromatic or absent. He indicated that there could be 4 or more courses, and indeed, subsequently the only 3-course plucked instrument we hear of is the Neapolitan colascione). The name *bandurria* was revived in 18th century Spain to be used for a miniature plectrum-played gut-strung version of the English guitar which had 5 doubled courses tuned all in fourths.

By the 1580s the *mandore* had become quite popular in France. The body could either have been carved out of a single piece of wood or built up in staves like a lute. According to Mersenne (1636), it had 4 strings tuned to *c' g' c" g"* (**hfh**), with two other tunings when the top string was two or three semitones lower (**hff** or **hfe**). It was 1.5 feet (49 cm) in total length, had 9 frets and was plucked with the fingers, a quill grasped by the fingers, or quills tied to one or more fingers.[296] Many had 6 pegs, but the two extra were only for decoration (he said elsewhere though that it could have more strings than the usual four). From around his time, mandore music for both 4 and 5 courses was being published. The mandore was popular through most of the 17th century, but by the end, it dropped to obscurity in France.

The names given to the instrument by Praetorius (1619) were *pandurina, mandürichen, mandürinichen, mandoër* and *mandörgen*. The tuning given in the text was *g d' g' d"* (**hfh**), but the 4-course one in the tuning tables was a fourth higher, *c' g' c" g"* (**hfh**). The latter tuning is too high for the 30 cm string length in his illustration at his Cammerthon pitch standard, but is fine at the French pitch. He mentioned that the instrument was very common in France. It is very likely that the tuning in the text was a alternative that worked at his Cammerthon pitch standard, while the tuning in the tables was that used in France. He stated before the tables that the tunings were in Cammerthon, but there are other instances of corrections in the text for errors in the woodcuts. In the illustration, there is a fifth string that made the first course double. The secondary tunings in the tables were both for an instrument with five strings: *c g c' g' c"* (**hfhf**) and *c f c' f' c"* (**fhfh**). From the table in Chap 1b, these tunings require a string length of over 36 cm, but it could be as low as 32 cm if the lowest string were

---

[294] M. Hodgson, 'The identity of 18th century 6-course lutes', *FoMRHI Quarterly* 14 (Jan. 1979), Comm. 175, pp. 25-7.

[295] J. Bermudo, *Declaración de instrumentos musicales* (Osuna, 1555).

[296] M. Mersenne, op. cit., Bk. 2 Prop. XIII.

an octave pair. In his experience, playing was by quill (like on the cittern) or by a single finger 'with the speed, clarity and precision that we would expect from the use of three or four fingers' (probably using a tied quill or the nail like a quill). Some used two or more fingers once they are familiar with the instrument.

The Talbot ms (c.1694) provides evidence of the same instrument in England late in the 17th century, where it was called a 'mandole'. One of his informants, Lewis, stated that the mandole had 6 (gut) strings in 5 courses with the lowest double and the rest single. Finger, another informant, stated that *c' f' a' d" g"*(**feff**) were the string pitches. This would be an instrument with a string length of about 30 cm. Shore, a third informant, was into larger 6-course mandoles, and he gave a 10-string tuning of *c f b♭ d' g' c"* (**ffeff**), with the lowest two octave pairs, the middle two unison pairs and the top two single. This differed little from a 16th century small octave lute. Talbot measured a mandole of Shore's, and the string length was 43 cm. He also measured an arch mandole of Shore's 'much as the Arch-Lute but less [in size]'. The 6 courses over the fingerboard were identical in tuning to his mandole, with a string length of 48 cm, and 7 single long courses with a string length of 108 cm, tuned to a diatonic octave below the lowest short course. When the arch mandole was discussed in another part of the ms, it differed in that the 2nd course was doubled.

Such instruments were also used in Italy. A *mandola* was called for in the 1589 Florentine *Intermedii*, which was the usual Italian name for it. In 1607, Agazzari (calling it a *pandora*) listed it as a melodic instrument, as opposed to a chordal one. Manuscripts from the third quarter of the 17th century indicate a tuning of *e' a' d" g"* (**fff**), with the instrument played either melodically with occasional chords or strummed like the guitar.

The final quarter of the 17th century saw some changes. While music specifically written for the instrument was previously written in tablature, an increasing amount was then written in staff notation. Five-course instruments (with 10 strings) became common, with the tuning *b e' a' d" g"* (**ffff**). The name *mandolino* started to be used before the middle of the century for an instrument with this tuning. The surviving design templates of Stradivari include some specified for mandola and some for *mandolino coristo* (coristo refers to the low pitch standard of stringed instruments and non-professional choirs). Stradivari's mandolas had a variety of sizes up to an estimated string length of 55 cm, while the mandolins were much more uniform in size, with a string length around 30 cm. His mandolini usually had the normal mandora viol-like pegbox with a flat emblem instead of a head or scroll, but some had a guitar-like peg plate. It seems that *mandora* was a generic name for lute-like plucked instruments that were either smaller than lutes or had characteristics (such as tunings) that were not lute-like, while a *mandolino* was a small mandora that conformed to the usual pitch standard for playing in ensembles.

From late in the 17th century, this finger-plucked mandolino was increasingly used in operatic arias and instrumental ensembles.[297] A 6th course tuned to *g* or *f♯* started to appear in the second

---

[297] Excellent sources of information on 18th century mandoras and mandolins are J. Tyler & P. Sparks, *The Early Mandolin* (OUP, 1989) and S. Morey, *Mandolins of the 18th Century* (Cremona, 1993).

quarter of the 18th century. The tuning then was *g b e' a' d" g"* (**effff**) or *f# b e' a' d" g"* (**fffff**). Early 18th century mandolini, mainly Roman, had an increased string length of about 33 cm, and since this happened before the expansion to 6 courses, we can conclude either that somewhat stronger carefully-selected gut was then available for such instruments. Mandolini with 6 single courses started to appear around 1760, but were not popular till the 19th century. During that century, this instrument, with a raised fingerboard and played with a plectrum, was called the *mandolino lombardo* or Milanese mandolin. It was played well into the 20th century. At higher modern pitches, it could be tuned an octave above the guitar. For bass strings it used guitar strings of metal wound on silk.

Around 1760, a gut-strung finger-plucked mandolino with 4 single strings tuned like a violin g d' a' e" appeared. It was called a Cremonese or Brescian mandolino, and was apparently made for the rapidly growing market of violin players opened up by the Neopolitan mandolin.

Wire-strung mandoras

Early in the 18th century, the Neopolitans developed and played at least one type of large mandora with 8 metal strings. Pinaroli called it a *liuto a penna,* meaning a plectrum-played lute. The lute at that time and place was called arciliuto, so the term 'lute' was free to refer to large mandoras or guitars with lute bodies. The illustration shows a body of lute/mandora shape with a plectrum scratch guard on the soundboard, a wide neck and a guitar-like peg plate with 8 pegs.[298] Bonani called it a *pandura* and the illustration shows a somewhat oversize normal finger-played mandora with 10 pegs in the pegbox, though the text indicates 'eight strings of metal'.[299] His text is generally more reliable than the illustrations.

The eight strings could have been in 4-course mandolino tuning, perhaps an octave lower than normal, *e a d' g'.* The string length would have had to be less than 51 cm. Two other possibilities are that it had 4 courses in the old bass violin (basso da braccio) tuning *G d a e'* (with string length less than 60 cm), or in cello tuning *C G d a* (with string length less than 90 cm), inspired by the new large violoncello (of modern size) that was rapidly growing in popularity. A fourth possibility is that there were 8 single courses. Evidence supporting the last of these possibility is the wide neck in the Pinarola illustration and a music manuscript which only contains repertoire from this period and earlier (though copied at a somewhat later date).[300] It states that it was for a *chitarra a pena* and its tuning was *C F D G c f a d'* or a tone higher. This is 5-course guitar tuning with added basses (the 6th course was related to the higher ones as on later guitars). The string length would then have had to be less than 60 cm. At this string length, the lowest strings would have to be of high-twist brass, medium-twist silver or metal-wound on metal or gut. The string lengths given here assume the corista pitch standard and that the first course was of iron.

---

[298] G. Pinaroli, *Polyanthea technica* Biblioteca Casanatense, Rome, Ms. 3006, c. 153 (1718-32), described in P. Barbieri, 'Cembalaro, organaro, chitarro e fabbricatore di corde armoniche nella *Polyanthea technica* di Pinaroli (1718-32)' *Recercare* I (1989), pp. 123-209.

[299] F. Bonani, *Gabinetto armonico* (Rome, 1722), plate 97; mod. edition ed. F. L. Harrison & J. Rimmer, Dover, 1964,

[300] Noseda 48/A in Biblioteca del Conservatorio 'Giuseppe Verdi', Milan; discussed in S. Morey, *Mandolins of the 18th Century* (Cremona, 1993), p. 93.

It is awkward to tie a metal wire onto a glued bridge designed for gut strings, and a stray end can draw blood. Traditionally as on citterns, wire strings have been attached to pins at the bottom end of the body, and the bridge was moveable. The string angle over the bridge has to be great enough for the pressure of the bridge on the soundboard to keep it from moving during vigorous play, and this has been accomplished by increased bridge height facilitated by a raised fingerboard. Mandoras , as lutes, always had the top of the fingerboard in the same plane as the soundboard so that the soundboard can be used for playing past the fingerboard frets. The glued bridge had to be low for this, as well as for minimising the torque of the string tension tending to twist it off. A low moveable bridge would be too mobile, but it can be stabilised by increasing the string angle over the bridge by building a bend in the soundboard at the bridge position.

All of the surviving wire-strung mandoras have this soundboard bend. From the 1740s we have 8-string 4-course instruments with string length around 78 cm, apparently with cello tuning, and 16-string 8-course instruments with string length 55-58 cm, apparently with guitar tuning with added basses. Manuscript music for a *mandolone* goes down to *C*, and both of these variants qualify for the name.

The Neapolitan mandolin appeared in the 1750s. It appears to have been intended to be a miniature cello-tuned mandolone for violinists to play. If it were to have an iron 1st course and violin tuning, the string length would have to be less than 30 cm. A few such mandolins survive, but most were made with a 33 cm string length to be like the violin, requiring the 1st course to be gut. The 2nd course was brass, each string of the 3rd course was two brass wires twisted together, and the 4th course was an octave pair having a low octave of metal wound on gut or silk and a high octave of brass.[301] In the 1760s and 70s, the Neapolitan mandolin became a great success, and spread to France and then all over Europe.

From the 1760s, 4-course mandolins with a string length of 45-50 cm appeared. They could have been tuned an octave lower than the usual Neopolitan mandolin (*G d a e'*) with gut on the 1st course, or an octave below the usual gut-strung mandolino (*e a d' g'*) with iron on the 1st course.

During the second half of the 18th century, mandolins with six double courses appeared, presumably to cater for guitar players. Small ones with a string length of about 31 cm were tuned to an octave above the guitar *(e a d' g' b' e'')*, and larger ones with a string length of about 53 cm were tuned like the guitar *(E A d g b e')*. They were usually made in Genoa and so were called Genoese mandolins.

---

[301] E. Segerman, 'Neapolitan mandolins, wire strengths and violin stringing in late 18th c. France', *FoMRHI Q.* 43 (April, 1986), Comm. 713, pp. 99-100.

The Development of Western European Stringed Instruments

Chapter 9: Renaissance and baroque plucked wire-strung fingerboard instruments

Citterns in the first half of the 16th century

By the end of the 15th century the Italian cetra had ceased to be fashionable and was, according to Tinctoris, mainly 'played by rustics to accompany light songs and to lead dance music'. A few decades earlier, it had the highest of reputations. A few decades later, a modified version of it became respectable again in Italy. Though the modifications didn't replace the Italian name for it (though *cetera* or *citara* were more commonly used), they led to an instrument that was exported to the rest of Europe, and we shall henceforth use the English name 'cittern' for it.

The earliest 16th century Italian evidence is in a painting 'Madonna Enthroned' by Gerolamo dai Libri dated 1526[302]. Like one of the larger 15th century cetras, it had nine strings, but they were equally spaced over an unusually wide fingerboard. Of course, the unusual spacing and width may be cases of the artist not appreciating the difference between strings and courses, but the possibility that this string pattern was real must be considered. The principle behind this tuning could be that of most cittern tunings, that the top 3 courses were for melody and chords, the 4th course was at a convenient pitch to enrich common chords, and the other courses were subsidiary and plucked mainly open when useful. The tuning given a century later for a 10-course Italian cittern by Mersenne[303] *c' b b^b a d f b g d' e'* illustrates this principle.

The dai Libri cittern played with a lute, and as with the lute, the neck fit into the player's palm with the thumb protruding. That was not possible with the cetra because of the protruding fret blocks. Nevertheless, the cetra way of holding the neck, rather than this one, persisted on the Italian cittern afterwards. What was new with this cittern, and did persist, was the continuous fingerboard with inset frets of varying length.

The next piece of evidence is the 8-string 6-course tuning given for the *cethara* in 1533 by Lanfranco[304].   The notes given were those of the hexachord, with *ut* being an octave-pair 3rd course, *re* being a single 6th course, *mi* being a single 4th course, *fa* being a single 5th course, *sol* being a unison-pair 2nd course, and *la* being a single 1st course. If we assume that *ut* was the lowest note *g*, the tuning would then be *a c' b gg' d'd' e'*. This 8-string version of the hexachord tuning *a c' b g d' e'* was not again reported. The only other version of the hexachord tuning that includes an octaved course was one that Praetorius included in his tuning table. He wrote that the 5th course sometimes had one string an octave lower, with the tuning *aa cc' bb gg d'd' e'e'*.

---

[302] In S. Giorgio in Briada, Verona, reproduced in G. Kinsky (ed) *A History of Music in Pictures* (Dent, 1930), p. 113.

[303] M. Mersenne, *Harmonie Universelle* III (Paris, 1636), Bk. 2, Prop. XVI; corrections of printer's errors in E. Segerman, *FoMRHI Q* 43 (Apr, 1986), Comm. 698, pp. 39,40.

[304] G. M. Lanfranco da Terenzo, *Scintille di Musica* (1533), Brescia, pp. 139-40.

The hexachord tuning given by Lanfranco could have been an abbreviated version of dai Libri's 9-string tuning. It became the basic Italian cittern tuning. When Virchi invented a new tuning, which was *d f b g d' e'* (in unison pairs), he explained how it related to the basic hexachord tuning. Cerone and Mersenne also gave the hexachord tuning for the cittern. With the predominance of Italian examples amongst the surviving instruments and in the iconography, we would expect that there was more cittern playing in Italy than elsewhere, and that the preponderance of that playing would have been in this tuning. Tuning in unison pairs was probably most common. Unfortunately, except for a few scraps, none of the repertoire for this tuning has survived.

Non-musical advantages of this tuning are easier to imagine than musical advantages. One of the former is that the hexachord was essential to music theory, and apparent knowledge of theory distinguished between high and low class (educated and uneducated) musicians. When in fashion, the cittern was an elitist instrument. Another is that everyone at the time with any musical interest played the lute, and if a lute-player picked up a cittern and tried to play it, he or she would be completely mystified. Thus the cittern was demonstrably in a class of its own, not to be compared to the more popular lute.

The strongest non-musical advantage is that the Italians involved then were in an early music movement resurrecting the spirit of ancient Greek music, and they believed that this tuning's resonance with theory (believed to be ancient) must make it historically correct, and the instrument, derived from the cetra (supposedly the direct descendent of the kithara) was historically appropriate. They were doing their best to be both practical and authentic. The early carved Italian cittern design is what almost always appeared in paintings with ancient associations[305]. Almost every cetra and cittern before the middle of the 17th century (non-Italian as well) had protuberances on both sides of where the body and neck joined, and a reasonable case has been made that these were considered to be vestigial wings symbolically referring to those characteristic winged parts of the kithara[306].

The 5th and 6th courses were the most expendable, and a degenerate 4-course version of the Italian cittern could have left them out. I know of no evidence of an Italian 4-course cittern played in Italy. Praetorius (1619) discussed 4-course citterns as common instruments which had 'the vilest of associations, fit only for cobblers and tailors'. They had the tuning that was either 'French' (*a g d' e'*) or 'Italian' (*b g d' e'*). It is most likely that he was referring to instruments currently being played in Germany (as confirmed in the A. S. ms), and whether there were Italian ones in Italy was not mentioned or implied.

The third piece of evidence on early 16th century Italian citterns is a surviving instrument dated 1536. It has the typical frying-pan body shape (with the back considerably smaller than the top) that was typical of subsequent Italian citterns with the body and neck carved from one piece of wood. Most such citterns had their pegs plugged in from the front into blind holes in a peg block, but this cittern has

---

[305] P. S. Forrester, 'The cittern in Italy', *FoMRHI Q* 50 (Jan. 1988), Comm. 858, pp. 59-62.

[306] E. Winternitz, 'The Survival of the Kithara and the Evolution of the Cittern', *Music Libraries and Instruments* (Hinrichsen, 1961), pp. 209-14.

a pegbox (into which pegs went in from the sides) with a central ridge so that the pegs did not go through the full width of the peg box. If it had hexachord tuning, its 10 strings were probably organized onto 4 pairs and 2 singles.

In Germany there is a reference to a book of cittern tablature by Schlumberger[307], now lost, that dates from 1525 or 1532. The instrument was not mentioned in Virdung's 1511 book[308] or the one in 1528 by Agricola[309], but it is referred to obliquely in Agricola's 1545 revision by the comment 'cithara media' on the bass side next to the third fret of a fingerboard diagram for a 4-string Tenor and Alt viol[310]. The comment could possibly refer to the $d^{\#}$ on the c 4th viol string, but it is much more likely to refer to the g on the e 3rd viol string.

No evidence has come to my attention of cittern activity in France in the first half of the century, but it must have been there for the French 4-course cittern to have been imported from there to England and become popular amongst young London gentlemen by 1548[311]. Also, the close relationship between the 15th century cetra tuning and French cittern tuning suggests a relationship independent of the 16th century Italian hexachord tuning.

Citterns from the second half of the 16th century and from the 17th

The cittern's main period of popularity was the second half of the 16th century and on well into the 17th. Let us start with characteristics of the citterns of that time.

Sizes

About a couple of dozen Renaissance and early baroque citterns survive, and the vast majority of them are Italian. Peter Forrester has reported[312] that about half of them have string lengths about 45 cm, about a quarter of them have string lengths of about 60 cm, with the rest divided into clusters near 50 and 55 cm. Citterns were soloistic instruments, and those of different sizes at different pitches very rarely ever played together, as was very often the case with other types of Renaissance instruments. Citterns were not called by voice or size names except for one source from the middle of the 17th century in Germany[313]. Thus the appearance of different sizes probably largely represents the individual preferences of players in their compromises between rounder tone with larger instruments making simpler playing more satisfying, and the versatility of smaller instruments making the expression of varying musical ideas and virtuosity much easier. Matching comfortable vocal pitches with easy familiar chords must also have been important.

---

[307] J. Tyler, 'A checklist for the cittern', *Early Music* 2/1 (Jan 1974), p. 27.

[308] S. Virdung, *Musica Grtutscht* (1511), Basel, facs. edition ed. L. Schrade (1931), Kassel.

[309] M. Agricola, *Musica instrumentalis deudsch* (1528), Wittemberg.

[310] M. Agricola, *Musica instrumentalis deudsch* (1545), Wittemberg, p. 38.

[311] J. M. Osborn, ed. *The Autobiography of Thomas Wythorne* (Oxford, 1961), p.19.

[312] P. S. Forrester, 'The cittern in Italy', op. cit.

[313] See below under 'German citterns'.

There probably was a cittern smaller than these surviving ones that was popular in Italy around 1570. The evidence that supports this suggestion is that 'slight' citterns as well as normal ones were imported into England in 1568[314], and that a book of music published by Virchi in 1574[315] has stretches for chords indicated in the tablature that are seen elsewhere only in the music for the small English cittern (with a string stop of 35 cm). Praetorius discussed a cittern of this size but only knew of it as English. Such an Italian cittern would have gone out of fashion in Italy before he could have become aware of it.

Fretting

The Italian cittern transferred the cetra's slots in the neck (for the large wooden fret-blocks) to a continuous fingerboard, where the slots became much smaller. Into each slot was slipped a fret of folded-over hammered sheet metal (generally brass) backed by a wooden strip. The fingerboard was only supported by a thin but relatively deep neck underneath the first two or three courses, making the fingerboard imitate the cetra where the wooden fret blocks stuck out on the 'bass' side well past the neck. So on the cetra and the Italian cittern, the player's thumb provided the counter-force to the pressure of stopping the strings on the fingerboard. This was different from other plucked fingerboard instruments (such as the lute) at the time, where the counter-force was provided by the palm of the hand in the 15th and early 16th centuries.

The cetra had wooden block frets only for notes in a diatonic scale. The early citterns had a semi-diatonic fretting system, i.e. a compromise between the cetra's fully diatonic system and the fully chromatic system found then on lutes, guitars, viols, etc). In this fretting system some frets extended across the full width of the fingerboard, some lay under some courses and not others, and a few were missing completely. An advantage of this fretting is that one can often reduce hand stretches in chords by pressing some strings against the fingerboard a considerable distance behind the active fret, such as where the next lowest-sounding fret would have been if it were there. Another is that it reduces the risk of discord by fingering the wrong fret inadvertently.

There was one basic type of semi-diatonic fretting pattern, but with many variations in which courses each partial fret went under[316]. The usual pattern of fret positions that had full-length frets was: 1, 2, 3, 5, 7, 9, 10, 12, 14, 16, 17 and 19 semitones from the nut. If we omit the first fret (as was the case with the implied fretting in the tablature of the earliest surviving publication of cittern music[317]), this is a repeating sequence of a tone, a semitone, a tone and a tone. It is likely that this was supposed to represent some ancient Greek mode. That the pattern is symmetrical across the whole fingerboard, and that it does not repeat at the octave, suggests that non-musical considerations were very important. If the nut is included as the 0th fret, and ignoring the general decrease in fret spacings as they progress towards the bridge, the pattern looks something like this: | || | | || | | || |. When the fretting became

---

[314] London Port Book entry, *JLSA* X (1977), p. 116.

[315] P. Virchi, *Il primo libro di tabulatura di cittara* (Venice, 1574).

[316] L. P. Grijp, 'Fret patterns of the cittern', *Galpin Soc.J.* XXXIV (1981), pp. 62-97.

[317] G. Morlaye, *Quatriesme Livre ... en Tabulature de Guyterne & au jeu de la Cistre* (Paris, 1552).

fully chromatic, this pattern was usually retained in the wooden backing strips for the frets, which had one color for the previously full-length frets and a contrasting color for the others. The pattern is useful as a visual aid when moving from one fingering position to another. Semi-diatonic fretting on some citterns survived until the 17th century in Italy and France and well into the 18th century in the Netherlands, Spain and Germany.

Cittern fret positions usually deviated from equal-temperament ones in the direction of meantone intonation. The sound of metal strings includes more higher harmonics than gut strings, so common intervals are more noticeable when out of tune because of mismatch between audible harmonics which should be in unison. So, while equal-temperament fretting was acceptable on gut-strung instruments, on citterns, closer to pure thirds, as provided by meantone temperament, was preferred. The fretting patterns of most surviving citterns approximate the 'fifth comma' variety of meantone, where the deviations from pure of intervals of thirds and of fifths are equal. When a fret served desired notes on different courses that require a different fret shift, the shift was intermediate. With more chromatic fretting and the wider range of chords this implies, the compromises between different course requirements for each fret position led to fret positions closer to equal-temperament[318].

Construction and design

The cetra, all early Italian citterns, many later Italian ones and some non-Italian ones were tuned by pegs inserted from the front into holes in a head block that did not come out on the other side. All citterns followed the tapering body depth of the cetra (deeper at the neck than the tail). The peghead, neck, back and sides of these early Italian citterns were carved out of one piece of wood. This is called the 'carved' type of instrument making, and is rarely seen on non-Italian citterns. The sides sloped (like a frying pan) since the back was smaller than the soundboard. The upper part of the body shape outline had rather straight sides, leaving the neck at a clear angle, looking somewhat like two sides of an equilateral triangle. The sound hole was almost as low as half way down the soundboard. The crossbars under the soundboard usually rested in slots cut out of the sides; the slots for the longest bar usually went all the way through the sides, so that the ends were visible from the outside. When it was made, the ends of that bar were flush with the sides, but as the instrument matured and the wood contracted perpendicular to the grain, they protruded from the sides.

The carved type of instrument-making technology survived from medieval times when it was standard for fingerboard instruments other than lutes. It was well known for folk instruments in the rest of Europe and so was not respectable in affluent musical circles there. That is probably why Italian citterns were rarely brought home by the many visitors who went to Italy for musical guidance and inspiration.

The innovations that the French apparently made before 1550 upgraded the construction technology to what was currently fashionable. Their citterns had viol-like peg boxes (they also similarly changed the peg plate of the Spanish 4-course guitar to such a peg box soon after they adopted it). Both Italianate half-width necks and full necks appear to have been common. The sides

---

[318] For further information on this see *FoMRHI* Comms. 88 and 124.

were perpendicular to the back and were made of separate pieces of wood, glued to the back, the neck and the tail block. We call citterns made this way 'built-up'. On most of the surviving built-up citterns till well into the 17th century, the back was the starting body mould, and the sides are wrapped around it when glued. The back was the mold that determined the shape. It is likely that this feature was there from the earliest built-up citterns. Some Italian built-up citterns were made to look just like carved ones, and their sides were usually made first, with the backs glued onto them.

The built-up type of cittern had a more rounded upper body shape with the neck edge flowing smoothly into an outward-curving arc which blended into the inward curve of the rest of the body shape. It also had a higher rose placement on the soundboard. There were two bars on the back, one usually directly under the rose center and the other at or near the width maximum. This back barring was used on built-up citterns of all countries with any fretting pattern.

A minor detail that often appears on surviving citterns, and is easy missed on examination, is a slot cut out of the bottom of the fingerboard where it is glued onto the top of the soundboard. This slot forms a tunnel through which a ribbon for supporting the instrument could be threaded and tied around the neck end of the body.

A common method of mounting unison string pairs on citterns in the 16th century was to use the same piece of wire for both strings of a course. On built-up citterns, one starts by twisting one end onto one tuning peg, take it down past the nut and bridge, around the end pin, and then back by the same route to the other peg. On carved citterns, instead of an end pin, the tail fixing involved a protruding comb (with slots) carved on the body. The wire from the first peg went through one slot of the comb, around a metal or bone rod nestled under the comb, back through another slot, and then back to the other tuning peg.[319] This was very convenient for mounting the strings, but if a string broke, both strings of the pair were out of action and one usually had to stop playing, which can be quite inconvenient. This was not a problem with an iron course because iron strings very rarely break. Brass strings break much more often, and being able to continue playing in spite of a brass-string breakage is likely to be a major reason for triple unison courses on citterns. One of the three would be attached to the end fixing by itself. Thus the appearance of a triple course on a late 16th (or early 17th) century cittern suggests the likelihood that it was strung with brass.

French citterns

Over a dozen books of French cittern music were published in the second half of the 16th century. Illustrations in them tell us what that cittern looked like. The design looks like it had built-up construction. Measurements of a painting[320] indicate a string length 45-50 cm, like the usual Italian citterns. The fretting had the same semi-diatonic and mean-tone nature as the carved Italian cittern, so one must assume that one copied it from the other. It had 10 strings in 4 courses, with a relative tuning that may be expressed by the pitches *ee'e' dd'd' aa bb*. This is Tinctoris's 15th century cetra tuning with added low-octave strings on the 3rd and 4th courses. The high-octave 3rd and 4th courses were made

---

[319] P. Forrester, 'Some notes on cittern fingerboards and stringing', *FoMRHI Q* 32 (July, 1983), Comm. 466, pp. 19-22.
[320] E. Segerman, 'A Late 16th Century French Picture with Instruments' *FoMRHI Q* 101 (Oct. 2000), Comm. 1736, p. 24.

of iron, as were the 1st course strings. The 2nd course strings were copper. The low-octave strings on the 3rd and 4th courses were twisted metal (type unspecified), a newly invented rope type of string which extended range downwards because of increased elasticity. The tablatures indicate that the 4th semitone fret was missing, and the cittern for the earliest surviving printed book had the first fret missing as well.

Much of the early French repertoire was transcriptions of polyphonic music that were originally vocal, but were presented as dances. Comparison with the vocal originals shows that parts were generally given to the 3rd and 4th courses when the original pitch was both at the high and the low octave. Whether the original pitch was high or low was lost in the cittern tablature transcription, but there was no attempt to indicate that one could pluck a course at different angles to favor one octave or the other. Octave ambiguity for these courses was expected. One source said that theoreticians could find the sound objectionable (second inversion chords were not avoided), but most found it acceptable.

French citterns kept changing during the second half of the 16th century. Notes previously unavailable on the frets were wanted, so missing frets appeared and partial frets grew in length. The fretting gradually became more chromatic. Transcriptions of vocal polyphony lost favor, and then apparently so did octave ambiguity (Praetorius mentioned no octave stringing when he mentioned French tuning, and Mersenne wrote that unison brass triplets were usual, with one octave string in a course an alternative). A unison 3rd course would have led to stringing at a higher pitch for the first course, with twisted strings no more needed. On gut-strung instruments, octave stringing was used to reduce the loss of tone quality of thick gut strings due to inharmonicity. The problem that limits how low a wire string can be tuned is different. It is pitch distortion, in which the string sounds sharp from the stretching caused by pressing the string behind the fret. So octave stringing on a wire-strung instrument would only be chosen if the octave ambiguity was preferred, implying either lack of indoctrination in, or rebellion against, the injunction to avoid parallel octaves in the principles of polyphony.

<u>German citterns</u>

The Germans experimented with different tunings. Nevertheless, the relative tuning of the first three courses of all types of cittern involved a tone between the first and second courses and a fifth between the second and third courses.[321] In the 2nd half of the 16th century, there were books published of music for the 10-string 4-course French cittern[322] with semi-diatonic fretting and an 11-string 6-course cittern tuned *bb GG dd gg d'd' e'* with chromatic fretting.[323]

In the 17th century, Praetorius discussed and depicted a 4-course small English one and a 6-course apparently carved Italian one. The latter was called a *Chor Zitter*, implying that it was tuned at his preferred Chorthon pitch standard. Its string length was 48 cm. All of Praetorius's citterns had chromatic fretting, and all except the *Chor Zitter* were built-up. The remaining ordinary cittern was a 12-string 6-course one with a string length of 46 cm. The 6-course tunings offered other than the 'old

---

[321] An 18th century Spanish revival had a fourth between the second and third courses.
[322] S. Kargel, *Renovata Cythara* (Strassburg, 1578).
[323] S. Kargel & J. D. Lais, *Toppel Cythar* (Strassburg, 1575).

Italian hexachord one were those of Kargel, *b G d g d' e'*, and of 'VV', *G d b g d' e'*. An extraordinary large 6-course cittern with a string length of 75 cm had a tuning of *f# D A d a b*. The unfinished illustration shows 6 strings and 8 pegs. Another extraordinary cittern that was played by Dominicus, a court musician in Prague, had 12 courses, 8 of which were pairs that went over a fingerboard with fan-shaped fretting (like the bandora), and the remaining 4 were single and went to a peg box extension. The string length of the 1st course was 70 cm, and the string length of the strings on the peg box extension was 111cm. The tuning was $e^b B^b f c / g d a e b g d' e'$. Three tunings for 5-course citterns were given, *d b g d' e'*, *G f# d a b* and *F e c g a*. Tunings of the 'ordinary' 4-course cittern (fit only for beggars or tailors) were *b g d' e'* (Italian) and *a g d' e'* (French).

The mid-17th century south German manuscript *Instrumentalischer Bettlermantl* by A, S. in Edinburgh discussed only 4-course citterns with chromatic fretting. The French tuning was apparently considered more appropriate for solo playing, and the Italian tuning for continuo work. There were four sizes used for the continuo band. The *Discant* was tuned to *e' c' g' a'*, the *Alt* to *b g d' e'*, and the *Tenor* to *f# d a b*. They would have had string lengths of about 35, 45 and 60 cm. No information was given about the *Bass*, but it probably was tuned a tone lower than the *Tenor* and an octave below the *Discant*.[324] The *Discant* was apparently a German adaptation of the small English cittern.

The French-tuned English cittern

The cittern and gittern (Renaissance guitar) were new arrivals in England in 1548, played by young London gentlemen[325]. At least when it was established, the cittern had four unison courses, fully chromatic fretting, the fourth course tuned a tone higher than the third[326], about 45 cm string stop, and two strings per course except for three on the third[327]. The tuning was French without the octave ambiguity of the third and fourth courses, *aa ggg d'd' e'e'*. The fully chromatic fretting and unison stringing were new, but the repertoire apparently came from France. If the translation of a French instruction book[328] that appeared in 1568 had survived, its tablature probably would differ from the French original by assuming that the fingerboard had a 4th fret.

The Meuler steel revolution

Around 1580, a new kind of very strong iron wire became commercially available. It apparently only could be made in the workshop of Jobst Meuler in Nuremberg[329]. Meuler's strings

---

[324] E. Segerman, 'Violins, citterns and viols in the Edinburgh 'A. S.' manuscript', *FoMRHI Q* 91 (April 1988), Comm. 1576, pp. 38-44.

[325] Thomas Wythorne autobiography, see J. M. Osborn, op. cit.

[326] *Mulliner Book* (c. 1545-85) and *Lord Middleton Lute book* (c.1574). One piece in the Mulliner Book has a fifth course tuned to *d*, which would have required twisted wire.

[327] Eglantine Table at Hardwick Hall

[328] J. Rowbotham, *The breff and playne instruction to learne to play the gyttron and also the cetterne* (1568).

[329] That there was an anomalously strong wire available around 1600 became apparent in the analyses of pitches and string lengths reported by Abbott & Segerman in *Galpin Soc.J.* XXVII (1974). A few years later, Michael Morrow called my attention to a letter by Heinrich Schutz referring to Jobst Meuler, the string-maker, that seemed to be relevant. I mentioned this in *FoMRHI Q* 29 Comm. 438 (1982). That letter was the subject of *FoMRHI Q* 30 Comm. 439 (1983) by Karp. The evidence on strong wire was summarized in *FoMRHI Q* 30 Comm. 440 (1983) by me, and the story about Jobst Meuler was properly researched in *FoMRHI Q* 51 Comm. 866 (1988) by R. Gug.

could tune over 6 semitones higher than had previously been expected for iron strings (and higher than gut), and after 1600, he developed iron strings that could tune almost 10 semitones higher than previously (almost a fourth higher than gut strings)[330].

Meuler ran into trouble in 1608 because a rival obtained a privilege (monopoly) on all wire making from the Imperial Court in Vienna[331]. In 1610, the Nuremberg Town Council supported Meuler's claim that he had invented a new kind of wire, in great demand, that others couldn't make, and so was outside the specifications of the privilege. A more powerful privilege was granted in 1621, after which Meuler was only able to fill a wire order if he was given permission by a resolution of the Town Council. No business can survive in these conditions, and his specially strong wire became unavailable. Instruments designed for its use either disappeared or changed to lower tunings. Any wire strong enough to tune as high or higher than gut only appeared again late in the 19th century with the invention of steel piano wire.

This especially strong wire led to the invention of new instruments and adaptations of others. Two adaptations Praetorius discussed were the replacement of gut by metal strings on the violin and on lutes. English inventions included the Leero Viol, with sympathetic metal strings and the orpharion, a wire-strung instrument tuned like a lute at the usual mean-lute pitch (that viols usually played at) and even at the tone-higher pitch that treble lutes sometimes used (when playing with violins or recorders).

The new wire allowed a 50% increase in string length for the same pitch, and that increase could be used to add to the bottom of the range of the instrument. This is a basic factor in the design of the 12-course cittern depicted by Praetorius. Another cittern shown by Praetorius that used this wire to increase size with much less corresponding lowering of pitch was the large 6-course cittern. With this wire, it is possible to tune the largest surviving Italian cittern size (with about 60 cm string length) to the same pitches as the most common one (with about 45 cm string length).

The 'Italian'-tuned English cittern

Another instrument invented to use this wire was the small English cittern. It is likely to have been a 4-course version of the Italian 'slight' cittern that Virchi apparently wrote his music book for. At some point this instrument acquired a theatrical fool's head, and it could have been early, when the 'slight' cittern possibly became a common accessory for the all-singing-dancing clown. When the strong wire became available, it could be tuned an octave higher than citterns had usually been tuned to. With the new Italian tuning for the fourth course (a major third rather than the tone above the 3rd course of the French tuning previously used on English citterns), this cittern quickly became the standard cittern in fashionable musical circles.

At about this time there is a curious comment made by Vincenzo Galilei[332]: 'The cittern was used first, before other nations, in England, in which island they are already made to perfection.' The

---

[330] E. Segerman, 'Praetorius's plucked instruments and their strings', *FoMRHI Q* 92 (1998), Comm. 1593, pp. 33-7.

[331] R. Gug, 'Jobst Meuler or the secret of a Nuremberg wire drawer', *FoMRHI Q* 51 (1988), Comm. 866, pp. 29-36.

[332] Vincenzo Galilei, *Dialogo della Musica antica e della moderna* (1581).

date of Galilei's publication makes it unclear whether the English cittern he referred to was of the older larger French-tuned type or the later smaller Italian-tuned instrument that was mostly an octave higher. Galilei was not a bad historian and must have been aware of Italian citterns since his youth, which probably was earlier than the recorded introduction of citterns into England. Perhaps he came to his conclusion because he came across evidence of the citole in medieval England (Chaucer?) earlier than elsewhere. His observation 'made to perfection' could refer to chromatic fretting, or to a high general quality of workmanship in currently produced English citterns.

This opinion of high quality could well have been based on instruments by London makers in the circle of John Rose. Rose was primarily a lute and viol maker in London who was very interested in wire-strung instruments, having invented the bandora in 1562. He made the Helmingham Hall instrument, dated 1580, apparently originally as a 10-string 5-course cittern with many bandora characteristics, and soon, with Meuler's wire, converted it into what could well have been the first orpharion. It was most likely in this circle that the small cittern was created from combining the 'slight' cittern, Meuler's wire, a degenerate Italian tuning and a theatrical fool's head.

Members of this circle had been making citterns for the affluent because of the growing interest in the Consort of Six, an ensemble which very much impressed Queen Elizabeth. Its popularity could perhaps be associated with a tradition of its playing 'for the reception of guests and persons of distinction'.[333] That ensemble included treble and bass viols, a transverse flute, a treble lute, a cittern and a bandora, with likely variations including a recorder instead of a flute, a violin instead of a treble viol and an orpharion instead of a bandora. The Consort initially used the large cittern, but it blossomed in popularity (producing all of the surviving repertoire) when the small one replaced it.

Praetorius[334] wrote at length about the small cittern: *Klein Englisch Zitterlein*. He was attempting to be comprehensive, and since he mentioned no other small cittern and no other English cittern, we can presume that he was aware of no others. The tunings he offered were *f" a' d" g"* and *f" b♭' d" g"* (the latter named 'corda valle' after the popular French lute tuning). These tunings were also given in his tables of instrument tunings. He learned about the instrument in these tunings from an Englishman who came to Germany three years prior to his writing about it (c. 1614). These tunings were not previously recorded elsewhere for a cittern. They appear to be an exploitation of Meuler's later stronger wire which allowed a lute or gittern tuning an octave higher than normal. Praetorius admired the player's style, which was to play divisions using a tremolo technique. The likely repertoire played was the treble lute part of lute duets or of Consort lessons an octave higher than usual. Praetorius apparently had copies of this instrument made, and specified it in some of his large-scale vocal-instrumental compositions, playing from violin parts.

In this melodic style of playing in this tuning, the 4th course would be of minimal use at the given high pitch. It was thus probable that the reentrant aspect of this tuning was for ready conversion

---

[333] G. Schondonch, *The Custom Book of St. Omers College* (c. 1610); see J. M. Ward, 'Sprightly & Cheerful Musick', *Lute Soc. J.* XXI (1979-81), pp. 104-6.

[334] M. Praetorius, *Syntagma Musicum II* (1619), p. 55.

to standard cittern tuning. This would easily be accomplished by crossing the 2nd and 4th courses between the pegs and the nut and between the bridge and the tail fixing, and tuning the strings a minor third lower for English light-music pitch (the same as Praetorius's Cammerthon) that violins and recorders played in, or a tone lower than that for English Consort pitch that viols usually played in. Praetorius did not mention the normal tuning for the English cittern (*b' g' d" e"*), probably because it was of the degenerate Italian type, which was very disrespectful, and perhaps with wishful thinking, he believed that it was being permanently replaced by the octave lute/guitar tunings.

When the strong wire became unavailable, repertoire for the cittern and the Consort apparently ceased to be produced. Nevertheless, through the following few decades, the cittern (especially the cittern head, which was that of an ugly fool) was mentioned frequently in theatrical scripts, often associated with barbers[335]. Robert Fludd[336] writing in 1618, mentioned that citterns were played in Consorts and by themselves in barber shops. The tuning pitch given on his somewhat bazaar drawing of a cittern was an octave lower than the tuning with the strong wire. If this was not just another error (there were many, usually associated with poor communication between Fludd and his continental publishers), it possibly reflected an alternative tuning used by barbers when Meuler's wire was either difficult to get or overly expensive. The small cittern could be tuned this way strung in iron and brass, or just brass (Mersenne mentioned all-brass stringing as a possibility on citterns). Mention in the plays is understandable since barber shops and the theatre were frequented by the same kind of people.

The guittern and late cittern

As Meuler's wire became less available, we presume that a growing number of these citterns were retuned as Praetorius's Englishman did (but an octave lower), so that players familiar with lute or bandora fingering could play them. Soon cittern playing was abandoned, and the 4th course was tuned below the third, an octave lower (relatively) than previously. The actual pitch (considering that only normal iron wire was available) was probably an octave above the top four courses of the bandora (*g c' e' a'*). The Holborne and Robinson books were known and respected for what could be played on the cittern, but that music was no more played, and couldn't be played on the new tuning. The instrument with the new tuning was not a cittern, and it was then called 'guittern', an appropriate name because of the guitar tuning. The 4-course Renaissance guitar was seriously out of fashion then, and the wire-strung instrument was probably considered to be a transformed revival of it (as well as a 4-course octave bandora). This guittern was played in Germany and France[337] as well as England.

We find no further evidence of citterns in England till the middle of the 17th century. Then a larger instrument, with about 46 cm string stop and iron, brass and twisted-brass stringing appeared, apparently to resurrect the old highly-respected cittern in a new easily-playable form for beginning amateurs. It was called 'cittern', its tuning was an octave lower than the old cittern, and the larger size

---

[335] D. Abbott & E. Segerman, 'The Cittern in England before 1700', *Lute Soc. J.* XVII (1975), pp. 24-48.

[336] J. Godwin, 'Instruments in Robert Fludd's *Utriusque Cosmi ... Historia*', *Galpin Soc. J.* XXVI (1973), p. 3

[337] E. Segerman, 'A 1656 Tabley ms: On Viol Players, Cittern and Gittern', *FoMRHI Q* 46 (Jan. 1987), Comm. 774, pp. 34-5.

gave it the resonance needed to make very simple music sound well enough. Both cittern and guittern then had 8 strings in 4 courses, and were usually played with a quill, but finger playing was also acceptable. Playford published two books[338] of very easy music for the cittern, recommending finger-playing in the second to compete more effectively with the growingly popular Spanish guitar (which he disliked). The playing instructions were adapted from Robinson's book. His first book included a section of tablature music for the guittern as well.

The final three pieces in the guittern book required a tuning with a major 3rd on top followed by a minor 3rd and then a 4th, forming a minor chord. This tuning relates to a new growing fashion in tuning of amateur instruments with adjacent intervals of a major and minor third, with the open strings forming either a major or minor chord. The lyra viol and French baroque lute pioneered such tunings, and they spread to other instruments in the second half of the 17th century. They also appeared in the various versions of the viola d'amore.

5-course guittern and cithrinchen

Late in the 17th century the guittern acquired a fifth course, either by adding two strings (totaling 10) or by splitting the 4th pair into single heavier twisted-brass 4th and 5th courses. The 5th course also followed bandora tuning. This was also the basic tuning of the baroque guitar, so repertoire for that instrument could be played on the guittern by plucking and strumming with the fingers. Often the guittern also adopted the body shape of the upper end of the bandora with a sweeping cut-off curve below, ending up with a kind of bell shape, leading to the name 'bell guittern'. It became popular in northern Germany and Scandinavia as well as England, and took sizes between the larger cittern size and the original smaller guittern size. On the Continent it was called 'cithrinchen', where it usually took a new-style chord tuning.

In most of the first half of the 18th century, we have no evidence of either the cittern or guittern in England. Indeed, in 1697, William Turner[339] included these, as well as the orpharion and bandora, as old English instruments that were 'laid aside'. Popularity of the guittern (with the bell design) continued on the Continent. The courses of the cithrinchen were usually tuned with a 4th interval on top, and then alternating major and minor 3rds. Tuning and playing the instrument with fingers like the baroque guitar was not uncommon. All of the usual five courses could become pairs, or basses could be single when made of heavier twisted brass, making a 6th course possible[340]. So from 8 to 12 strings could be grouped in 5 or 6 courses.

Previously, except for Praetorius's English cittern, the name 'cittern' was associated with a tuning in which the second course was a tone lower than the first, and the third course was a fifth lower than the second. The names that the players give to instruments have usually been based on the technique needed to learn how to play it, in which tuning is a very important component, and

---

[338] J. Playford, *A Booke of New Lessons for the Cithern and Gittern* (1652) and *Musick's Delight on the Cithren* (1666).

[339] M. Tilmouth, 'Some improvements in Music noted by William Turner in 1697', *Galpin S. J.* X (1957), pp. 57-9.

[340] E. Segerman, '... the Wensler G30 cithrinchen stringing', *FoMRHI Q* 86 (Jan. 1997), Comm. 1498, pp. 25-6.

occasionally to project an image that the audience would respond to. The cithrinchen tuning was not a traditional cittern tuning, yet the instrument proclaimed that it was a cittern by imitating the cut-away bass half of the neck from Italian citterns, by the tapering of body depth characteristic of all citterns, by playing it with a quill and by its cittern-diminutive name. It is likely that the name was justified by Praetorius's book, which was well known in Germanic countries at the time, where the English cittern was called a diminutive of 'cittern' (zitterlein) though the tuning given was not that of a cittern.

English guitar or cistre

Around the middle of the 18th century, a screw-tuned finger-plucked six-course 10-string version of a larger sized cithrinchen (with string length of about 43 cm) was developed, most probably in France where it was called *cistre*. The bottom of the bell shape was filled out with a more cittern-like rounded curve and the body became wider and deeper (with near-uniform depth). The French tuning, from the top down, was minor and major thirds, two fourths and a tone (*c d gg c'c' e'e' g'g'* at a pitch standard about 3 semitones below modern). The bass strings were made of metal wound on iron, silk or gut. This differed from the cithrinchen, where they were made of twisted brass. It is much easier to make a lower bass string that frets in tune by winding metal onto a more flexible core than to put enough twist into a thicker twisted metal string without breaking it in the process. Thus this change in bass string construction allowed six courses to be consistently used without needing to obtain strings from a highly skilled metal string maker. This helped in the spread of this instrument's popularity.

The French aristocracy then were fashion leaders in Europe, and they treated musical instruments as fashion accessories. Instrument makers were encouraged to create new instruments or instrument designs to provide variety in amateur instruments to meet fashion needs. The recent invention of a lathe with a screw-driven tool holder by Antoine Thiout (for cutting threads on spindles used in clocks and watches) made the use of screws on musical instruments the commercial proposition it had never been before. French makers then started using screws in tightening the hair of bows and in tuning the strings of the cistre and in mounting a capotasto on it.

On the tuning head of the cistre, there was a brass plate holding and covering a set of screws, one for each string. The screws, turned by a watch key, were threaded into nuts with hooks which stuck out from the plate and rode along slots in it. The strings needed loops on both ends, one to engage the hook and the other to go on the tail pin. The neck and fingerboard had a number of central holes between adjacent frets through which a capotasto could be attached by a screw and wing-nut, allowing playing at various higher pitch levels with the same fingering.

The English aristocracy and affluent merchants that followed Paris fashions quickly adopted this instrument, and within a decade of its invention, local British makers were producing their own versions. In the English tuning, the fifth course was tuned a tone higher than in the French one (*c e gg c'c' e'e' g'g'*), thus including all of the courses in the C major open-string chord. These versions differed from the French ones by usually abandoning the shoulder shape at the upper end of the body that was inherited from the cithrinchen (and ultimately from the bell gittern and bandora), and replaced it by a more cittern-like basic shape (without changing the wide and deep French proportions).

In England, this instrument was called 'guitar', or occasionally 'cetra'. The latter was probably a more masculine-sounding substitute for 'cistre'. One possible contribution to the choice of 'guitar' as the usual name is a memory of the guittern a half-century earlier, which had similar size, shape and string materials. Another is that the baroque guitar was somewhat out of fashion in these circles at the time, but the guitar name was still associated with the position of primary domestic hand-plucked instrument, so the name helped this instrument to displace it in that position. The gut-strung guitar was then called 'Spanish guitar'.

The Portuguese 'guitarra' had the English shape modification (plus an added two strings to make all courses unison pairs). It was introduced to Portugal[341] via English merchants that had strong commercial ties there. The Norwegian 'sister' adopted the basic French cistre body shape, but otherwise remained a cithrinchen. The tuning had the 6th course tuned a fourth below the fifth, the rest being in standard 5-course cithrinchen tuning.

After its initial burst of popularity, the French offered variations on the basic cistre design to serve the fashion need of novelty. One was a small-lute or mandora body (it was then called a 'pandore'), and another was a compromise between the original and the pandore model, with the back rather smaller than the belly and sloping sides. The usual screw tuning device was not to everyone's taste. Extra care is needed in finding the right screw to tune with the watch key, the watch key can easily be misplaced, the extra loop on each string was a bother and there was little leeway in where it could be placed. So some players preferred ordinary tuning pegs, especially on the pandore model, where they looked much more traditional. Individual tuning machines were then invented so that strings could be tuned at their proper places on a peg box. They were of worm-gear type, clearly the ancestor of those used on guitars today. Tuning could still be by watch key, but more commonly by turning a metal ring, which could be considered to be a built-in watch key. That ring outlined a normal peg head, but it was not filled in during this period because the artifice of a metal machine was fashionable and disguising it as an ordinary peg was not.

The French instruments mentioned so far were mostly played there by women, so the makers developed a larger cistre to be predominantly played by men. It had a string length of over 50 cm with 6 courses on the fingerboard, and 2 or more courses of unstopped strings that were about half-again longer, tuned from a second peg box above (and offset from) the main one, like on a German theorboed lute. Body shape could be any one of those used on the smaller cistre plus an asymmetric variant of the sloping-sides one, where the body met the neck much closer to the bridge on the treble side than on the bass side. Tuning was either by ordinary pegs or by individual-string machines. The highest 6 courses were all tuned a minor third lower than the original smaller cistre, the 7th course was tuned a fourth lower than the 6th, and subsequent courses descended diatonically from the 7th. The first 2 courses were of iron, the 3rd of brass, the 4th of either brass or of metal wound on iron or silk. These courses were all unison pairs. Lower courses were usually single, made of metal wound on gut or silk, and if any were string pairs, they were in octaves with the high octave of plain gut.

---

[341] E. Segerman, 'Origins of the 'guitarra portuguesa'', *FoMRHI Q* 89 (Oct 1997), Comm. 1543, p. 39.

This new larger cistre had to be distinguished from the earlier smaller one, and since the men playing it wanted to claim the name *cistre* for their own instrument, new names all around were called for. These names became *guitthare angloise* for the original smaller one, and *cystre* or *guitthare allemande* for the new larger one. At least these are the names given by l'Abbé Carpentier in his method published in Paris c. 1771, where he only mentioned the *guitthare angloise* in passing, showing a not unexpected masculine disdain. It is likely that the name cistre was still widely uses for that smaller instrument.

The *angloise* part of the name *guitthare angloise* did not mean that the instrument originated in England. In 1758, Bremner wrote in his *Instructions*[342] that the instrument was 'but lately introduced' into Britain. By the time a name other than *cistre* was needed in France, that name could have reflected the great popularity that the instrument had already achieved in England. This could have also been the case with the *guitthare allemande* since German versions with 8 fingerboard strings and 8 or 9 long strings survive from 1756 and later. But primarily, the *angloise* was a domestic-fashion model name, just as *allemande* was.

The names 'English guitar' and 'cittern', as widely used in recent times for these instruments, are historically justified as English translations of 'guitthare angloise' and 'cistre'. There has been some feeling that we should stop using 'cittern' for them to avoid confusion with earlier citterns with 'proper' cittern tuning. The term 'late 18th century cittern' should be perfectly acceptable because 'cittern' is what so many musicians then called it.

In the 19th century, gut-strung versions of the English guitar became popular as amateur instruments in England and France. Names used included the word 'harp', with the other word being 'guitar' or 'lute' or 'dital'. The 'harp' part reflected either that the tuning mechanism was like that on a harp, or its design included a pillar and an arm for the tuning pins like on a harp. The earliest design had just a fretted neck, and subsequent designs had a tuning arm between that neck and a pillar (like on the polyphont described below).

Archcittern

With the invention of the archlute in Italy at the end of the 16th century, the principle was applied to the cittern. Robinson (1609) wrote music for and drew a 14-course (7 doubles on the fingerboard and 7 singles off it) archcittern version of the small English cittern that was based on an Italian model that he altered. Its tuning was $G\ A\ B^b\ c\ d\ e\ f\ /\ g\ d'\ f'\ b^b\ g'\ d''\ e''$. The sole surviving example of an Italian archcittern could be related to that model. It is by Canpi and is in the Museo Bardini in Florence (no. 137). It has 7 double courses over the fingerboard and 4 single courses from the second peg box. In 1607 Agazzari mentioned the *ceterone* (archcittern) as a continuo instrument.[343] In the same year Monteverdi included two *ceteroni* in the continuo band in *Orfeo*. The term *ceterone*

---

[342] cited in A. Baines, *European and American Musical Instruments* (1966), p. 42.

[343] A. Agazzari, *Del sonare sopra il basso* (1607), trans. O. Strunk, *Source Readings in Music History* (1950).

means 'large cittern' and need not imply a second neck. A 1616 Italian publication provided tablature for a *citara tiorbata* that used strings tuned to *A B c d f / b g d' e'*.[344] Praetorius apparently never came across an Italian archcittern, but his 12-course Prague cittern qualifies as an archcittern because of the four strings on the peg box extension. Mersenne mentioned a 15-course *Cisteron ou Guiterron* that was like a theorbo but had a flat back.[345] We hear no more of archcittern activity until the second half of the 18th century when the German guitar was played in France and Germany.

Bandora and orpharion

In 1634 John Stow wrote that the bandora was invented by John Rose in 1562. The earliest contemporary mention of the instrument was in 1566, when it was specified in the music directions of a play. Though usually called 'bandora', this late 16th and 17th century instrument was also called 'pandora', with sometimes either of these names ending in 'e' instead of 'a'.

The earliest English name for it was 'bandurion' which seems to imply 'large bandurria'. 'Gitteron' meaning 'large gittern' would have been appropriate, but that name was probably already being used in English for the vihuela and viola de mano. The *bandurria* was a small 3-string Spanish instrument of the time with a round back, tuned with intervals of a fourth and a fifth. It possibly could have been known in England from examples brought home by travelers or pirates, or from the book by Bermudo published in 1555. Any relationship between this instrument with the English instrument is far from obvious. The name 'bandurria' could have just been considered attractive, being so different, and the bandora was certainly very different.

The bandora's invention and early popularity can readily be understood in terms of the relationship between the cittern and gittern when they both first appeared in England just before 1550. It was then fashionable, as stated in Wythorne's autobiography, for young gentlemen to learn both instruments. Both being treble instruments, they could not play together in the usual lute fashion of treble and bass. A wire strung instrument such as the bandora, tuned like a gittern (but an octave lower) could play duos with the cittern, and such a pair could easily be formed from the same circle of players.

Besides the four courses tuned an octave below the gittern, the bandora also had a fifth course tuned a 4th lower than the fourth, and a sixth course tuned a tone lower than the 5th. The paired unison strings were then tuned: *C D G c e a*. This added bass range was made possible by the recent invention of metal bass strings twisted into ropes, as used on the French cittern, the first music for which was published in 1552. A seventh course tuned a fourth lower than the sixth (tuned to *GG*) became possible when high-twist twisted brass strings became available, and someone thought of angling the frets and bridge to give one or two semitones of extra range. Praetorius offered an alternative tuning for the 7-course bandora: *C D G c f a d'*. If it was the same size as the one depicted, the *d'* string would have had to be of Meuler's steel. Otherwise, the size would have had to be 3/4 that of the usual bandora, rather like that of an orpharion.

---

[344] P. P. Melli, *Intavolatura di liuto attiorbato*, iv (Venice, 1616).
[345] M. Mersenne, op.cit. Bk2, Prop 12.

Praetorius also mentioned and depicted a 9-course bass orpharion, which he called *penorcon*, with the tuning *GG AA C D G c e a d'*. The design of the instrument depicted was the same as that of the bandora, but it was about 10% smaller. At that size and the given pitches, the lowest string would not fret in tune. It should have been as large as the bandora or tuned a tone higher. Since this is the only mention of such an instrument, it might have been an experiment of only limited success.

There are no surviving bandoras. A French painting, now in the Louvre, made in 1609, shows a bandora being played as viewed from behind. There one sees a dark-light striped back with apparently seven stripes.

The orpharion was developed around 1580 as a smaller version of the bandora to be tuned like the lute. The name was apparently a conflation of Orpheus and Arion. It was a response to the availability of very strong steel strings made by a secret process developed by Jobst Meuler of Nuremberg, which allowed a wire-strung instrument of lute size to be played at lute pitches. There are two surviving English orpharion examples before 1621, when Meuler was prevented from freely selling that steel, and it became unavailable. Both of these orpharions have a seven-staved back. The 6-course Rose orpharion could well have been the first one ever made. It has a considerable arch in the back, and the 9-course Palmer orpharion probably did as well originally (since it never had cross bars on the back, and much of the current severe distortion of the body shape can be associated with a flattening of an originally arched shape).[346] When discussing the orpharion (but calling it 'pandora'), Mersenne wrote in 1635 that it was no more in use, and 'as for its back, it is flat, or at least it is not as convex as that of the lute'. Praetorius discussed an 8-course orpharion, giving one tuning *C F G c f a d' g'*, and another a tone higher.

The name Mersenne used indicates that there was some ambiguity in distinguishing between the orpharion and the bandora. If one omits the first course of a 8-course orpharion, one has the tuning of a 7-course bandora. If one shifts the strings of a full-sized bandora down one course (on the bridge and nut) and adds a Meuler steel first course tuned a 4th higher than the original first course, one has the tuning of a bass lute or bass orpharion (called 'penorcon' by Praetorius). If we neglect pitch standard (which could not be done for ensemble music, but possible for vocal accompaniment or solo purposes), retuning the third course by a semitone could convert one to another. Thus, to some extent, whether an instrument played like a bandora or an orpharion was the player's choice. That choice could have depended on the player's musical aspirations. The bandora was played mainly as an accompaniment instrument, where the technical demands were usually rather limited, so it could be an attractive fretted stringed instrument for the use of a player who was not a fretted strings specialist. A lute specialist would choose an orpharion to offer variety in playing the extensive and complex lute solo repertoire. In the surviving wills that mention instruments, we find numerous orpharions or bandoras, but only once do we find both, and that was after the orpharion became largely redundant because Meuler's wire was unavailable.

Unique features of the bandora and orpharion were metal pins for string attachment set into the

---

[346] E. Segerman & D. Abbott, 'On the Palmer Orpharion', *FoMRHI Quarterly* 3 (Apr. 1976), Comm. 16, pp. 48-56.

bridge and an undulating body shape formed by a number of indentations set into an essentially egg-shaped outline (this shape was sometimes imitated on viols). These indentations were either smooth curves or inward points. The number of indentations on each side was sometimes three but usually four. The earliest orpharion, the one by Rose, dated 1580, has the peg holes going through a wavy peg plate. The other examples, which include the other orpharion, plus all of the depictions, show a viol-like peg box, with pegs coming in sideways. All examples have a carved head on the end.

On all examples (except for one French painting of a bandora) the fingerboard extends over the soundboard. The 15 frets were made just like those on citterns, of brass strips backed by hardwood strips. Before about 1590 it seems that the bridge, frets and nut were all parallel as in lutes and citterns, but after then it became increasingly fashionable to have all of these angled in a fan shape, giving the lowest strings up to two frets greater length than the highest strings.

This angling is necessary for the open-string range of a sixteenth used on a seven-course bandora to give acceptable intonation on maximum-twist roped brass lowest strings without iron first strings breaking too often. With the same type of stringing as bandoras, orpharions would have been tuned a third or fourth higher than bandoras. But orpharions generally used specially strong steel higher strings which allowed them to be tuned up to about an octave higher than bandoras. This allowed them a fifth more bass range which they often utilized by adding more bass courses.

The neck cross-sectional shape was usually symmetric across the full width of the fingerboard, sometimes almost like a somewhat rounded triangle with a point down the middle (as on the Rose orpharion and implied by the line down the back of the bandora neck in the Henry Unton painting depicting a Consort) and sometimes quite rounded (as in the Van der Venne painting in the Louvre). The Palmer orpharion (1619) has an asymmetric neck like Italian citterns and a separate heel and neck as on the Spanish guitar (that was popular mostly in Italy at the time). These features, apparently untypical of English instruments, could well have been the result of it being made for a Danish court musician going through the standard training of the time, which involved spending some years in Italy for learning music theory and performance practices (where he probably learned to play the cittern), followed by a stay in England to learn the kind of repertoire most popular at home.

Most depictions show the height of the ribs noticeably less at the neck end than at the tail end. Talbot's measurements possibly imply uniform rib heights, as is found on the Palmer orpharion. The Rose orpharion is cittern-like in that the rib height is greater at the neck. It is likely that it was originally made as a rather large 5-course cittern (the inscription on the side says ten strings and the peg placement in the peg plate implies that there were originally ten pegs, but two were added afterwards) incorporating bandora features, and then very soon converted (probably by the maker) to a 6-course instrument that could play like a lute.

Details of the body construction can be found on the surviving orpharions, but these involve some guesswork since these instruments have been much repaired. Soundboard barring was parallel on parallel-fretted instruments, and when the frets and bridge were angled, the bars were angled to the same fan pattern. The barring was very lute-like but much lower in height, with six main bars and several thinner bars under the rose, plus a diagonal bar from the treble end of the bridge to the edge. The soundboard was purfled along the edge. The rose, backed with vellum, could either be carved from the soundboard (as in the Rose instrument) or set in (as in the Palmer). The Rose instrument never had a tail block but the Palmer instrument has one now. The back was made with seven staves often alternating dark and light, without supporting cross bars.

The bandora was strung with iron, brass and twisted brass. Orpharions used the same string materials except that Meuler's steel was needed for the first course. There were from six to nine courses with lute tuning. Six course instruments usually had parallel fretting, and instruments with more courses usually had fan-shaped fretting. The Talbot ms mentioned that there were orpharions with 7 courses over the fingerboard and a theorboed neck of the English style with 5 nuts, each for an octave pair.

Before the middle of the 17th century, it appears that each course of a bandora was a unison pair. It used a double first course and unison bases before this became usual on English lutes. The playing technique on the bandora as well as the orpharion was essentially that of the lute, but with gentler plucking strokes to avoid clashing of the strings.

When Meuler's specially strong strings became unavailable around 1620, the orpharion could no more substitute for the usual mean or treble lutes at the same pitch, and so it went seriously out of fashion in England. Another reason for its redundancy is that if tuned at a lower pitch, the low extra basses could not fret in tune. In the time of its popularity in England, all courses of the orpharion seem to have been unison pairs. There is a surviving continentally-made (possibly by Tielka) 8-course orpharion in the Frankfurt Museum apparently from around 1700 that is small enough to play at the usual lute pitch using iron for the first course. The low basses would only sound well with metal-winding, which was available by then.

The bandora was popular in England as well as France and Germany throughout the 17th century, but no specific repertoire for the later period survives. Bandora players then probably played from general instrumental bass parts, either following the figures or previously memorizing the harmonic sequence. An early 18th century German engraving showing a musical performance in a church shows a bandora hanging on the wall.[347]

After the middle of the 17th century, octave stringing on the lower four courses of the seven-course bandora was also used. The instrument was then often played strongly with a quill. Roger North wrote that 'there was once a company of itinerant musitians fitted for a consort equal with any of the same numbers now celebrated: consisting of 2 violins, a base, one loud hautbois and 2 wire pandoras. ... the pandoras had a better effect to fill and adorn the sound than any harpsicord I have ever heard since. For the strings are mostly of twisted wire, the touch with a quill strong and guittar fashion, full accords at every stroke, and not a little *arpeggiando*, and all open and above board.'[348]

---

[347] J. G. Walther, *Lexicon* (1732), Engraved frontispiece, reproduced ed. G. Kinsky, *A History of Music in Pictures* (Dent, 1930), p. 255.
[348] ed. J. Wilson, *Roger North on Music* (Novello, London, 1959), fn. p. 272.

The Talbot ms mentioned that in the time of King James I, bandoras played bass in 'wire consorts' with a cittern playing treble, a wire-strung guittern playing a second part, and an orpharion playing thorough bass. This statement could have been possible if the cittern used Meuler's wire and the guittern (of the same size) used iron treble strings. Though there is no report of such a consort from that time, there is no reason to suppose it didn't happen.

All of the surviving bandora repertoire dates from the last quarter of the 16th century plus a few years afterwards. Also from this period is all of the music for the Consort, an ensemble of several accompanying instruments (cittern and bandora or orpharion) and several melodic instruments (treble viol or violin, flute or recorder and bass viol). It also included a treble lute tuned like a mean lute that alternated between playing a highly divided melodic part and an accompaniment part. A feature of the Consort was the contrasts in type of sound produced by the different instruments. The term 'Consort' then implied an ensemble with different types of instruments involved.[349] When the violin and recorder were played, the pitch level played at was probably a tone higher than when the treble viol and flute played.

Polyphont

The polyphont or polyphone was an English instrument strung with brass wire, of which no example survives. It was mentioned and described in several sources from the second half of the 17th century. One[350] claimed that it was invented by Daniel Farrant early in the century, and another[351] stating that it had 'something of the Harp, Lute, Theorb &c: it was a sweete Instrument', knew of only one player, the physician Sir Francis Prujeane. It was described in two sources. The manuscript notes Randle Holme wrote[352] for a continuation of his book on armory[353] included a description and a drawing. The Talbot ms includes a description and some measurements. The Holme drawing shows essentially a rectangular body with rounded corners and many small bandora-like undulations around its edge. The Talbot measurements indicate that the body was over a meter long and 8 cm deep. The Holme drawing shows two necks protruding from the body, with an arm joining their ends (reminiscent of a lyre). The shorter neck on the right carried a fingerboard, and the longer one on the left didn't. A bridge (or bridges) formed a long S shape from the lower left of the body to the upper right. The Talbot information indicates that the nut and frets on the fingerboard were angled like on the bandora, and the fingerboard, which had 8 frets, was 18 cm long, so the string length of the longest fingered string (assuming that the fingerboard end was where a 9th fret would be) was about 46 cm. This makes it likely that this string was tuned to *d'*. Thus if it was tuned somewhat like a lute, it was like a bass lute.

No tuning information survives. There were basically three sets of strings: the numbers of strings listed with (H) and (T) afterwards denoting whether they were from the Holme and Talbot information respectively. The set over the fingerboard was 4 (H) or 5 (T) single strings. The second set was tuned from pegs on the arm between the ends of the two necks, and had 9 (H and T) single

---

[349] The modern use of the term for a set of instruments of only one type started with the first edition of the Grove Dictionary.

[350] J. Playford, *Musicke's Recreation* (London, 1652, 4/1682).

[351] John Evelyn diary 1661, quoted in M. Tilmouth, 'Some improvements in Music noted by William Turner in 1697', *Galpin Soc J.* X (1957).

[352] British Library Harl. 2034, reproduced in 'Polyphont' entry in The New Grove Dictionary of Musical Instruments 3 (Macmillan, 1984), p. 137.

[353] R. Holme, *Academy of Armory, or A Storehouse of Armory and Blazon* (Chester, 1688).

strings. The left thumb plucked strings in this second set (like on the barytone), while the other left-hand fingers stopped the strings over the fingerboard.

The third set of strings were for a wire-strung harp, and they were in three sections. The high section, to the right of the neck with the fingerboard, was tuned from pegs on the top of the body, and had 3 (H) or 6 (T) single strings. The middle section, between the two necks, was also tuned from pegs on the top of the body, and had 8 (H) or 7 (T) pairs of strings. The final section, tuned from pegs part-way up the second neck, had 9 (H) or 3 (T) single strings. The total number of strings was 41 (H) or 37 (T). In 1655 Sir Francis Prujeane mentioned that one had 'above forty single strings'.

This instrument could play two independent lower lines, one by the left thumb on the second set, and the other by the right thumb on the middle and low sections of the third set. Higher lines would be played by other right-hand fingers on the fingerboard strings and the high section of the third set.

An earlier instrument that has some characteristics of the polyphont survives in the Vienna K. M. (Schlosser Cat. No. C.67). It was made in the Wendelin Tieffenbrucker workshop in Padua around 1600. It has 9 double and 2 single (on the bass side) courses over the fingerboard (of string length about 80 cm), 15 single treble strings tuned from the top edge of the body, and 20 single bass strings tuned from an arm that comes out of the neck near the nut, curves up, and then curves down and embeds itself into the side of the body. The original gut frets on the fingerboard and the normal bridge design for this set of strings indicate that the fingerboard strings were originally gut (metal strings would wear gut frets too quickly to be practical). The other two sets of strings had individual bridges appropriate for metal strings. With this design one can much more readily pluck the bass strings both by the left and right hand thumbs than one can on theorbos and archlutes.

Another possibly related instrument was one with silver strings that Piccinini's brother played, which he called *Pandora*.[354]

---

[354] A. Piccinini, *Intavolatura di liuto, et di chitarrone* (Bologna, 1623), p. 5.

Appendix 1: Development influence charts

The lines represent an important initial influence such as playing style, tuning, size, body design, or it could represent a change of name for essentially the same instrument. The dates are estimates of the first appearance of each instrument, and can be quite approximate.

Descendants of the earliest stringed instruments

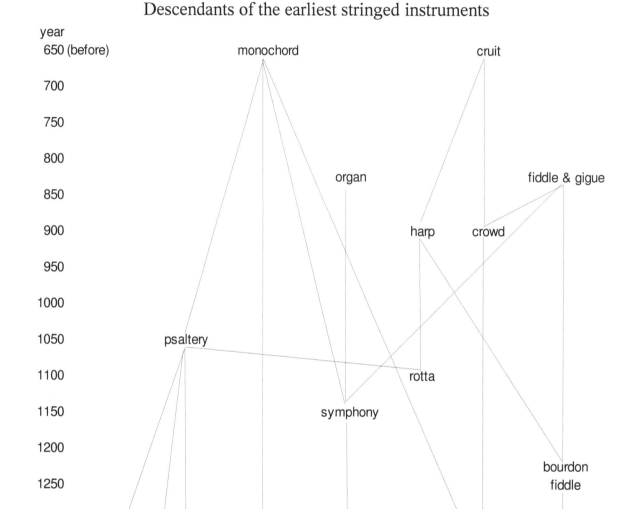

Development of the more modern bowed instruments

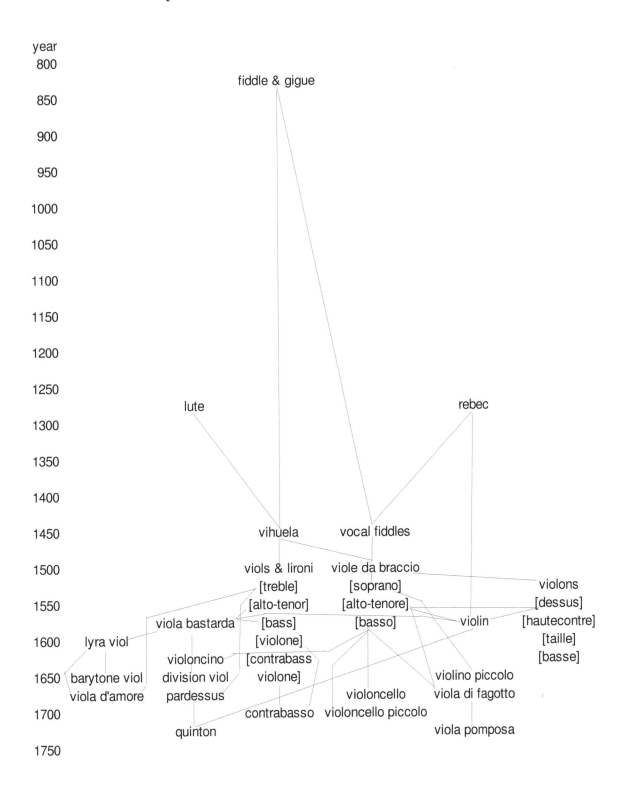

Development of the more modern plucked instruments

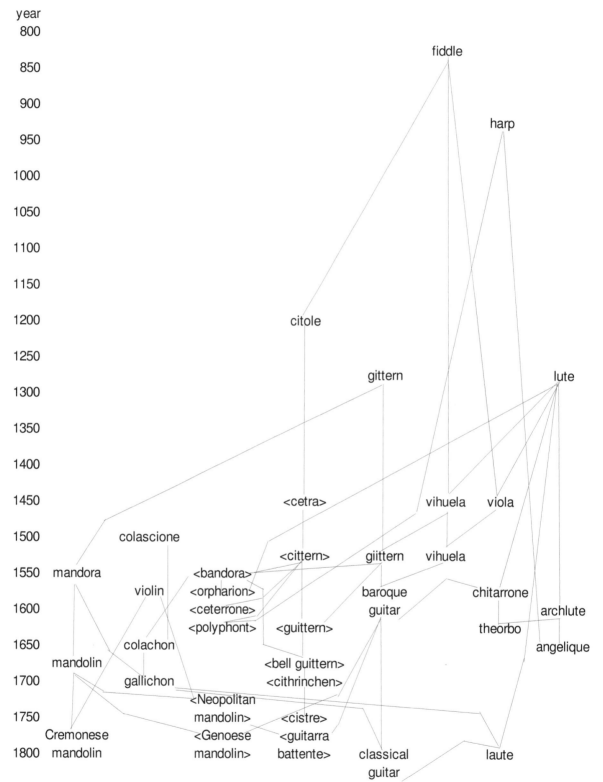

Pointy brackets < > indicate instruments with metal strings

The Development of Western European Stringed Instruments

Appendix 2: Some topics involving string and wood technology

Polnische geigen, fingering past the fingerboard and violin fingerboard length

The 1545 edition of Agricola's *Musica instrumentalis deudsch* mentioned *polischen geigen*, which were fingered by the fingernails pressing against the strings in mid air, as opposed to the usual method of being pressed against the fingerboard by the fingertips. The same fingering method is currently used in playing the Cretan lira and the Indian sarangi. In each of these modern cases, the strings are much thicker, and thus under higher tension, than those on similar instruments that are fingered normally. This could well also have been the case with Agricola's polischen geigen. The fingering on these instruments stops the string from vibrating at the fingering position by pressure on the string from one direction only. To be effective, this requires more finger pressure than clamping the string between the finger and the fingerboard. For fluency in fingering, the distance that the finger needs to move to stop a string needs to be limited, and this is provided by high tension, which gives greater resistance to the finger pressure. A similar preference for thicker strings on the trumpet marine is also to allow more finger pressure to properly inhibit vibration at the finger position. An advantage of this choice of type of fingering on polischen geigen is that sliding the finger along the string while bowing (producing a pitch slide) is particularly easy because there is less friction. Portamento playing was probably popular at other times than its heyday in the late 19th and early 20th centuries.

The modern violin has a fingerboard long enough to finger two octaves and a fourth on the open string. Galeazzi wrote in 1791 that modern compositions of his day could not be played on a fingerboard that is shorter than two octaves for the open string. This has been adopted as the normal fingerboard length on a modern baroque violin. A generation earlier than Galeazzi, in Leopold Mozart's time, the highest a violinist was expected to play was *a'''* in 7th position, which is an octave and a fourth above the open string, and depictions from this period confirm the predominance of this fingerboard length. Nevertheless the virtuoso Locatelli of that generation wrote music that went much higher, up to the 14th position in one caprice. It is most likely that he fingered past the fingerboard in mid air, as modern violinists do for very high music, like the polischen geigen was fingered, but without the nail. It is much less likely that he had a special instrument with a fingerboard of modern length. I asked an eminent modern baroque violinist about this, and he said that it is much harder to finger in mid-air in the second octave than in the third. In the third octave, the string gives more resistance to finger pressure because the fingering is so close to the bridge. So what was Locatelli's trick? There was no trick at all, since string tensions on Italian baroque violins were considerably higher than on modern violins (which are somewhat higher than on modern baroque violins), making off-fingerboard fingering in the second octave easier.

Twisted and roped gut strings, and catlins

The making of gut strings became professionalized in the 15th century.[355] One type of traditional machine for twisting the gut after it was cleaned involved a wide deep trough with a V-shaped cross section that drained the water dripping from the guts. On one side of the trough was the twisting device that had a crank that turned a large gear which turned two small planetary gears. The small gears were on shafts, with hooks on the other end. These hooks stuck out over the edge of the trough. On the opposite side of the trough were vertical holes in the edge into which wooden pegs were plugged.

The string maker made a loop on one end of the gut and placed it on one of the hooks and threaded it loosely across the trough, around the peg on the opposite side of the trough, back to the other hook, back to the peg, back to the first hook, back to the peg, etc. When the required thickness to make the string was reached, the gut was cut, a loop made, and placed on one of the hooks. There could have been a stick at the bottom of the trough that was lifted whenever the gut was threaded across the trough, and then dropped, to provide a uniform degree of looseness to allow for shortening when the string is twisted. The stick would have been removed before turning the crank twisted the string. Since the two hooks turned in the same direction, the part of the string going around the peg is not subject to rotating forces. This system allows twice the length of string to be made than would be made if the string were built up between only one hook and the peg. After twisting, the string was stretched between pegs on a long rack. As the string dries and contracts, the amount of twist decreases relative to the maximum twist it can take, so if the string was intended to be a high twist string, its twist could be periodically topped up on the rack.

In a twisted string, the individual guts (or gut fibers) wander between the center and outside of the string to even out the tension because where a fiber is near the outside, its helix takes a longer path, pulling in the ends. This increases its tension, so if it can, it wanders inwards to relieve that tension, pushing other strands outwards.

To make a roped-gut string, one puts a maximum amount of twist in each of a number of strings on the above twisting machine, storing the previously twisted ones between additional pegs around the trough.   Then the loops of one end of each string are put on one hook and the loops on the other end on the other hook, with the strings threaded around the peg on the other side of the trough. They are all twisted together as much as possible. If there is no initial twist in each component string in the rope-making process, each fiber has the same scope of wandering as it would have with a high twist string with more material in it. The string becomes smooth, but the elasticity is no different from that of a high-twist string. For the expected increased elasticity, the fiber path for the length of string needs to be longer than the wandering in a high twist string of the same thickness. This requires an initial twist so that a fiber goes from the outside to the center of the whole string (the other side of the strand) and back to the outside more often than the wandering in a high-twist string. This makes the string show the ridges or bumps of rope construction.

---

[355] K. Dorfmuller, *Studien zur Lautenmusik..*, (Tutzing 1967), p. 32 cites evidence of a Munich string maker in 1431.

English players appear to be the only people who gave names to different strings that could be purchased, and these names generally indicated where they were imported from. The name 'catlin', which first appeared in the middle of the 16th century, probably came from 'Catalan', indicating that it came from the string-making center in Barcelona. By Dowland's time, Spain was no more a significant source of strings, and thicker strings of good quality were made in Nuremberg, Strassburg and Bologna, with those from Bologna the best. These latter strings were transported from Venice, and so were called 'Venice Catlines'. Why were they not just called 'Venice strings' (as there were 'Venice lutes')? Put another way, what was the significance of including 'Catline'? It appears that the word was associated with the highest quality. There was no unique type of construction implied since the strings from Nuremberg and Strassbourg also had adequate musical properties (needing rope construction), and they were not called 'Catlines'. Also, the Mary Burwell lute tutor (c. 1670) did not mention catlins at all, with the thin strings coming from Rome and the thick ones from Lyons. Thomas Mace (1676) prescribed Venice catlins for mid-range strings and the basses from Lyons or Pistoy. In 18th and 19th century usage, catlins were what thin strings of high quality was called. From the baroque onwards (at least), quality has always been the only defining characteristic of catlins.

Mace wrote that Pistoy basses were the best, like thick Venice catlins, and they were smooth and well twisted. His criteria for goodness for all strings were clearness to the eye, stiffness to the finger, and smoothness. I have previously interpreted this reported smoothness of Pistoy basses and Venice catlins, as not showing the bumps of rope construction, while the implied less-smoothness of Lyons would indicate that they showed such bumps. But Mace's criteria, including smoothness, applied to Lyons as well. And the Burwell tutor indicated that the criteria for goodness were clearness and transparency, being smooth and well twisted, and hard and strong. These included the thick Lyons strings as well as the thin ones from Rome. These apparent contradictions with my interpretation of smoothness make it untenable, and showing the bumps of rope construction was not a distinguishing factor. Smoothness probably referred to unevenness in the surface of the string, ignoring the regular ridges of rope construction when they were there. I have seen much of such unevenness in roped strings made by our trainee string makers.

Mace's goodness criteria of clearness to the eye and stiffness to the finger, and Burwell's criteria of clearness and transparency and hardness, imply that there was strong binding of the fibers to one another in the string, and that there was a minimum of spaces between fibers in the string to scatter light which stops the light transmission of translucency. The obvious way of accomplishing both of these effects would be to treat the string with a drying oil which both bonds the fibers and fills the spaces. We have found that a film of linseed oil inhibits the transmission of water vapor more effectively than any other oil or wax commonly available in early times, so treatment with linseed oil should also effectively resist tuning instability on humidity changes. Mersenne (1636) mentioned that there was some type of oil treatment in the making of strings. Dowland (1610) mentioned that fresh strings appear clear and oily, but that this can be counterfeited on old strings by further treatment with oil. Specifically of thick strings, he wrote that if they are fresh and new, they will be clear against the light, though their color is blackish.

We have concluded that the thicker gut strings that increased the open-string pitch range by half an octave from the third quarter of the 16th century onwards had rope construction. They either all had the surface ridges of such construction or these ridges had been polished smooth. Such polishing would require considerable skill and time to end up with really smooth strings that are fairly true, making such polished strings rather expensive. The statement by Mace that Venice catlins were at the same price as minikins (the recommended thinnest strings, the name implying that they came from Munich) argues that they were not polished smooth. So the rope construction would probably have been obvious, easily copied and universal for thick strings by all makers. We need to consider what happened earlier in the 16th century:

There is evidence of superior strings early in the 16th century. Around 1517, Vitali, recording the wisdom and compositions of Capirola, wrote that superior strings from Munich 'give' more (presumably meaning that they were more elastic) and did not have thicker and thinner ends.[356] He did not indicate that Capirola used them, outlining rather his satisfactory methods for using strings with one end thicker than the other. This could imply that the Munich strings were rather expensive. The reports of a 7-course 14-string lute by Virdung (1511) and the indication of a 7-course viola da mano in the Bologna fragment[357] could imply an open-string range greater than the usual 2 octaves. In the middle of the 16th century, when these superior strings were available from Spain, the vihuela (see chapter 8) relied on them, especially the 7-course vihuela, which had an open-string range like later lutes that relied on roped-gut basses.

The Barcelona regulations controlling the making of strings survive.[358] At least 2 years of apprenticeship was required. There were serious penalties for revealing the secrets of the craft. These secrets surely included the methods of achieving the high standards consistently and efficiently. The Munich-Barcelona makers appear to have had no competitors in the quality-strings market. This could have been because what was needed to make such strings was obvious and could be developed, but others did not find it worthwhile to do so (i.e. they couldn't sell them at the price appropriate for the work), or what was needed was not obvious, and others would not know what to do (i.e. there were important secrets to keep). Examples of the former could have been to carefully select the pieces of gut to be twisted so that the final thickness would be uniform and to top up the twist of thick ones to maximum as the strings dry (if other string makers did not routinely top up twist while drying). An example of the latter could have been to make roped-gut strings and to polish away the ridges to make them look like normal high-twist strings (if there were obvious ridges of rope construction, others would have realized that this leads to better strings and would have found ways to copy it).

If the last hypothesis above is correct, no strings before the 1570s showed any ridges of roped construction, and all low bass strings did after then. What might have led the main-stream string makers to appreciate the advantages of rope construction? I suggest that the inspiration came from the success of twisted metal wire strings first used on French citterns around 1550.

---

[356] O. Gombosi (ed), *Compositione de Meser Vincenzo Capirola* (Nevilly-sur-Seine, 1955), p. xcii.

[357] Bologna University Library MS 596. HH. 2^4 (c. 1500).

[358] J. M. Ward, *The Vihuela de Mano and its Music* (1953 - unpublished PhD thesis), p. 22.

Modern misconceptions

Many modern early musicians believe that early strings were very flexible to bending. They find this idea attractive because a string that is soft and flexible to the touch can lead one to expect that it offers a warm sound and musical flexibility to the player. One type of evidence in support of this idea is that very old gut found preserved with museum instruments are often not as stiff as modern strings. The bonding between fibers deteriorates with time (as Dowland noticed), which leads to such flexibility, so it is most unlikely that this was the way these string were when new. Since the fibre bonding in these old strings has deteriorated, they are completely opaque. Another type of evidence cited is that quite a few paintings show wiggly strings radiating out of peg boxes. The wiggly pattern looks somewhat like what one can see when one drops a flexible sewing thread on a table. But the strings in the pictures are supporting similar shapes against gravity in three dimensions in mid air, with free ends not drooping. Bending flexibility could not have generated the shapes seen, but we need to consider what might have done so. A good possibility is that players stored old strings in their peg boxes under the tuned strings, and it was not easy to tuck all parts of them in. Coils in the old string could readily have been from where it had originally been wound around a peg. The storage could be of strings that had been replaced but were still usable in an emergency, or of parts of strings to be used to tie to a good-sounding string that had broken at a place that left enough length to do this, thus giving it some more life. It is also possible that the painting of strings radiating out of pegboxes was a fashionable artistic fancy that was not necessarily accurately drawn from real life.

There is a current Italian string maker who sells lower-pitched gut strings loaded with metal powder and/or heavy metal salts folded in with the gut fibers when the strings are twisted up. Some modern early musicians find these strings more acceptable than the equivalent roped-gut strings because they have a richer sound (more like metal-wound strings), they have more bending flexibility and their surface is smooth. So this type of string seems to be an attractive possibility for what was originally used. That maker has a patent on his process, and I've heard that a threat to sue has induced an American string maker to stop making this type of strings. If his presumption that this type of strings was originally used were true, then the patent would certainly not be valid on the grounds of prior art!

From an historical point of view, the claim that the original strings had much bending flexibility is falsified by the evidence on stiffness. The early evidence is presented above, and later evidence is from the writings of Galeazzi (1791)[359], who wrote that a good string is supremely elastic and strong and not limp and yielding, and Savaresse (in Maugin & Maigne, 1869)[360], who wrote that when you squeeze a packet of thin strings (chanterelles) they must feel elastic and return promptly as a steel spring would do. The claim that it is possible (with a reasonable probability) that they were usually loaded with metal powder and/or heavy metal salts is falsified by the above evidence of clearness or translucency, since that property requires that any material added to the gut must have an index of refraction close to that of gut, a requirement not met by any metal or heavy metal salt I know of.

---

[359] F. Galeazzi, *Elimenti teorico-practici di musica...* (Rome, 1791).
[360] Maugin & Maigne, *Nouveau manuel complet du luthier* (1869 ed.).

Bowed strings, bridges, sound posts and bass bars

A bowed string vibrates almost exclusively in the direction of movement of the bow, and it drives the bridge at the string notch back and forth in that direction. This oscillating force mostly drives the bridge to oscillate rotationally about some axis perpendicular to the bridge. That axis goes through a point in the bridge plane. The feet of a bridge can only move perpendicular to the soundboard, so the point about which the bridge oscillates must be on the line between the bottoms of the bridge feet. We are here neglecting the arching under the bridge and assuming that the bridge is rigid, so the frequencies involved are lower than the resonant frequencies of the bridge itself (which start at several kilohertz).

Where between the feet that axis point is located depends on the relative resistance of the soundboard to being driven by the bridge feet. A bass bar under the soundboard offers great resistance to being driven at high frequencies, and low resistance to being driven at low frequencies. A sound post under the soundboard offers low resistance to being driven at high frequencies, and higher resistance to being driven at low frequencies. The angular amplitude of oscillation about the axis point applies to the whole bridge, so the distance between that axis point and each foot must be proportional to the linear amplitude of vibration pumping the soundboard at that foot. So when an instrument has both a bass bar and a sound post, at low frequencies, the axis point is much closer to the treble foot than the bass foot, and at high frequencies, that point is much closer to the bass foot than the treble foot.

Now let us consider the forces of vibration on the bridge at the string notch due to the string's vibration. The bridge's rotational oscillations are driven by the component of the string vibration forces perpendicular to the radius line between the axis point and the notch. The remaining component of the string's vibrational forces gets transmitted along that line. That transmitted component has components parallel and perpendicular to the line between the two bridge feet. The perpendicular component drives both feet together (in contrast to the angular oscillation which drives them in a see-saw fashion), and the parallel component is fully resisted and does not lead to soundboard vibration.

The component of the string vibration forces at the bridge notch that drives rotational oscillations provides an oscillating angular force called 'torque' which is proportional to the forces themselves and the radial distance between the notch and the axis point. That same oscillating torque drives the bridge feet, with the oscillating force driving the soundboard being proportional to the distance between the axis point and each foot.

Since the forces that drive the bridge feet are proportional to the radial distance between the axis point and the notch, we can conclude that with the same string forces on the bridge and distance between bridge feet, the higher the bridge is, the stronger are the forces with which the bridge feet drive the soundboard. We can also conclude that when the axis point is nearer one foot than the other, vibrations of strings on the side of the bridge away from that foot have an enhanced effect in driving the soundboard (because of the greater radial distance).

The bass bar enhances the sound of the treble strings by this latter effect when an instrument has only a bass bar under the bass bridge foot. This was the case with some surviving mid-16th century viols with arched soundboards and cross-bars. If there is a similar bar down the center of the instrument, as a few surviving 16th century viols have, there is no such enhancement. This effect also enhances the sound of the bass strings when there is only a sound post under the treble foot. This appears to have been the case with the French fiddles and the early violin. This also works for a sound post integral with the treble foot that goes through a hole in the soundboard, so only the bass foot drives the soundboard and the axis point must be on the sound post. This was the case with some German viols in the 1530s, and with other instruments (like the Cretan lira and the crwth).

Sound absorption by creep in strings and instruments

When a piece of rigid material is subjected to a force that changes its shape (deforming it), the deformation can be elastic or inelastic. When the force is removed, if the deformation is all elastic, it immediately returns to its original shape. An example is a steel string, which returns to its original length when it is detuned. If the deformation is both elastic and inelastic, there is only a partial recovery of its original shape. An example is a new gut or brass string, which becomes longer (and thinner, since the volume doesn't change) than it originally was when it is tuned up for a while and later detuned.

Inelastic stretching is demonstrated by the dropping of pitch after a new gut or brass string is tuned up. After some days, the inelastic stretching essentially stops (in any useful string material), and the string 'settles down'. Many players observe that 'playing in' a string makes settling down faster. The same phenomenon occurs with the wood when a new stringed instrument is strung up. Its body immediately deforms somewhat in an elastic way in response to the string tension, but then it deforms inelastically slowly for some time until it settles down. Similarly, 'playing in' the instrument makes it reach its full resonance more quickly.

When a piece of a material slowly deforms inelastically, that deformation is called 'creep'. In creep, the microregions in greatest stress (capable of slipping relative to their neighboring microregions to relax that excess stress) do move, and do so suddenly, redistributing the stress to other regions, some of which then become overstressed and subsequently slip themselves. Each of these microregion movements produces a 'ping' that is audible with equipment that is sensitive enough. Since creep produces vibration energy, it is capable of absorbing vibration energy that will speed up what it is doing. Thus when a string or instrument is played while it is creeping, the creeping material will absorb some of the vibrating energy, making the sound duller than it would be without creep. This playing also speeds up the creep so it more quickly reaches the point when almost all of the microregions are locked in, unable to move (i.e. it settles down).

When the piece of material has settled down in response to the force on it, and then the force is removed, the elastic part immediately recovers, followed by a slow creeping recovery of some of the creep generated by the force. The deforming force had crammed some microregions into environments which, with the force removed, are at high stress relative to their neighbors, and those stresses are relieved by an amount of reverse creep. So a settled down string that has been tuned down to a low tension for a while will increase its tension. And an old instrument that has been stored with tuned-down strings may need a bit of playing-in before it regains the full resonance it had before.

Players have noticed that the resonance of a gut string often deteriorates just before it breaks. The sequence involved in the breaking of a string starts with the breaking of a few gut fibers. With the portion of the tension that they supported gone, the remaining fibers have to support a greater portion of the tension, increasing their stress (stress is the tension divided by the cross-sectional area, which is the relevant parameter when discussing material strength). As a result they stretch further, and that new stretching absorbs vibration energy by creep. The increased stress breaks a few more fibers, and this process continues until the remaining fibers become over-stressed and they all break.

Moisture content and swelling in gut strings and wood

Gut strings and wood are hygroscopic materials, and they either absorb moisture from the air (and swell) or they dry down (and contract) towards an equilibrium point of balance between the relative humidity in the air and the moisture content of the gut or wood. The relative humidity of the air is the percentage that the air actually has of the maximum amount of water that the air can hold at that temperature, and the moisture content of the gut or wood is the percentage of the total weight that is water. Tables exist for wood that relate moisture content with relative humidity, and similar tables can be made for gut. Such tables apply only to materials that are not stressed. When outside forces constrain the contraction or expansion, the equilibrium moisture content shifts towards what is normal at that state of contraction or expansion, with variation in the relative humidity having much less of an effect on moisture content.

Gut strings are made from two layers of collagen molecules that are in the walls of intestines. These layers are strong for resisting the pressure of digestive gasses (splitting of the intestines would be fatal). In these two layers, the axes of the helices wind around the intestine in opposite directions. These molecules are long polymers grouped in shallow triple helices with their surfaces studded with a coating of polysaccharide molecules that attract water molecules. When the other intestine material (such as muscle, fat, nerves, blood vessels and connective tissue) is separated away, the remaining gut stretches out and the axes if the helices end up at a small angle to the direction of stretching. A number of the cleaned gut fibers are then twisted together in making a string. String making is a wet process, and when the string dries, the diameter contracts much more than the length. When dry and tuned up on an instrument, and then the instrument is moved to a place of high humidity, the pitch first goes up because the fibers swell, but since they are twisted and fiber lengths change little, swelling pulls the ends in, increasing the tension. On picking up more water, the increased total weight lowers the pitch.

The different strings on a musical instrument don't vary much in tension. So the fibers on the thinner strings tend to be under higher stress than on the thicker strings. Because of the twisting and little-varying fiber length, higher stress along the length leads to more compressional stress across the width. Thus the variations in moisture content and sensitivity to humidity of the thinner strings tends to be less than that of the thicker strings.

Wood is a collection of long thin cells, and the long direction of most cells is along the direction in which the tree grows (the grain direction). The walls of each cell are stuck to the walls of neighboring cells, and the interior is filled with water when the tree is growing, and with air when it is used in instruments. There are pores (also called 'pits') in the cell walls that allow water or air to move from one cell interior to its neighbours.

The strength of wood is due to long cellulose molecules of the polysaccharide type. Their strength along their long direction gives wood most of its strength. These molecules aggregate in semi-crystalline bunches (called 'microfibrils') that wind around the cell in several distinct layers in the wall. The bunches are held together (within each layer and between layers) by a mixture of hemicellulose (a variety of shorter molecules which are saccharide and uronide polymers and copolymers) and lignin (a phenolic type of polymer). This mixture also acts as the adhesive between the walls of adjacent cells. Of these three materials, only hemicellulose swells or contracts by adsorbing or losing water by any significant amount.

Cellulose, hemicellulose and lignin constitute about 99% of the chemicals in wood if we ignore the water, with about half being cellulose and about a quarter of each of the others. The hemicellulose is distributed fairly evenly throughout the cell walls and the adhesive layer between walls, so slow swelling and contracting with varying water content does no create significant internal stresses, but gradients of water content would induce such stresses.

The hemicellulose is orientated in and between the cell walls in such a way that the expansion and contraction of wood with changing moisture content is greatest in the tangential (or circumferential) direction of the tree in which it grew, less than that in the radial direction, and comparatively very little in the grain (or growing) direction. The amount of contraction from fully wet to fully dry ranges from about 5 to 10 % in the tangential direction, about 3 to 6 % in the radial direction, and less than 0.1 % in the grain direction. The higher values are generally associated with denser woods. Thus if two pieces of wood with different orientations are attached firmly to one another, when the relative humidity becomes much different from what it was when first attached, stresses between them will develop.

The medieval method of instrument making avoided such problems by carving most parts out of one piece of wood. The grain direction of the soundboard and fingerboard (if there was one) were the same as that of the body, so strain on humidity variations was no problem. When the built-up construction method was introduced, the problem of strain on joints due to differential dimensional change with humidity change had to handled. Any component made of hard less-compressible wood was thin, and any thick piece of wood (such as a neck block or tail block) was of an easily compressible softer wood. And most important, these strains were minimized by 'stabilizing' the wood.

The maturing and ageing of wood

Stabilizing wood involves treating the wood in a way that reduces the dimensional changes caused by humidity change. A modern way is to make plywood, where thin layers are glued together, with the grain direction perpendicular in adjacent layers. Alternatively one can replace the water molecules attached to the hemicellulose molecules by other molecules that hold tighter than water does. A modern chemical, polyethylene glycol, works very effectively, but it is not used in instrument making. An historical way was to impregnate the wood with inorganic salts (and perhaps sugars). These materials were applied to wood in the fully swollen state (such as after the tree has just been felled), and are called 'bulking' agents because they prevent the wood from shrinking the normal amount as it dries. The intention is to maximise the amount of agent that is incorporated in the cell wall material and minimise the amount that is deposited in the open spaces inside the cell walls.

The stabilization process of most importance in instrument making involves degradation of the hemicellulose molecules so that a considerable fraction of the sites onto which water molecules dock are removed. Hemicellulose is considerably less chemically stable than cellulose or lignin, the other main components of wood. When dry, it undergoes thermal degradation where bits of the molecules break off, giving off carbon dioxide and water into the air in the cells. The higher the temperature, the faster this occurs. It happens faster when oxygen is available, but it still happens without, so it is not just an oxidation reaction. Data on weight loss of dry wood as a function of temperature and time collected by Stamm[361], when extrapolated to 20^0 C, suggests that wood would lose 1% in weight per century due to thermal degradation.

Another degradation mechanism, called 'hydrolysis', usually applies to cell walls of wood in contact with liquid water. In this type of degradation, larger chunks of the hemicellulose molecules break off as sugars, and go into solution in the water (the water goes black at higher temperatures because the sugars caramelise). This happens faster at higher temperatures and with more acidity (lower pH) in the water. When there is no liquid water in the cells but the walls are not dry, hydrolysis also occurs when there are stresses created by moisture-content gradients in the cell walls.

For making built-up instruments, old wood has always been favored over fresh wood because it is more dimensionally stable. Modern makers prefer using wood that has 'matured' for at least 5 years, with it being exposed to all the humidity changes provided by the weather for at least some of that time. This degrades some of the hemicellulose with the help of stresses produced by gradients in moisture content due to humidity cycling. Kiln-dried wood is less-well stabilised since it has not been exposed to humidity cycling. Aside from offering greater dimensional stability, maturing the wood also makes the instruments made from it sound better. This apparently is because adsorbed water on the hemicellulose, and the hemicellulose itself, make significant contributions to the amount of absorption of vibration energy when the wood is vibrated, and with some of both reduced, there will be less sound absorption.

Bowed instruments hundreds of years old have the reputation of being better than modern copies. The observation that it is easier to get the sound one wants from antique instruments could be

---

[361] A. J. Stamm, 'Wood Deterioration and its Prevention', Preprints of the IIC 1970 New York Conference on *Conservation of Stone and Wooden Objects*, Second Edition, Volume 2 (1971), p. 1.

explained by there being less absorption of vibrational energy resulting from there being less water and hemicellulose. Total sound power is not an issue since that is easily controlled by the player's bowing. Old wood with much of the hemicellulose degraded does not lose much in strength, and the wood quality index[362], which is sound-transmission velocity divided by the density, apparently improves.[363] But there is considerable loss in abrasion resistance and toughness of the wood. These losses are due to the loss of hemicellulose in the layer between cell walls, so less cohesion allows many of these layers to be fractured. The losses also weaken the adhesion between the microfibrils. Light scattering by the spaces left from lost hemicellulose is probably the cause of the loss of translucency of spruce with age.

My suggestion for the main advantage of old wood is that the loosened microfibrils and cell walls rattle at very high frequencies, and such motions absorb these frequencies from the soundboard vibration. This will reduce harshness and give a warmth to the sound of bowed instruments. This would also explain the bad reputation had nowadays by old soundboards on plucked instruments, since the very high frequencies are important for projection of the plucked sound. The 17th century French who preferred old Italian lutes (re-barring the soundboards) played their lutes only in intimate circumstances, and didn't need the projection modern pluckers do for the concert stage.

Many modern bowed instrument players prefer to play on antique instruments than new ones. The availability of such instruments is very limited and prices are very high, so many buy new ones that simulate antique instruments in as many aspects as possible. Some makers of such instruments simulate the ageing of the wood by stewing it, like in the salting process except for a longer time, and not necessarily using salt.

There is no simple relationship between the amount of degradation of the hemicellulose and the age of the wood since the amount of degradation depends strongly on the amount and nature of the cycling of moisture content in its history. It can vary considerably in the same piece of wood. Where firmly glued to another piece of wood that prevents the expansion and contraction due to humidity changes, the moisture content had not been varying as much as other parts not so constrained, so there has been less degradation, and so less age contraction. We can thus often see the location of the original bars on a museum lute soundboard by noticing where the cracks in the soundboard end.

Peg Fitting

Probably the most influential invention in the history of stringed instruments was the friction-operated turning tuning peg. It happened in the first few centuries AD, drastically reducing the space needed for the tuning arrangement, making compact instruments more practical.

For strength, the shaft of a peg is along the grain direction. Perpendicular to that direction,

---

[362] For the same instrument design, this index is a good indication of the sound output to be expected.
[363] The transmission velocity / density = sqrt(stiffness/density³), where the stiffness = sqrt((stiffness along the grain)(stiffness across the grain)). Stiffness is the modulus of elasticity (E). The loss of hemicellulose lowers both stiffness and density, but the effect of the density is stronger.

where its cross-section should be circular, are the radial and tangential directions, which differ by a factor of 2 in dimensional change with humidity changes. So when the humidity differs from that at which the peg was fitted, the shaft cross-section is no more circular, but elliptical. Hard woods such as ebony or boxwood expand and contract at least as much as softer woods. The grain-direction situation with the peghead is worse: one direction in the wood around the peg hole that determines its shape is the grain direction, which hardly changes, while the other direction changes much more with humidity.

When both the peg cross-section and the peg hole are elliptical, and the woods of both are relatively incompressible, the peg will not turn properly. It can only work if the wood of at least one is fairly compressible. Medieval instruments found in archaeological digs often had bodies (including pegheads) of rather incompressible oak, and pegs of very compressible lime or willow. In the Renaissance and early baroque, both woods were of medium compressibility, such as maple, beech and fruit woods. Since the baroque, the fashion has changed to pegs of rather incompressible wood like ebony or boxwood, while the pegbox remained with wood of medium compressibility.

In practice, well-fitted hardwood pegs work reasonably well in a variety of humidity circumstances. This is helped by a few factors that make the physical properties of the more compressible pegbox wood more uniform. One is that the presence of the pegs inhibits changes in moisture content when humidity changes, and another is that figure in the wood mixes up the directions somewhat. Of course, it is very important that the wood of both pegs and pegboxes is well seasoned. An oval peg in an effectively round hole still works, as will a round peg in an oval hole. The range of humidities within which the pegs would work could possibly be increased some by fitting the peg at a different humidity than reaming the hole.

Index

The Author

Ephraim Segerman was born in New York in 1929. From teenage years, he has been an amateur lute and viol player. He spent his early professional life working as a crystallographer and physicist in the soap industry, initially in the U.S. and then in the U.K., during which he earned a PhD in physics. In the U.K., he has formally taught courses in biophysics (U.M.I.S.T), acoustics (R.N.C.M and Univ. of Manchester) and instrument making (Manchester Coll. of Building). Since the 1970s, he has been devoted to music history scholarship, trying to solve outstanding problems in understanding how the music originally sounded.

This quest was started when an instrument-maker friend, David Rubio, asked him, as a materials scientist, to look into what original gut lute strings could have possibly been like. Rubio was disappointed at having to mount obviously anachronistic nylon strings on the lutes which he made as authentically as he could. The available gut strings, made for harps, broke when used for the highest string and sounded like dull thuds when used for the lowest strings. This led to an extensive study of the history of strings and string technology that still continues. Segerman realised that bass sound depended on elasticity, which depended on string twist, so he reinvented rope construction of thick gut strings. He also realised that the original pitch standard for lutes was about a tone lower than modern, at which the highest gut strings would last at least as long as gut violin Es.

With Djilda Abbott, he set up Northern Renaissance Instruments (NRI) for making the instruments and kinds of strings (including gut, silk and various metals) that were historically indicated according to their findings. This business has been invaluable, with the help of musician customers, in developing a deeper technological and practical understanding of historical instruments and strings.

FoMRHI (The Fellowship of Makers and Researchers of Historical Instruments) was founded with Jeremy Montagu and Djilda Abbott, and he was the editor of its Quarterly for most of its first quarter century, to which he also made hundreds of contributions.

To clarify the relationship between highest pitch and the longest string lengths of instruments strung with gut, he had to look at the relationships between nominal (reported) pitches and absolute pitches in Hz. This led to an extensive study of the history of pitch standards, starting with Praetorius's evidence, and then analysing the large amount of evidence collected by Arthur Mendel that had not previously been understood. His conclusions have been disputed by some wind-instrument and organ specialists who rarely trust any evidence other than from the surviving instruments they study. The early-music movement had accepted their conclusions generations ago, and any change in historical recognition is understandably avoided.

An extensive study of the history of tempo standards was undertaken when Michael Morrow pointed out that there was some historical information on tempo that was not understood, and David Fallows showed him a lot more. His conclusions have helped to understand problems that musicians were having with quickness of response of some reproduction original types of strings, i.e. it is a problem with modern tempos being much faster, and not with string quality. Musicologists have not accepted them since their understanding of the music has always assumed faster modern tempos.

This book results from the conjunction of two recent studies. One is a theoretical understanding of the lowest pitches that stringed instruments could be tuned to for their string lengths, thus allowing a calculation of the acceptable range of string lengths for the reported open-string tuning range of an instrument. The other is a reexamination of the development of stringed instruments from an ordering of the evidence in chronological sequence. His results offer new insights into the development of most of the instruments discussed.

Lightning Source UK Ltd.
Milton Keynes UK
UKHW050628290123
416116UK00009B/134